Islam *Versus* Gandhi Mahatma

Islam
Versus
Gandhi Mahatma

P. A. RAMACHANDRA RAO

SERIALS PUBLICATIONS
NEW DELHI (INDIA)

First Published: 2009

ISBN: 978-81-8387-225-6

Published by

SERIALS PUBLICATIONS
4830/24, Prahlad Street, Ansari Road
Darya Ganj, New Delhi-110002 (India)
Phone : 23245225
Fax : 91-11-23272135
E-mail: serials@satyam.net.in

CONTENTS

Preface

This book is for the ordinary person with a general interest in history and politics, and not for the specialist. It covers a crucial period in Indian history.

The title is not to be understood in the sense Mahatama Gandhi was opposed to Islam. Never. Gandhi's broad outlook with regard to religion is well known and he is lauded for it. The title simply means that Islam in its extreme form was represented by Jinnah and his followers, and they stood against Gandhi and his work to emancipate the country as one entity.

The first chapter mainly deals with Christianity and Islam. Their impact on India is great, and Indian history can be appreciated much better than now if we know more about the 2 religions. Not only their origin and subsequent expansion across the globe but also their strength and weakness. In this context the weakness of Hindu religion is obvious: the proliferation of gods and image worship without restraint. Along with monkey god and other lesser gods, in our romantic India, even Mahatma Gandhi in the future will be worshipped as a god.

I am obligated to Mythic Society in Bangalore and Nehru Museum Library in New Delhi for providing me the needed research materials. For a researcher, at heart imbibing the spirit of Christopher Columbus, has to search for facts and without the help of concerned people he cannot do much.

P.A. RAMACHANDRA RAO

1

A GLOBAL RELIGION

The religious thought of a people is made up of diverse ideas, and new ideas sprout up in opposition to them, so that at any time there is in evidence the "struggle of the thing achieved, to hold the new, the new-born individual, the new-born idea, the widening needs of the species, in thrall.[1]" One such idea that gained ascendancy by conflict is future life; in which Gandhi Mahatma as a Hindu subscribed faith unequivocally, and which Jesus admitted to his religion promising his followers the Kingdom of Heaven.

The doctrine of immortality of the soul, being ignored by the early Aryans, was developed and propagated in Gaul, Assyria, Egypt and India by the priestly class. The Egyptians were taken with its novelty, and it was represented by the cult of Serapis, the saviour of souls after "leading souls to the light and receiving them again." More or less, this is similar to raising of the dead preached by Christianity. Among the polytheists of Greece and Rome, however, the idea of future existence made no headway, and their prayers before the altars of gods anticipated their temporal happiness without caring for that bliss which transcends earth fixation. Further, the Mosaic law did not recognize the immortality of the soul, but some Jews known as Pharisees added to their beliefs a future state of existence on the strength of tradition.[2] Their approval of such a mind-expanding doctrine, however, was not based on evidence, and it was ordained that it should obtain the sanction of divine truth from the example of Christ's life.

Celibacy had its attraction even before Christ embraced it, but he made it more desirable with this view: "For while some are incapable of marriage because they were born so, or were made so by men, there are others who have themselves renounced marriage for the sake of the Kingdom of Heaven.[1]" Since celibate life was presumed to be related to Divine perfection, things which gratify the sensual and lower the spiritual were abhorred. So even the copulation of human sexes, notwithstanding its joy in the labour of creation, was grudgingly tolerated while the virtues of a passionless life were lauded to the skies. The loss of commonplace sexual pleasure was compensated by spiritual acquisition not without value; in fact, the Indian sages of bygone times wallowed in vainglory, and their overbearing attitude testified to the fact that people by and large looked with awe at what was obviously their creative spiritual energy which was difficult for others to possess. Similarly, celibacy was an essential part of the power of the Christian clergy.

The monasteries were set up, maybe originally, by Gautama Buddha and his followers, and their secluded life provided an ideal environment to promote chastity. The democratic leanings of Buddha who had his roots in one of the republican tribes of North India is well known; yet even he was disinclined at first to see the existence of female ascetic order, perhaps fearing its potential to subvert monastic principles.

Obviously, too much stress on continence by a religious order tended to encourage segregation of sexes, leading to discrimination against women. There is no sexual discrimination in Plato's ideal society, and women could occupy any office including the highest position in the state on the basis of ability. Plato drives home the point of equality between sexes in the form of a question: "Are dogs divided into hes and shes, or do they both share equally in hunting and in keeping watch and in the other duties of dogs? or do we entrust to the males the entire and exclusive care of the flocks, while we leave the females at home, under the idea that the bearing and suckling their puppies is labour enough for them?[3]" Much before him, Herodotus, observing that the Egyptians in their manners and customs seem to have reversed the ordinary practices of mankind, cities their everyday routine: "Women attend market and are employed in trade, while men stay at home and do the weaving."

It is usual to connect the idea of immortality of soul with the belief in God. The Christians did so, but the primitive Buddhists took no trouble to couple them. The Hindus being similar to Christians in this respect are ready to accept their religion, provided it declares that it is possible to have access to God and by that means to find salvation not only through the intercession of Jesus but others as well. The countless deities of the Hindus, notwithstanding the monotheistic view of the *Upanishads*, got reduced over a period to two, Vishnu and Shiva, both complementary in their function and antithetical in their existence. This happened very long ago, and subsequently in the passage of time the Hindu religion failed to achieve one absolute universal God, who is omnipresent and omnipotent.[4] A failure obvious from the fact that the above polarized Gods, because they lacked jealously to each other, have always shown a capacity to co-exist.

The Hindu religion extended to the Gods of other religion such a principle of co-existence, but they could not be won over by that means as tolerance was not one of their virtues. The Christian and Islamic idea of God was influenced by Jewish Yahweh, an extremely jealous God who would not let a rival exist. Absorbing this exclusive and uncompromising spirit the God of Christianity and of Islam, in the war against polytheistic cults, would settle for nothing less than total victory "because anything less would be, for Him, a denial of His very essence."

In point of aggressiveness and the consequent expansionist tendencies, Hinduism was not on a level with foreign cults mainly because it had never been a missionary religion. It had no church, nor its power was organized on a hierarchical basis in order to exert influence over a demesne. The monarchs of India to satisfy their desire for pomp and glory often took high sounding titles of transcendent power, somewhat like the bombast of the Roman pontiff who once on behalf of the church claimed supremacy over the whole world, but the Hindu priest in his own field never deluded himself with such a claptrap.

The Christian Church hierarchy was built on the model of Roman civil service, with the autocracy of the pope at the top resembling more or less Caesar's power. The word "pope" means papa or father thereby underscoring the patriarchal control of the Church since its inception. The Twelve Apostles who assisted Jesus in his mission were all men, and among them Peter received "the keys of the kingdom of heaven" from Christ himself. Though the date on which the Church at Rome was founded is not clear, according to universally accepted tradition, the Apostle Peter ruled over it when paganism reigned supreme everywhere.

At the spiritual level, there is not much difference between Jesus and Buddha in so far as they thought how to take the people from this world to a futuristic utopia. Hence, Christ's rebuke to Peter when he got enamoured of mundane things: "Away with you, Satan; you are a stumbling-block to me. You think as men think, not as God thinks." Jesus did not wish to establish any sort of earthly power, an equivalent to Cyrus' Persian world-empire, and his Kingdom of God was transcendental in nature. So, having adhered to non-violence, he asked Peter to sheathe the sword he had used to protect one who would rather die on the Cross than win by force.

While Christ stood for separation of the Church from the state, the pope at Rome in the footsteps of Caesars ruled his spiritual and temporal domain with absolute power. A small beginning in this direction was made by St. Gregory, who on the crumbled edifice of the Roman empire founded the Papal Monarchy. True, the Church at first not deviating from Christ preferred spiritual power to physical force; however, in circumstances when the spiritual authority did not produce results, the Church militant succumbed to the temptation to fight the Devil with the opponents own weapon, that is to fight fire with fire regardless of the moral consequences. This backward step was taken by Hildebrand (later Pope Gregory VII) who to make the Papal treasury safe raised an armed force and defeated the brigands.

The threat to the existence of divine institutions was not unique to Europe, and in India the sporadic chaos during the period between the demise of Aurangzeb (1707) and Ranjit Singh (1839) gave a boost to the zeal of warrior ascetics to safeguard religion. Finding that the spiritual sword was ineffective against mercenary rogues, Damodra, a worshipper of Krishna and the chief abbot of the famous Nathdvara temple at Mewar in Rajasthan, made shift to military force to defend the wealth of the temples. He therefore putting aside his sacred duties for a while, and, at the head of a force made up of hundreds of horses besides foot solidiers and two field pieces, galloped around his "extensive diocese" to keep bandits away.[5]

As Hinduism with its distinct features based on caste lacked the monolithic edifice of the Church, the existence of warrior ascetics more extensively than cited above, and their recourse to violence now and then passed for a non-event, in the background of Indian cultural diversity.

Christianity fared otherwise, for having enthroned St. Peter in Caesar's chair; in fact, Hildebrand set the Church on a course "which was to end in the victory of his adversaries—the World, the Flesh and the Devil—over the City of God which he was seeking to bring down to Earth." Hence, the devotion the Church and its prime agent pope once received from the hearts of the people was shifted towards parochial states the idolization of which, similar to the worship of man-made objects denounced by Paul in his speech to the Athenians, was at the expense of God and the solvency of the Church. In spite of this setback, the Roman Catholic Church exists as a divine institution with vast number of hierarchical offices propagating spiritual values.

It is well known that much of Christianity is altered since its origin, so that if Peter could walk into the Vatican he would not recognize the Deity worshipped there; however, amidst the changes one thing transfixed by dogma has remained the same, for eternity: the Church is still a citadel held by men as in the days of old. In justification the dogma puts things in this way: if it is not possible for a man to conceive biologically, likewise it is impossible for a woman to become a priestess theologically. Pope John Paul II sees the work of Providence that women should not be called as apostles, hence as priests. Furthermore, he said the synod had recognized woman's "dignity and vocation as a daughter of God, as a wife, and as a mother," and it had asked that "society be so constituted that women should not be forced to engage in external work." So that "the mother might devote herself fully to the family.[6]"

John Paul's above expressed thought, nevertheless, is not far removed from what Pericles said on the role of women in his funeral orations as it is recorded by classical historian Thucydides: "Perhaps I should say a word or two onw the duties of women to those among you who are now widowed. I can say all I have to say in a short word of advice. Your great glory is not to be inferior to what god has made you, and the greatest glory of a woman is to be least talked about by men, whether they are praising you or criticizing you.[7]"

In fact, "woman was considered in pagan culture to be merely an object of pleasure, of possession and of labour, and in Judaism was subordinated and humiliated." Especially to an Arab, she constituted a sort of wealth on a par with camels and palm trees, and when a man died his son inherited his wife too which meant he disinherited whatever was due to her from the ownership of her dead husband. Further, once an Arab chief desired to possess the prophet's wife Aisha through barter, that is exchange of wives, but Muhammad coldly turned down the audacious proposal as it was against his notion of religion.

Of Muhammad, one favourable view was concerning the loyalty of his followers who stooped to collect his spittle, or even a hair that settled on the ground as if these possessed his spiritual virtues. True, there never was "a king among his subjects like Mohammed among his companions." Not so flattering was another view that illustrates how he was much harassed by the siege of those looking for divine help to redress their grievances, so that he begged them to give him a modicum of peace. Sura 49:2 of the Koran betrays his melancholy situation:

> You who believe! Lift not your voices above the voice of the Prophet, nor shout when speaking to him as you shout one to another.

In the war of the sexes that went on then, Muhammad's hands were constrained mainly because the divine voice enshrined in the Koran upheld the prerogatives of men saying: "women are your tillage, so go to your tillage when you like." Taking the aforesaid verse as licence to indulge in kinky sex, some justified intercourse with women from the reverse side, that is from behind like animals in the field do.[8] The prophet's ennobling ideas of equality and brotherhood so far as women were concerned did not help much in freeing them from the shackles of regressive custom and tradition. For, unlike Jesus, he, a part prophet and part ruler, was compelled by the reality of his situation to balance the higher principles of morality against the practical needs of statecraft.

About Jesus, it is said that moral instruction was the main content and the very essence of all his talks. He was not only a Jewish teacher peregrinating in Judea but a reformer wishing to revolutionize the outlook of mankind. A few Galilean women always accompanied Jesus, and strove with one another for the sweet pleasure of listening to his voice and attending to his needs. Of all the women, Mary Magdalene was deeply attached to the young Rabbi, after he, through the influence of his ethereal beauty, had cured her distempered mind.

Jesus was born to reconcile in his consciousness the antithesis which perplexed the Jewish mind, namely the dichotomy between God and man. Born out of wedlock he was predisposed to ecstasy, that carried him up to the dizzy height of spiritual communion with the Father in heaven. From such ascending dreams he came down to face diurnal sufferings, rendered unbearable by the asperity of his people. He had his share of fame and ill fame that comes with it in the imbalanced society he was destined to live. For, when Jesus spoke in the synagogue of his home town, it so happened that the large congregation which heard him were filled with astonishment and said, "Where does he get it from?" and, "What wisdom is this that has been given him?" and, "How does he work such miracles? Is not this the carpenter, the son of Mary, the brother of James and Joseph and Judas and Simon? And are not his sisters here with us?" Here his spell was broken, and so he fell out of favour with them.

To speak of a man as the son of his father was Jewish custom, and their reference to him as the "son of Mary" was perhaps to undercut his reputation.[9]

About this episode Jesus said: "A prophet will always be held in honour except in his home town, and among his kinsmen and family." So ended tragically Jesus' Galilean preaching, and his being rejected in such a dramatic manner by his townspeople of Nazareth foreshadowed the greater rejection of Israel.

Indeed the use of parabolic method of teaching by Jesus represented a turning away from the people, to whom his speech was intended to be a riddle, so that "seeing they might see and not perceive, and hearing they might hear and not understand." Not this mystification to his twelve disciples, since they were expected to know the truth of the Kingdom of God. Among the names of the twelve apostles, "first Simon, also called Peter", of whom Jesus once said: "You are Peter, the Rock; and on this rock I will build my church, and the forces of death shall never overpower it." And the last Judas Iscariot, the dissembling man who betrayed his master that too after a kiss.

The late-Jewish eschatology sees the Messiah as the supernatural Lord of the heavenly Kingdom of God. It did not perceive him first descending on earth as a Servant in human form; but this idea took birth in the consciousness of Jesus. Hence, at Caesarea Philippi, Jesus, seized with a desire to know what others thought about him, asked his disciples, "who do you say I am?" Peter replied: "You are the Messiah." He was the first to recognize, or at least to acknowledge openly his messiahship, not yet his divinity. Then Jesus prohibited his disciples from revealing who he was; told them that he had to go through much sufferings, and to be rebuffed by the Jewish authorities, to be put to death, and to rise again.

Nobody had ever come forward openly on Palestinian soil to claim the title of Messiah or had been recognized by the people as such. Jesus was sensitive about his messiahship, since he did not want to engender political enthusiasm. Had he made obvious his messianic claim, there would have been such an upheaval that Pontius Pilate, the Roman Procurator of Judea, would have had to use military force.[10] So his messiahship was a secret, and yet no secret as it was known to his disciples besides others.

Not that his disciples understood his messianic ideal, which, being founded on love, on equality, and on human fellowship, was spiritual in nature. They coveted the gains of relationship, and if they had given up anything to follow him, it was only in order to receive it again an hundredfold when they should occupy positions as the friends and ministers of the Messiah. They hoped that he would establish his power in Jerusalem, after overthrowing the existing dispensation.

Hope, that sure comforter of one and all, spurred the two disciples, James and John, to ask Jesus a favour: "Grant us the right to sit in state with you, one at your right and the other at your left." When the other disciples heard this, they were filled with indignation, and observing their spirit of contention Jesus said, "You know that in the world the recognized rulers lord it over their subjects, and their great men make them feel the weight of authority. That is not the way with you; among you, whoever wants to be great must be your servant, and whoever wants to be first must be the willing slave of all. For even the Son of Man did not come to be served but to serve, and to surrender his life as a ransom for many."

Jesus made his triumphal entry into Jerusalem, riding upon an ass, which symbolized a non-political messiahship. The crowd was puzzled, but penetrated his meaning sufficiently to realize that he was not the Messiah of their hopes. Many spread their garments on the road; others plucked down branches from the trees and strewed them in the way, while those that went before and those that followed after, cried "Hosanna!" Then he went into the temple, and began driving out those who bought and sold in the precincts of the sacred ground. Whereas the temple was a "house of prayer for all the nations," he said, "you have made it a robbers' cave."

Born out of indignation, as a result of the intolerable living conditions of the people, the pessimism of Jesus is not metaphysical.[11] It cannot be related to the speculative pessimism of the Indian philosopher Buddha.

The purification of the temple by Jesus, exercising his authority as the Messiah, was a challenge to the Jewish ruling oligarchy, especially to Caiaphas, the incumbent High Priest. The rulers, "sought some means of making away with him; for they were afraid of him, because the whole crowd was spellbound by his teaching." Before that, some people inimical to him came to trap him with a question, and they asked: "Are we or are we not permitted to pay taxes to the Roman Emperor? Shall we pay or not?" Jesus saw through their cunningness, and replied, "Pay Caesar what is due to Caesar, and pay God what is due to God."

As the final conflict was drawing near, Jesus at Bethany met a woman carrying a bottle of costly perfumed oil, which she poured over his head. Looking at this, some exclaimed in anger, "Why this waste? The perfume might have been sold for thirty pounds and the money given to the poor." And they turned upon her with fury. But Jesus intervened, and spoke these prophetic and imperishable words: "Why must you make trouble for her? It is a fine thing she has done for me. You have the poor among you always, and you can help them whenever you like; but you will not always have me. She has done what lay in her power; she is beforehand with anointing my body for burial."

It is probable that Jesus had a prevision of his death. Among the New Testament Jews, it almost seems none had ever thought of a suffering or dying Messiah. But the explicit utterance which the Synoptists impute to Jesus describing his death as an atoning sacrifice, might well be stuff interpolated after the event.[12] The Last Supper too, considered as a historical scene, is an interpolation of early Christianity. Giving thanks during supper, Jesus gave bread to his disciples, with the words: "Take this; this is my body." Then he gave a cup to them, and they all drank from it; afterwards he said, "This is my blood of the covenant, shed for many."

Such a abominable scene is revolting and inconceivable. "To demand from others that they should, while he was actually present, imagine the bread and wine which they were eating to be his body and blood, would be for an actual man wholly impossible. It was only when Jesus' actual bodily presence had been removed, and only when the Christian community had existed for some time, that such a conception as is expressed in that formula could have arisen."[13]

At the supper Jesus said, "I tell you this: one of you will betray me—one who is eating with me." Hearing such words the disciples were dismayed, and they said one by one to him, "Not I, surely?" Jesus answered: "It is one of the Twelve who is dipping into the same bowl with me." Then, to bolster his master's confidence, Peter said, "Everyone else may fall away, but I will not."

Apart from betrayal, what Jesus might have apprehended was "an attack by hired assassins." And it is to this he refers in his talk with his disciples concerning the two swords, which would have provided enough security against such an attack, and which were in their possession. It is to the advantage of Jesus, as well as his followers, that he should be officially arrested and put on trial by the Sanhedrin, the Jewish council, under the shadow of the Roman power.

This episode in the life of Jesus came about in the following way. While he was engrossed with talking to his disciples about his inevitable destiny, Judas, one of the Twelve, at the head of a mob armed with swords and cudgels descended on him.

Judas Iscariot, having become a disciple of Jesus at twenty-five, had black hair, sported a red beard and on the whole could not be labelled ugly. His mother had been a dancer, and his father was a military tribune, and he was born to unwed sexual partners. After squandering all his wealth, he stumbled into the fraternity of Jesus, with which to ingratiate himself he was useful on all occasions and he even did the menial work of cleaning the shoes.

Now, in conformity with a prearranged signal, he kissed Jesus, thereby exposing his identity in the darkness. In the sequel, they seized him and held him fast, seeing which act of outrage Simon Peter drew the sword he was wearing and cut off the right ear of the High Priest's servant. Jesus to pacify raised temper said to Peter, "Sheathe your sword. This is the cup my Father has given me; shall I not drink it?" The sequel to this high handed act against Jesus was the desertion of the disciples, who had stood by him till now. Indeed one follower had nothing on him but a linen cloth, and when they tried to seize him "he slipped out of the linen cloth and ran away naked."

Jesus was led by night to "the high priest" Annas, who, though not "the high priest of that year," had once been such and kept the title. In the trial that followed, the Jewish ruling class first tried to secure his death on flimsy grounds, but met with a check owing to lack of agreement between witnesses. Nevertheless, Jesus was condemned to death because two of his disciples gave utterance to his innermost thoughts: Peter when he made known the secret of his messiahship to the other disciples at Caesarea Philippi; Judas Iscariot by telling it to the High Priest. It is the betrayal of this secrecy by Judas that contributed to the arrest of Jesus and later his death. The Gospel of Mark is explicit on this point. "Then Judas Iscariot, one of the Twelve, went to the chief priests in order to betray him to them. And when they heard it they were glad, and promised to give him money. And he sought an opportunity to betray him."

At the trial, since he was the sole witness, Judas was not of much use to the High Priest, who made good this weakness by extracting a confession from Jesus himself with this million dollar question: "Are you the Messiah, the Son of the Blessed One?" Jesus said, "I am" reinforcing what he told with an allusion to his Parousia, upon which the High Priest cried blasphemy, and the Jewish council decided on his death.

For carrying out this decision the Jews approached Pontius Pilate, the Roman governor, and handed over the prisoner to him. Here, no charge of blasphemy was levelled at him, but the interrogation had an overtone of political sedition, which very much concerned the governor. "Are you the king of the Jews?." Pilate asked him. Jesus replied, "The words are yours." And he made no further reply though many charges were brought against him. It so happened that a certain Barabbas was in custody, and since it was the custom of the governor to release a prisoner on a festival day to humour the people, a crowd was at hand to make the solicitation. Pilate desired to play off the people against the priests, by releasing Jesus. But the fickle Jerusalem mob turned against Jesus, and asked for the freedom of Barabbas owing to the machinations of the priests. When Pilate asked what he should do with Jesus, the assembled shouted, "Crucify him!"

This type of capital punishment having originated in Persia, the Romans, since the Punic Wars, used against the slaves and non-Jews. It was the most cruel and repulsive punishment, as it prolongs the death agony. Upon the cross, which became a symbol of Christian inspiration for centuries to come, Jesus cried aloud, "My God, my God, why hast thou forsaken me?"

He died in the reign of Tiberius Caesar, and was believed to have risen again. It is known that in Judea interment took place three hours after death, so that many seemingly dead people who were in a coma might have returned to consciousness in their graves, and then died horribly. Hence, the view is put forward that the resurrection of Jesus, in fact, was deliverance from premature burial when he was in a coma.

After Jesus was brought down from the cross, Joseph of Arimathea, a member of the Essene Order, removed him to a tomb and then resuscitated him. Peter, on that night of terror, having fled from Jerusalem to Galilee, Jesus went before him. He manifested before Thomas, one of the Twelve, who was allowed to put his hands into the marks of his nail wounds. "Now," Jesus says, "thou, Thomas, art convinced because thou hast so unmistakably seen me. It is well for those who now or in the future shall not see Me; for after this they can feel a firm conviction, because thou hast convinced thyself so completely that to thee, whose hands have touched me, no possible doubt can remain of My corporeal reanimation."[14]

Consequently, "for a Jew crucified under Pontius Pilate there was certainly no resurrection." But still the death and resurrection of Jesus represent experiences of the then embryonic Christian community.

The worship offered to Jesus after his death by the Christians is derived from a Judaism influenced by oriental religions, especially the cult of Mithra. Had it not been for the human sacrifice of the Mithra cult, the fundamental idea of the Last Supper, obvious in the ritual practice of eating and drinking the flesh and blood of Jesus, could not be explained.

The followers of Christ fed themselves with the pleasing but misbegotten thought, that his reign on earth was imminent. The reigning sentiment of the orthodox believers of Christ was rooted in the Millennium, a doctrine well calculated to bolster the hopes and quieten the fears of mankind living in the so-called crooked age. An age whose social anomalies were highlighted in one of the Pauline epistles: "You must face the fact: the final age of this world is to be a time of troubles. Men will love nothing but money and self; they will be arrogant, boastful, and abusive; with no respect for parents, no gratitude, no piety, no natural affection; they will be implacable in their hatreds, scandalmongers, intemperate and fierce, strangers to all goodness, traitors, adventurers, swollen with self-importance. They will be men who put pleasure in the place of God, men who preserve the outward form of religion, but are a standing denial of its reality.

This description fits well the evils of kaliyuga, which according to the Hindus reflects the degeneration of the present age in comparison with the idyllic conditions of bygone times. To escape from such ever present miseries, the followers of Christ looked towards the future, perpetually waiting to see the arrival of the Kingdom of God. Gandhi's escape route, however, took him to the past, and his thoughts settled in the epoch of god king Rama, whose utopian state energized him to fight against the contemporary ills.

But after winning over adherents and building the edifice of Christianity on the strength of the coming new age, the doctrine of Christ's reign on earth was cast aside as heresy. Consequently, the two indisputable facts relating to Christianity were non-occurrence of the Parousia, and the abandonment of eschatology.

True, that Jesus could not set up an earthly kingdom of God, through a metamorphosis, but he had established the Christian community which aimed at bringing in a change. His followers worked in a favourable background; for, in the epoch of Christ's birth, there existed in everyone's mind uncertainty about his origin, uncertainty about his final destiny, and in his heart a ceaseless struggle between his ideal self and the counter-cravings of his lower self. In consequence, there was spiritual fervour, a thirst for religious enlightenment, in order to escape from the routine of existence. The spiritual thing Jesus begot was expected to answer his doubts, settle his anxieties, and take him to a higher level than the existing culture of the Graeco-Roman world.

From very early times the Christian community was aware that the gospel had universal application, and that Jesus had the potential to expand into the God of the universe.

At first, what prevented a movement in that direction was the power of the Roman state, and no matter "how an apologist like Justin might point to Heraclitus, Socrates, and Musonius Rufus as pre-Christian Christians," there was no improvement in church-state relations.[15] As the ties of the Christian movement with Judaism gradually weakened, it looked for some kind of understanding with the Graeco-Roman culture embodied in the pagan society, but the state perceiving it as foreign superstition turned against it.

The Roman Emperor absorbed in his own self all the powers of the state; he was besides the supreme pontiff, receiving homage from his subjects as the personification of god. The Christians, on the other hand, professed a belief that could not coexist with any other cult, thereby exasperating the rulers of a state where "a thousand forms of religion" lived in amity.

The Jews at least deserved some mercy and got it at the hands of the state, because they were a nation, and were pursuing the religion of their forefathers from generation to generation regardless of the antipathy of others. But the Christians were a sect, which had abandoned the religion of their fathers; consequently, to the state they were no better than apostates, or rather atheists, meriting severest punishment.

The Homeric gods struggled only for ascendancy, not unlike men enamoured of power, but the Christian faith gave birth to the one true God who would not live with other gods and their images, and in fact was the terminator of their existence. The Jews having initially entertained the aversion to visual representation of god, the primitive Christians with their Jewish pedigree could not help inheriting this intellectual trait, as well as their uncompromising attitude in reference to it. The Christian apologists, in order to make the way clear for Christ's doctrine, pointed the finger at the stupid idolators, who bowed to the images of brass and marble produced by their own hands.

Neither Socrates before them nor Gandhi afterwards had any objection against bowing to the images of deities, although their views on God were intellectual as well as abstract. The few in all ages were wise enough to know that it was impossible to define "by forms and colours the infinite Spirit, the eternal Father, who pervades and sustains the universe." But the ordinary people especially the superstitious minds, with limited intellectual horizon, were more easily reconciled to see in human shape their venerated gods.

But now the tide had turned against them. The apostle Paul, charged with the task of upholding the divinity of Christ Jesus, was vehement in his attack on the pagan gods and their images, obvious from his address to the Romans: "For all that may be known of God by men lies plain before their eyes; indeed God himself has disclosed it to them. His invisible attributes, that is to say his everlasting power and deity, have been visible, ever since the world began, to the eye of reason, in the things he has made. There is therefore no possible defence for their conduct; knowing God, they have refused to honour him as God, or to render him thanks. Hence all their thinking has ended in futility, and their misguided minds are plunged in darkness. They boast of their wisdom, but they have made fools of themselves, exchanging the splendour of immortal God for an image shaped like mortal man, even for images like birds, beasts, and creeping things."

Paul, a Roman citizen, known also by his Jewish name Saul, was not the founder of the Christian movement, but joined it after missionary work aimed at conversion had started.[16] He did not see Jesus in his earthly ministry, nor could it be thought that Paul was given a cinematic view of that ministry at the time of his conversion. His credentials obviously did not inspire confidence, so the charge was made against him that he was not a real apostle, and that he was preaching a diluted version of the gospel. He therefore took pains to stress the divine origin of his undelegated apostolic commission. For Paul originally had been a despicable character, persecuting the Christians as nobody else did, but once on the road to Damascus he experienced a visionary encounter with Jesus. In the sequel, the revelation of Jesus inspired the theology of Paul, and made him an apostle as well as a zealous missionary destined to change the face of Christianity.

As Paul, the great evangelist, made his journey across the Aegean Sea sprinkled with fish haunted islands and into the seaboard towns on the mainland close by, an area divided as East and West on the basis of geography, but united on the strength of the ruling pagan culture, he met with success but there was opposition and persecution as well. His mission was to take the people, away from their attachment to non-existent gods, the mute and lifeless idols of paganism, and to the real and living God of the Christians.

He was in Athens, which about this time had lost its fame as the center of Hellenic culture, but it was the same idol-ridden city of bygone times, exciting in the sequel the missionary ardour of Paul. The Athenians, however, spoke of him disparagingly; some thought he was on a mission to promote foreign gods, while others looking at him as a smooth-tongued gossip said, "what would this babbler say?," in expectation of receiving some newfangled ideas from him. As their curiosity got the better of their skepticism, they let him speak in the assembly. Here, Paul made known his faith in one God, but when he came to the well-known theme of "resurrection of the dead" their patience expired. Some scoffed at him, but others politely saying, "We will hear you on this subject some other time," abruptly put an end to his talking.

The next scene of Paul's crusade against idolatry and the diverse gods it represented was at Ephesus, a city in Asia Minor famous for its temple of Artemis, one of the seven wonders of the ancient world. Here one Demetrius, a silversmith, perceiving the danger to his trade from Paul's rejection of idols, explained to the other craftsmen, "how this fellow Paul with his propaganda has perverted crowds of people, not only at Ephesus but also in practically the whole of the province of Asia. He is telling them that gods made by human hands are not gods at all."

He incited them to riot, so that the whole city was in a uproar, till the town clerk quietened the boisterous mob, after telling how the law could be used against the Christians, if they were really at fault.

Soon Paul leaves Ephesus hurriedly, but the setback he met with here did not weaken his spirit, and it was mainly owing to him that Christianity made rapid progress in the lands of pagan culture. How he died remains a mystery, and he was probably killed in Rome during the reign of maverick emperor Nero Caesar, who, after a fire devastated Rome, made a scapegoat of the Christians and executed a lot of them, in eccentric ways, which agreed with his capricious life.

The era of persecution for the Christians came to an end, when Constantine the Great ascended the throne; at first, he was the protector rather than the proselyte of Christianity, to which he was initiated by the hands of a heretic on his death bed. His pro-Christian tilt to be thought a shrewd policy; for, the Christian movement from its small beginnings in Palestine had penetrated the vast network of countries that represented the then Roman world, providing in consequence the unifying force at the moral level which the empire otherwise lacked.

The Edict of Milan of Constantine, and his co-emperor of the East Licinius, symbolized the great charter of toleration, by which an individual of the Roman world had the right to choose his religion.[17] At this hour of triumph, the Church was torn by religious factions, and the hate of the Christians to each other surpassed their enmity towards the pagan gods. The casualty of this discord over theological issues, too abstract for the emperor with a soldier's background to penetrate, was his policy of toleration, since it was denied to those who differed from his views of the official Church.

Looking at the kingdom of heaven reduced to chaos by contending parties, Constantine, ever solicitous for the peace of his realm, bemoaned that the Christians, "who had the same God, the same religion, and the same worship," should be divided on matters of little weight. This was a moment for him, besides the clergy, to reflect on the example of Greek philosophers who knew how to argue without losing temper, and how to maintain freedom of speech without endangering friendship. But the advantage of temperance was lost on the clergy, no less on Constantine himself, who after imbibing the heat of controversy was so much unsettled as to resort to harsh measures against the dissenters.

On the whole, the first of the Christian emperors, still uninitiated to the new religion, unacquainted with the Greek language, unsophisticated to know the metaphysical language of the faith, and consequently, "unskilled in the stratagems of theological warfare," was unequal to combat Christian heretics, whom he never understood at their face value.

He thought that the glory of this reign was the general council of the whole Christian world, held in 325 at Nicea, under his presiding authority, though he was not yet a genuine Christian. The sequel to Nicea "was a half-century of ecclesiastical anarchy from which Eastern Catholicism never really recovered, and the establishment of imperial interference in ecclesiastical affairs as a permanent part of the Christian tradition."[18]

Though Constantine was partial to Christianity, he did not openly suppress paganism. He thought he was a model to his subjects, but those who refused to follow his path of enlightenment were allowed to enjoy their temples and fancied gods.[19] Such a policy was guided by a desire not to alarm the followers of polytheism; but this was cold comfort to them, because in the guise of reforming the old religion he aimed at its ruin. The opulent temples of Greece and Asia were sacked, and to some extent the treasure so obtained went to build the city of

Constantinople. The images of gods having lost their potency got no better treatment, and they were moved from place to place like merchandise.

The destruction of pagan temples not only continued but celebrated as auspicious events, by the successors of Constantine, or rather his sons; one among them, Constantius II, issued this edict: "It is our pleasure that in all places, and in all cities, the temples be immediately shut and carefully guarded, that none may have the power of offending. It is likewise our pleasure that all our subjects should abstain from sacrifices. If any one should be guilty of such an act, let him feel the sword of vengeance, and, after his execution, let his property be confiscated to the public use. We denounce the same penalties against the governors of the provinces, if they neglect to punish the criminals."[20]

But the English historian Edward Gibbon confidently asserts that "this formidable edict was either composed without being published, or was published without being executed." It is obvious that wherever pagans were numerically strong and influential, these laws having remained defunct, the temples opened to receive the customary worship of the devotees. Indeed Constantius himself, curbing his reformist zeal, visited the old temples of Rome, and the Senate consecrated the memory of his predecessor, Constantine, by associating his name with those gods whom he had rejected and insulted during his reign. The ancient gods still held their ground, and it was only by a slow process Christianity displaced them.

The successor of Constantius II is generally known as Julian the Apostate; while persecuting the Christians, he tried to revive paganism by opening the temples everywhere, but his restoration work was aborted when he was killed in battle. Subsequently, the gods of yore who had embellished the airy world of pagan imagination were doomed to extinction, as the reign of Theodosius the Great (379-395) saw the culmination of anti-pagan movement, with the Senate at Rome voting for the abolition of pagan cults. Theodosius was the first truly Christian emperor, and his empire was Christian as well.

It is natural to suppose that the triumph of Christianity was also the triumph of anti-image movement, the root cause of all the hubbub and ill-blood in the religious world of the past. But this was not so, and the image worship was destined to return, which certainly, represented the victory of superstition over reason, in conformity with the views of early Christians. The very destruction of pagan image worship, by removing any sort of invidious comparison with it, facilitated the move towards Christian image worship for the benefit of superstitious masses. The symbolic worship first came into vogue in the veneration of the cross and of relics. The saints and martyrs had the rank of demigods, and the devotion, as well as the innate prejudice, of pilgrims expressed itself by visiting, touching and kissing their tomb. A more fitting memorial to the departed was a copy of his features, delineated by an artist, and before long people prayed in front of the image of a Christian saint, while the Catholic church made use of the pagan rites of genuflexion, incense, and luminaries, all of which besides those ceremonies devised to inspire awe in beholders. It was imperative that Christ should not lag behind saints in regard to veneration shown to image worship, lest his memory might be obliterated, and his place in the church usurped by others; however, the early Christians did not know the true features of Christ, his mother and the apostles. This obstacle the Christian artists got over, after having recourse to their imagination, which was aided by some heathen model.

Before the end of the sixth century, the use and even the worship of images was firmly established in Christianity. "The Olympian Jove," Gibbon says, "created by the muse of Homer and the chisel of Phidias, might inspire a philosophic mind with momentary devotion; but these Catholic images were faintly and flatly delineated by monkish artists in the last degeneracy of taste and genius."

About two centuries later, some pusillanimous Greeks realized to their consternation that, under the guise of Christianity, they had brought back their forefather's pagan religion. Much to their grief, they were targeted as idolators, by the Jews and Muslims, who inveterately hated graven images and all relative worship. Well, the taunt of the Jews did not count much as the weight of alien tyranny had broken their spirit; but the conquering Muslims, invigorated by their new religion Islam, stood on a different level. Against their invading forces, the cities of Palestine, Syria and Egypt had been fortified with the images of Christ, his mother, and his saints, but to no avail.

The fight for one God, and against the images, was taken up with new vigour by the Muslims, the adherents of a new prophet, Muhammad.

The word Islam means "submission," and this religion owes its birth to prophet Muhammad, who at one time was seen as anti-Christ, though the reality is different. In fact, Muhammad was humble enough to acknowledge that he was the last of the six prophets, and that Jesus Christ who preceded him was one among them. The revelations of God, or rather Allah, made to Muhammad are enshrined in the book Koran, which in Sura 5:82 says: "Certainly, you will find the most violent people in enmity to the believers are the Jews and the polytheists, and the nearest in friendship to the believers are those who say, We are Christians."

Expatiating upon the perennial theme of God's compassion and mercy, Koranic Sura 2:59 says, "Believers, Jews, Christians, and Sabians – whosoever believes in God and the Last Day and does what is right – they shall have their reward with their Lord, they have nothing to be afraid of and shall not be grieved." This reflects the tolerance of Muhammad, above many of his followers, who in conformity with tradition aver that the above mentioned Sura is set aside by another, 3:85, which gives out: "And whoever chooses a religion other than Islam, it will not be accepted from him, and in the future world he will be one of the lost."

However, "those who repent after that and amend, then surely Allah is Forgiving, Merciful."

The non-Muslim is known to the believers of Islam as an infidel; but it is not right to say, without scriptural authority, that a person born in pre-Islamic times is an infidel. True, the Koran does not mention of Krishna and Rama, whom the Hindus see as the incarnation of God, or avatar, which in the language of tradition may be read as messenger, prophet, or saint.

The following Sura 40:78 endorses the belief in the existence of many prophets before Muhammad: "And certainly We sent apostles before you: there are some of them that We have mentioned to you and there are others whom We have not mentioned to you." It is evident from Koran that no community was deprived of prophetic guidance, and prophets were also sent to India.

Until the mission of prophet Muhammad, it was incumbent on the Indians to follow their prophets, and the pejorative term "infidel" could not be imputed to them, in the absence of scriptural evidence.

But, according to the views of Muslim scholars in the heyday of Islamic culture in India, the advent of prophet Muhammad changed everything. All former religions were rendered inoperative, and though Islamic tradition mentions only Judaism and Christianity, the doctrine of abrogation has much wider application.[21]

Consequently, the fact that India in bygone times had its prophets does not extenuate the guilt of those Hindus who have lived since the coming of Islam.[22] The orthodox view is that these "infidels" are culpable for their failure to embrace Islam. Even a Hindu monotheist is an infidel, if he does not acknowledge the prophethood of Muhammad.

Arabia before Muḥammad was a land of polytheists, and a very sacred city in it was Mecca, which from the surrounding areas attracted pilgrims. It is certain that the pagan Arabs of Mecca knew Allah as the supreme being; besides, there existed female deities: Al-Lat, al-Uzza, and Manat, which symbolized the Sun, the planet Venus, and Fortune, respectively. While Allah means "the god," Al-Lat means "the goddess," or rather the mother goddess, originating in so remote times that Herodotus mentions of her.

Idols made by hand were probably imported from nearby countries to Arabia. The ancient Arabian idols, according to one Islamic tradition, came from India where idolatry originally flourished.[23] In pre-Islamic times, it is said that the Brahmins of India in order to show their devotion to idols were accustomed to making a long journey to Mecca, and its famous sanctuary Kaaba they thought the best place of worship.

The Kaaba was a temple of black stones which had for its corner-stone a meteorite, but heathenism of Arabia had elevated it to a god. Later, thanks to the progress of Christianity, the inner walls of the Kaaba were embellished with the painted images of Christ and the Virgin Mary; when Mecca fell to Muhammad, he got all the paintings erased, except the Virgin Mary and Child.[24]

Not much is known about the ceremonial practices of the pagan Arabs; however, certain long enduring beliefs at variance with monotheism persist to this day. Some trees supposedly inhabited by a deity were venerated as sacred, and neither Judaism, nor Christianity, nor Islam was successful in eliminating completely such a belief. Furthermore, it is an age-old custom to honour god by a kiss, or by running the hand over the rock or the stone, in order to absorb holiness by contact. About kissing of the black stone embedded in a wall of the Kaaba, Caliph Omar according to a tradition once said, "Had I not seen the Prophet kiss you, I would not kiss you myself."

Islam, the religion Muhammad established, was a simple creed made up of things borrowed from Judaism, and, to a less extent, from the heresies of the Monophysite Christians of Arabia.[25] There is only one God, and Muhammad is his prophet; the revelations of God to him form the basis of a set of performances and prohibitions imposed on the believers, thereby distinguishing them from the unbelievers. The faithful was not loaded with vexatious and perplexing theories about the nature of God, and all his energy was directed towards his duty to propagate his religion, as well as to wage a holy war aimed at the destruction of the unbelievers. The Koran exhorts him thus: "Fight those who do not believe in Allah and the Last Day, and do not prohibit what God and his apostle have prohibited, and do not follow the true religion of those to whom scriptures were given, until they being brought low pay the tax. The Jews say Ezra is the son of God, while the Christians say Christ is the son of God. That is what they say with their mouths, imitating the speech of those who disbelieved before. May God destroy them, how perverse they are!"[26]

The above passage downgrades the Jews and Christians for being polytheists. Of course, Judaism and Islam have much in common in so far as they put faith in monotheism, prophetic revelation, the religion of the Book, and a radical eschatology. Muhammad, who at first prayed with his face towards Jerusalem, had thought well of the Jews, and "happy would it have been for their temporal interest had they recognized in the Arabian prophet the hope of Israel and the promised Messiah." The Jews were somewhat flattered, when Muhammad elevated Abraham and Moses to the rank of prophets, but the same honour extended to Jesus nettled them. Above all, they rejected Muhammad's claim to be an apostle sent by God, in the sequel, arousing his implacable hatred.

The offence of the Christians was their doctrine of trinity. The title "Mother of God" accorded to the Virgin Mary was perceived by the Arabs as the sexual trinity of the pagan world, in opposition to the unity. The Koran is clear on this point: "And say not, Three. Desist, it is better for you; Allah is only one God: far be it from His glory that He should have a son."

The Jews and the Christians with so much common between them, but having differed on what is true religion, hated each other. Muhammad hated both, thinking that they had deviated from the revelations of God. The Koran went a step further in binding them together against their common enemy, in the following verse: "O you who believe! do not take the Jews and the Christians for friends; they are friends of each other; and whoever amongst you takes them for a friend, then surely he is one of them; surely God does not guide the unjust people."[27]

By connecting Islam with the Jew Abraham, whom the Koran calls Ibrahim, and by ascribing to him the honour of building the Kaaba, Muhammad in one stroke was able to establish the respectable pedigree of his religion; of this man, the Koran sings in laudatory terms: "Abraham was not a Jew nor a Christian but he was an upright Muslim, and he was not one of the polytheists."

The Koran closely follows Jewish and Christian thought in respect of the day of reckoning, or rather the Judgement Day. Such a momentous event will happen so suddenly as in the twinkling of an eye, with absolutely no margin of time on hand "to make a bequest." The trumpet will sound, the graves will disgorge the dead, and all will stand before God to be judged on their merits. Obviously, the unbelievers, as well as the hypocrites, have more to fear on this day of chastisement, since they did not repose faith in the God Muhammad had espoused.

While distributing the opposite sensations of pleasure and pain, one to the faithful, and the other to the unfaithful, respectively, Muhammad has painted a colourful picture of heaven and hell, contrived to move the imagination of, and to bring into line, his people, otherwise prone to intramural strife. Hell is the common lot of the infidels, and their punishment will be commensurate with their errors. The habitations of the Jews, the Christians, the Sabians, the Magians, and the idolators are sunk below each other in the abyss, "and the lowest hell is reserved for the faithless hypocrites who have assumed the mask of religion."[28]

The believers, however, in the footsteps of Muhammad will enter paradise, whose peculiar virtue being that there is neither toil nor fatigue; besides, its inhabitants can adorn themselves with costumes and ornaments fit for royalty. Further, its door is not barred to the opposite sex, but Muhammad is tight-lipped about their male consorts, "lest he should either alarm the jealousy of their former husbands, or disturb their felicity by the suspicion of an everlasting marriage."

It is right to recall how Jesus confronted with a similar perplexity got over it by an apt reply to his critics: "At the resurrection men and women do not marry, but are like angels in heaven."

Not so the prophet's heaven, synonymous with shady groves, silken robes, rich wines, artificial dainties, marble palaces, numerous attendants, blooming youths, flowing rivers, and black-eyed girls, amidst which men with their wives "reclining on raised couches" abandon themselves to every kind of carnal delights. It does not appear, however, that Muhammad gave himself over to sensuous enjoyments; "on the contrary, his personal habits were very simple, and he described this heaven of earthly delights during that happy period when his love for Kadija was one of the stays of his life."[29]

Muhammad, the son of Abdullah, was born in A.D. 570 at Mecca and had blood ties with Medina, a city about 280 miles to the north of his home town. His father was dead at his birth, his mother too passed away when he was young, so that he was put under the care of a surrogate mother. He was brought up by his grandfather, a kindhearted man who died a pagan, and then by his uncle Abu Talib. Their help was a source of comfort to Muhammad, who belonged to an indigent family, and he was sensitive to distress brought about by his straitened circumstances his soliloquy extracted from the Koran makes obvious:

> Did He not find you an orphan and give you a home?
> Did He not find you in want and free you from it?[30]

Facts about Muhammad's early life are scanty, but it seems he was influenced by a monotheist, who censured his idolatry and turned him against idol worship. Whether this is true or not, it is certain that the young impressionable mind of Muhammad was exposed to the influence of Jewish and Christian ideas concerning the deity. Meanwhile, the turning point of his life came, when, at the age of twenty-five, his employer Khadija, a prosperous widow much older than him, fell for him and then married him. Now, the husband of a rich wife, he got security he had longed for, but until the age of forty when he took up his prophetic mission, he languished in obscurity, with his life having no focus.

Muhammad from this marriage begot two sons and four daughters; of all the daughters, Fatima was dearest to the memory of Muhammad; she ranks above others on one more count: she married the cousin of the prophet, Ali, and the progenies of this union are looked upon by a group as the true heirs to the Caliphate, thereby polarizing Islam.

Islam encourages polygamy by letting a believer marry as many as four wives, but in reality this licence to hunt prospective bridgs is almost cancelled by a Koranic (Sura 4:3) verse:

> If you are afraid that you shall not do justice among them then marry only one.

The sexual urge of the Arabs, however, is intensified by the heat of the climate, and early writers have observed their libidinous complexion. True, the humane ordinances of Koran to some extent cushion the sexual despotism of an Arab over his petty domain of wives, which in the past was replenished with captive women treated as war booty. The affluent are warned that on the Last Day their power and wealth is of no consequence, and they will be questioned why they did not help the orphans and the poor.

Furthermore, an Islamic marriage cannot be solemnized without the groom agreeing to give the bride a piece of property, known as *mehr*, which in its true sense is more than dowry as it is commonly understood.[31] It is the exclusive right of the wife, and wife alone, and nobody else is allowed to put a finger in that pie.

In consequence of marriage she becomes a woman of property; hence the practice of giving dowry, instituted in Islam from a realistic point of view to support her in the event of marital discord, helps the larger interest of liberating women.

Not only women are segregated, and screened from inquisitive eyes but love marriage is discouraged, on the ground that love must bloom as a result of marriage, and should not be a pre-nuptial manoeuvring of both sides to hit the right mate.

Muhammad had so great a passion for women, that he indulged his desire for sex without restraint, and since he was a prophet, "a special revelation dispensed him from the laws which he had imposed on his nation." Well, if the prophet is no ordinary mortal, his wives too are cut above the usual type of women, a fact made obvious by Koran:

> O wives of the Prophet! You are not like any other women.
>
> And stay in your houses and do not show your finery like the displaying of ignorance in bygone times.[32]

According to Islamic law, the husband at any time may divorce his wife, not vice versa even if he beats her. Further, the husband cannot take back his divorced wife until she marries a second husband who in turn divorces her. About the wives of the prophet, his threat of divorce was enough to give them the shivers, because they were forever excluded from the hope of another marriage after having once shared the bed with him.

Notwithstanding the egalitarianism of Islam, Sura 4:31 firmly establishes the superiority of men over women by saying: "Men are in charge of women because God has made the one superior to the other and because they spend their wealth (to maintain them). So good women are obedient, guarding the unseen (parts) because God has guarded (them). As for those from whom you fear rebellion admonish them and banish them to beds apart and beat them; then if they obey you seek not occasion against them."

Celibacy, the treasured virtue of Gandhi, is no virtue in Islam. The prophet Muhammad is believed to have said that marriage makes a full man, and that one must marry when the occasion for it is favourable.[33]

Though polygamy is said to be preferable to the kind of prostitution existing in the west, the ideal of Islamic society is neither polygamy nor monogamy, but justice. Besides regulating the sexual energy of Muslims, justice in Islam aims at providing the felicity of marriage to such women who would otherwise remain unattached. The Koran (Sura 2: 187) extols the joys of wedded life in the following verse:

> It is made lawful to you to go into your wives on the night of the fast: they are an apparel for you and you are an apparel for them.

While adultery looked upon as evil invites capital punishment, fornication, in both sexes, is chastised with a hundred lashes. But incestuous alliances, of course not deserving similar penalty, were not discouraged.

In one respect a Muslim woman can hold her head high, as she cannot be forced into a polygamous relationship, and her right to say "no" to such an existence that belittles her as one among the many women is accepted.

Muhammad's sexual peccadilloes notwithstanding, which never occasioned a scandal, he was venerated among his devout Muslims, and despite his rank he had only about fifteen wives to attend on him. "If we remember the seven hundred wives and three hundred concubines of the wise Solomon," Gibbon says, "we shall applaud the modesty" of the prophet. Moreover, except for the young and beautiful Aisha, the daughter of his trusted ally Abu Bakr, the rest of his married partners were widows.

Aisha, because Muhammad doted upon her, had an ascendant influence, and later was revered as the mother of the faithful. Once by her indiscretion she occasioned to Muhammad heartburning; she during a night march became lost to her guardians, and presented herself in the morning in the company of a man. It is well known that Arabs jealously guard their wives, and concerning the prophet, the believers were told not to enter his houses without permission. So her getting lost aroused suspicion, and Muhammad, being too fond of her to give her up, got convinced of her innocence after divine revelation, with the result he published a law which effectively sealed the lips of scandalmongers. Accordingly, no woman should be condemned unless four male witnesses had surprised her in the act of adultery. The Koran (Sura 24) makes clear the punishment for perjury:

> And those who accuse free women then do not bring four witnesses, flog them, (giving) eighty stripes, and do not admit any evidence from them ever; and these it is that are the transgressors.
>
> Why did they not bring four witnesses of it? But as they have not brought witnesses they are liars before God.

Whether wives, or concubines, or women of a different kind, Muhammad's dalliance with them might look remarkable in a prophet, but the religion he founded did not come in the way of such pleasures. Even for a prophet, however, everything in relation to women was not always pure delight. Once his wife, Hafna, the daughter of Omar, caught him that too on her own bed, while he was embracing his Egyptian captive; in the sequel, a divine revelation let him do what he desired regardless of the tantrums of his wives. In the sale of captives, Muhammad had a soft heart for children, so that he forbade their separation from their mothers. When his own baby son died, his little Ibrahim born to Mary his Egyptian mistress, the prophet overwhelmed by passionate grief wept over his grave, and levelled the earth above it with his own hands.

Such a kind heart in Muhammad, not only a prophet but also a conqueror, is praiseworthy; more so when he, abjuring the right of polygamy, was completely loyal to his wife Khadija for about twenty-four years of their wedded life.

His love for her even after her death did not subside, despite his preoccupation with exotic women, and he had elevated her memory to a spiritual level became obvious from his talk with his wife Aisha, who harboured such haughty pride that was natural to her blooming beauty.

Aisha: Was she not old? Has not God given you a better in her place? Muhammad: No, by God, there never can be a better! She believed in me when men despised me; she relieved my wants when I was poor and persecuted by the world.[34]

True. Khadija was a faithful wife, believed in his words, and cherished the glory of Muhammad, when he was without followers, yet a prophet, endowed with a pious and contemplative mind. Till the age of forty he had lived minus fame, and would have died so, had not unity of God and had not the desire to rescue his people from sin and error seized his imagination.

His first conquests in the path of ushering in the Islamic revolution were Khadija, his adopted son Ali, servant Zeid, and friend Abu Bakr. Later, the question who was the first convert to Islam became a matter of some importance, and the contenders for this distinction were Khadija, Abu Bakr, the first Caliph, Muhammad's subsequent father-in-law, and his cousin and later son-in-law Ali. The name of Ali is backed by Shia Muslims, but it is almost certain the honour belongs to Abu Bakr. While Ali was a child at his conversion, and therefore had little weight, Abu Bakr was a rich merchant high in influence even before he evinced interest in Islam. Obviously, his conversion signified much to Muhammad, at a time he had nothing to fall back upon against the world, excepting his unitarian ideology of divinity.

Almost from nothing Muhammad saw the increase in the strength of his adherents. Some leading citizens of Mecca came to his side, for which loyalty they were rewarded with the command over armies and governorship of provinces in the subsequent progress of Islam. But the majority of converts in Mecca were of low rank, especially slaves cruelly exploited by their masters. At first, the polytheists of Mecca were complacent, did not see the danger looming large from the infant community of Unitarians, but later took the bull by the horns to protect their interest.[35]

Mecca was held by a tribe, to which Muhammad also belonged, known as Quraysh, which managed companies to share their profits. This tribe with its vested interest was for preserving the *status quo* of the city, against the religious innovations of Muhammad. Generally speaking, the unbelievers mocked at his claim of having been commissioned by God to reveal the truth, and asked: "Why was this Puran not revealed to an important man in the two towns?"

Furthermore, the Arabs of the generation of Muhammad did not entertain a strong conception of life after death.[36] Hence his words about the resurrection of the dead met with disbelief, and they rebutted him in the following way:

> What! When we shall have become bones and decayed particles, shall we then certainly be raised up, being a new creation?
>
> There is nothing but our life of this world, and we shall not be raised.[37]

The age-old conservatism and traditions of Mecca held their ground, and despising him they asked: "What! Shall we indeed give up our gods for the sake of a mad poet?" They feared, at least those with vested interest, if they abandoned their gods they and their city would face ruin. So there was resistance to change, and under the influence of their persecution nearly a hundred Muslims including eighteen women migrated to Abyssinia. One timely acquisition to Islam was the service of the indomitable and much feared Omar, a fine companion of Muhammad in his days of travail.

Muhammad, meanwhile, was zealous to convert more people, and consequently, invoking his freedom of conscience, he visited the Kaaba on the occasion of festivals to accost the pilgrims, and to enlighten them about the reality of one God. Of all the people who should oppose his pious exhortations at the temple, but his own venerable uncle. "Citizens and pilgrims," Abu Talib said, "listen not to the tempter, hearken not to his impious novelties. Stand fast in the worship of Al Lata and Al Uzzah." This odd critic, however, spurred by deeply ingrained loyalty to family and tribe, a well known trait of the Arabs, loved Muhammad and protected him from the wrath of the Quraysh, who on the pretext of defending religion hated the ascendancy of his Hashim family. Nourishing the flame of hate in their bosom, the leaders of the Quraysh denied food and water to Hashim progenies, stopped intercourse with them, and pressed hard on Muhammad wishing to deliver him to the justice of their gods.

Muhammad under the stress of circumstances deviated from his principle, and seemed to reconcile himself to the existence of paganism after all. The reason for this conclusion is he recited (Sura 53:19) the following verse: "Al-Lat, al-Uzza, and Manat are the exalted virgins whose intercession may be counted on." By this concession, he doubtless made peace with the Meccans, but Gabriel descended to censure him for uttering words not revealed to him. The virtue of Islam as a religion is that it does not recognize any mediator between God and the believer, except prophet Muhammad. At the price of increased hostility of the Meccans, he recanted his words, and the epilogue for the above revealing story concerning prophetic visions is that the sin of Muhammad may be used as an evidence to prove his sincerity.

So long as the moderate chief, Abu Talib, a Nestor among the Arabs, was alive, their mutual illwill did not reach the point of extremity. But after his death, the truce was at an end, and Muhammad was abandoned to the fury of his enemies at Mecca.

True, a prophet is never held in esteem in his home town; so looking for a congenial ground to spread his message, Muhammad went to nearby Taif; however, pelted by the people he with cuts and bruises fled the town and was back in Mecca.

About this time a certain Abu Sufyan had come to power in Mecca. He was the very antithesis of Muhammad, because he was a zealous worshipper of idols, and because he hated the Hashimite family of the prophet. The feud between the pagans of Mecca and Muhammad was irreconcilable, more so now as he was negotiating clandestinely with the people of Medina to establish his power in that quarter. As the situation turned potentially dangerous, Abu Sufyan summoned a meeting of the Qurayshites to decide how to deal with the prophet; neither exile nor imprisonment was thought the right step in the deliberation as it would not contain the mischief thoroughly well. Not like death, which was decided upon as the most suitable option. It was agreed that a sword from each tribe should pierce his heart, in order to apportion equitably the guilt of homicide, in the process perplexing the retaliatory steps of the Hashimites. Muhammad somehow came to know of the plot, and in the still of the night, with his friend Abu Bakr, gave his enemies the slip by abandoning the house. The assassins at the door waited, but they were taken in by the presence of Ali, who slept on the bed covering himself with the green robe of the prophet.

Not far away from Mecca, in the cave of Thaur, Muhammad and Abu Bakr hid themselves, and were in touch with the outside world as the family of the latter gave them food and information.

They had gone towards the south and in the wrong direction to Medina to baffle and confound their enemies; yet the pursuers on the trail of them came near their mountain hideout, but supposing it to be untenanted did not search it. Abu Bakr despairing of safety thought of the weakness of the two in the cave; however, Muhammad in the selfsame place reflected on the strength of the three, in which he counted his omnipresent God.

The life of Muhammad from this stage onwards is linked with the tale of two opposing Arabian cities, and the first episode in this tale is as one city squeezes him out the other city beckons him. At Medina, a substantial chunk of the population was Jewish, and their presence was enough to infect others to some extent with the doctrine of monotheism, thus paving the way for the reception of Muhammad.

Moreover, some people from Medina who went to Mecca on pilgrimage had been meeting Muhammad, and these came under his spell. Once they got back to their town they diffused among their people the message of one God, and one prophet, with whom they had formed an alliance to abide by his faith for eternity. A big catch of the prophet was seventy-five people of Medina, who after conferring with him and his fraternity promised on behalf of their city to take him as their leader if he were thrown out from his city, and to defend him against all danger.

> "But if you are recalled by your country." They asked overcome with anxiety, "will you not abandon your new allies?"
>
> "All things, said Muhammad affably, "are now common between us; your blood is as my blood, your ruin as my ruin. We are bound to each other by the ties of honour and interest. I am your friend, and the enemy of your foes."

"But if we are killed in your service," replied the leaders of Medina, "what will be our reward?"

"Paradise," said the prophet.[38]

After having courted him with servile flattery, in a situation where the desire of each side for the help of other more or less balanced, they saw in his exile a good omen, but fearing for his safety looked forward to his arrival. He came indeed, sixteen days after he quitted Mecca, enduring a hazardous journey along the seacoast, and then moved towards the Medinans, void of pomp except he rode on a camel with an umbrella shading his head. He had left the hate of a city behind him, and while receiving the spontaneous love of the people of Medina he was hailed as their chosen leader.

The flight of Muhammad from Mecca, known as hegira, in A.D. 622, represented the dawn of a new era for the Muslims, in so far as the age-old connection with the paganism of Arabia was broken. Muhammad was a gifted man, and knew how to strengthen fraternal relationship among the brotherhood, before he ventured to change the timeworn idea of religion. With he himself the center of the world he was fashioning, there came into existence around him as if pulled by his magnetic attraction, three orders of men to distinguish them for having assisted him in such a task. Of these, *Ashab* (Companions) were his early associates; *muhajirun* (Exiles) were people who accompanied him in his flight to Medina, and Ansar (Helpers) were the men of Medina.

At this time the prophet thought it right to build a mosque, the very first of its kind, and the plot he chose for this belonged to two orphans. Their guardians were ready to give it freely, but Muhammad would not entertain such an offer, and the deal was finalized after fixing a price.[39] That he refused a gift is conceivable in view of the fact that the prophet was always touched by the situation of the orphans and widows; doubtless, he got this sensitiveness through his own personal experience as an orphan. The prophet is believed to have said, "I am he who takes care of the orphan," and the Koran denounces those who with a heart of stone embezzle the property of the orphans, or exploit the forlorn of the community.

The divine law has its say even in the distribution of plunder, and a fifth of the spoils was kept by the prophet for pious and charitable objects. About the several uses to which charity is directed for the dispersal of wealth, the Koran (Sura 2: 177) explicitly says: "It is not righteousness that you turn your faces towards the East and the West, but righteousness is this that one should believe in God and the last day and the angels and the Book and the prophets, and give away wealth out of love for Him to the near of kin and the orphans and the needy and the wayfarer and the beggars and for (the emancipation of) the captives, and keep up prayer and pay the poor-rate."

Such a well-intentioned concern in the weak has to be seen in the background of Islamic concept of organized charity, a peculiarity of the Judaeo-Christian world.[40] Obviously, in view of Koran's antipathy against paganism and polytheism, the beneficiaries of Islamic charity are mainly the Muslims. The Christian Church too once suffered from such a narrow outlook, but after the Enlightenment, and with the separation of Church and state, it has embraced a broad humanitarian approach. But the apologists of Islam maintain, whether rightly or wrongly, that it is a seamless whole in which religion, politics, economics and morality are fused together. Islam in other words is not just a formula for worship, but such a comprehensive social system that religion and politics cannot be divorced from each other.

About economics, Islam is opposed to the glut of materialism, which sucks people into a bottomless abyss in the unending desire for wealth. To check the avarice for quick and large returns, the Islamic economy avoids paying interest, though banks exist on the foundation of profit and loss sharing concerns. According to Koranic commandments of inheritance, or *wiratha*, the property of the deceased should be distributed among not only the nearest surviving relatives such as wife, sons and daughters, but also other near relatives as parents, brothers and sisters of the defunct, and the list of beneficiaries is pretty long when it includes less prosperous relatives, indigent neighbours and the chronic poor of the community.[41] On the whole, Islam is in favour of capitalism shorn of its material obsessions, and its distributive justice lies midway between the extremes of capitalism and socialism.

Having the perception that humans succumb to the temptation of settling at extreme positions, the Koran to forestall such a thing aims at the "Middle Nation" society. In which neither ascetic spiritualism nor runaway materialism, neither selfishness nor altruism, neither freedom nor restriction in sex, neither polygamy nor monogamy, and neither democracy nor authoritarianism is the ideal, but the mean between the two extreme points.

The mosque in question was built in a rather uncouth style, in contrast to the opulent architectural wonders that followed the zenith of Islamic power. Muhammad, with no disposition to the pomp and vanity of the high, fitted well to such austere surroundings as he leaned against the trunk of a palm tree in order to preach in the assembly of the believers. He saw himself transformed in Medina from a preacher to a sovereign as well, but he was unlike other potentates exercising power; for he attracted so passionately the devotion of his subjects that they bent down to take even his spittle.

Nevertheless, he was in one respect like other potentates as power got into his head, and changed him. So he gave up his former moderation which was the outcome of his weakness, and assumed a fiercer aspect to fit into his new role as the messenger of war. He thought that his message of one God was for the Arabs, and perhaps even for all humanity, but till now his words were lost on the unbelieving world.[42] Hence the art of persuasion was at an end, and by the sword he wanted to destroy idolatry in Arabia, to clean the Kaaba of its impurities, and to convert the pagans to Islam. Wherever he showed a modicum of mercy, in what otherwise was a merciless war inspired by fanaticism, it was guided by interest so that he let his defeated enemies on the payment of a tribute follow their accustomed worship.

Muhammad, in the war against paganism, turned his avenging fury on the Jews too, fighting them off and on as his inclination guided him. Their original sin had been that they mistook a metallic calf which gave a mooing sound for a God. They besides no longer retained their erstwhile religious purity, and the fact that they were monotheists did not extenuate their guilt in other respects. Expatiating upon this the Koran (Sura 4:160. 161) says:

> Wherefore for the iniquity of those who are Jews did We disallow to them the good things which had been made lawful for them, and for their hindering many (people) from God's way.
>
> And their taking usury though indeed they were forbidden it and their devouring the property of people falsely; and We have prepared for the unbelievers from among them a painful chastisement.

Muhammad's coldness towards the Jews reflected their superior economic strength, which made them enemies with the Arabs. The

Jews had a big say in the economy of the Hijaz and likewise the market at Medina was under their control. Their economic prosperity was at the expense of the Arabs, especially the Quraysh at Mecca, and the Aus and Khazraj at Medina. Muhammad was supported by the last two tribes, while he himself belonged to the former tribe. The Jews became wealthy through their enterprising spirit, and their expertise in agriculture and irrigation. After establishing roots as homeless refugees, they in a few generations amassed so much wealth as to own extensive lands and to control trade and finance of the country. Moreover, the iron trade was in their grip, so that they were sellers of arms, coats of mail and farm tools to their neighbours.[43] The Jews were an insular race, and their affluence incited the envy of the Arabs, no less their plundering instinct for which war served as an excuse.

In fact, the Arab combined the role of a businessman with that of a freebooter; his defence of his caravan imperceptibly schooled him for the attack of the caravan which belonged to the opposite side. Muhammad, to this inborn trait, added his religious fervour and his grudge against the Meccans for compelling him to live an exile from his native town. Even then it was no easy task for Muhammad to turn the war energies of Medina against the other city, as both were knit together by blood ties, and the Arabs always held in esteem such relationship. But as the holder of apostolic office, he superimposed the more honourable brotherhood of Islam over ties of blood, and succeeded in hammering into their head the concept of *jihad* or holy war against the infidels of Mecca.

The warrior prophet fought at the head of his faithful zealots, and from diverse places the Arabs came to him attracted by religion, as well as plunder. It was no little matter for the wandering Arabs, with their predatory habits, to have been allowed a fair share in the spoils, and besides the prophet let them appropriate women captured in war; that is either as wives or concubines, a foretaste of the joys of heaven kept in reserve for them on a mightier scale. "The sword," said Muhammad, "is the key of heaven and of hell: a drop of blood shed in the cause of God, a night spent in arms, is of more avail than two months of fasting and prayer."[44] Believing in all he said, the Arabs were so enthusiastically converted to his faith that they showed a contempt for death in battle, and longed for the bliss of yet to come world. The Koran urged the prophet to war, and the prophet under divine obligation urged the believers to war, echoing His message, that "if there are a hundred of you they shall overcome a thousand of those who disbelieve, because they are a people who do not understand."

But the first step towards conflict with the infidels resulted in a minor engagement, a few against a few, which was in the nature of a skirmish. Even when it was in the real sense a war, of the Arabs against the Arabs, the combatants involved were limited to a few thousand, although in its effect it was a big revolution. It was more like the war of the Greeks against the Greeks in respect of numbers, described by the historian Thucydides; like them, Muhammad kept no standing army, and his fighting men came together under his standard when a battle was imminent.

In the skirmish mentioned above, the Muslims while attacking a caravan of the Meccans had spilt blood, during the sacred month when war was prohibited. Since the Arabs felt revulsion at this impiety, Muhammad took some pains to justify his hostile act in Sura 2:214: "They will question you (O Muhammad) with regard to warfare in the sacred month; say: Warfare therein is a serious matter; but to turn (men) from the way of God and to disbelieve in Him and in the sacred temple and to drive his people from it is more serious with God, and infidelity is more serious than killing."

The Syrian trade of Mecca had to pass through the territory of Medina, and since the threat to it from the Muslim fighters was too obvious, Abu Sufyan himself guided a rich caravan of a thousand camels to get the better of a difficult situation. Muhammad with some three hundred men, and a cavalry with a ludicrous strength of two horses, waited their approach to intercept them. His enemies were about a thousand strong, and the opposing forces met at Badr. As the Quraysh men sallied out from the hills, Muhammad looking up for divine help said, "O God, if these are destroyed, by whom wilt thou be worshipped on the earth?" The Muslim troops held their ground, and when they seemed to waver, the thundering voice of the prophet so bolstered their courage up that their enemies leaving their bravest dead on the field took to their heels. Their victory despite comparative weakness in the size of the army was attributed to their faith in the religion of Muhammad, and now their elation was proportionate to the despair of their foes at Mecca.

About this time Muhammad took steps to eject the Jews from the Hijaz.[45] He knowing well that the Jews were his enemies, particularly because they denied his prophetic mission, would not tolerate their existence in his proximity. At his behest one or two Jews were killed, and in fact, Muhammad permitted the assassination of idolators and Jews who had escaped from the battlefield. The Qainuqa Jews of Medina were mostly goldsmiths, and on their refusal to embrace Islam, were forced to surrender after an unequal conflict. Muhammad grudgingly spared their lives at the intervention of his allies, and seizing their wealth he let them go with their wives and children out of the country to a melancholy exile.

The Quraysh were still smarting from their defeat, when the buccaneers of Medina gave one more injury to them by seizing a valuable caravan. The people of Mecca were resolved on exacting vengeance, and once again Abu Sufyan took to the field with an army about thrice in its strength to the previous one he fielded, to face adversaries roughly a quarter of his strength, thus between rivals large disparity in number existed as in the previous contest. But size mattered this time swinging the balance in favour of Abu Sufyan.

Muhammad had put faith in such a defensive strategy that would let his men remain in the town, but against this he was influenced to prefer the very opposite thing owing to the importunities of his troops. So they moved out, and the two forces met at Uhud, close to Medina. The pagans marched in crescent shape, and the right wing of their cavalry was led by their famed warrior Khalid bin Walid, who later changed sides to become in the next reign of Abu Bakr the first commander-in-chief of the Islamic Army. The thrust of the believers firm attack broke the center of the enemy phalanx, but the subsequent events were their undoing. So the Muslims who had disobeyed their prophet, disordered their ranks, and were looking for spoils got safety in flight. Khalid having so manoeuvred his cavalry as to get around the flank of the Muslim forces, cried out that Muhammad was killed. This was wishful thinking; for a spear attack wounded him in the face, and he was taken to a place up the hill with Abu Bakr sticking around.

The Quraysh in spite of their victory did not follow the Muslims and lacking confidence to lay siege to Medina saw the advantage of success dissipated by inactivity.

For Muhammad, if Badr was a triumph Uhud was a disaster; yet such was his spirit that amidst the chaos of the battle he had censured the infidels for the murder of a prophet; that after the troops rallied round him he marched towards Mecca, and pitched camp before the Quraysh. His tactical move was a proclamation of defiance by which he again habitually robbed, of course not the material things of the Meccans, but some of the glory of their recent deeds.

Notwithstanding his bravado, Muhammad felt the miseries of his followers occasioned by the death of loved ones in the battle, and tried to console them in Sura 3 whose relevant summary is given here:

> If you have suffered a blow (at Uhud), so did the enemy at Badr, and wars come to provide martyrs and that God may prove those who believe. Paradise is only to be attained when God knows who will really strive and endure. Certainly you were desirous of death before you met it, and now you have seen what it is. Every man dies when God permits—it is all written down—and the best of this world and the next is only for those who are steadfast in the way of God. Don't think that the idolators will ultimately triumph. Victory was in your hands until you disobeyed God's Apostle and the archers left their post to plunder the enemy's camp. You were put to flight because you sought worldly gain. God allowed you to be defeated in order to test you, and now He has forgiven you. If God helps you none can overcome you: if He abandons you who then can help you? So let the believers rely upon God.[46]

In the next stage of the conflict, those in power at Mecca made one more attempt by an act of aggression to humble the prophet. They were helped by a dominant Jew who used his influence to attract Bedouin tribes, and altogether a confederation of ten thousand betook against Medina. It was not possible for them to storm the town without heavy casualties, because where it was vulnerable Muhammad, taking the counsel of a Persian convert, had dug a trench to make it otherwise. So the invaders were left high and dry, and after sending long distance arrows at the position of their enemies retired to a camp.

With no breakthrough in war, diplomacy meanwhile got the upper hand to put each other at a disadvantage, the fruit of which nefarious diplomacy was the Jews backed out mistrusting their allies who likewise mistrusted them. Finally, the Quraysh retreated to Mecca after the allies deserted the confederacy, and after Muhammad refused to come out to give them a fight as he was safe in the town.

The Jews had sided with the Quraysh, and Muhammad without loss of time proceeded against them. They put up resistance for a while, and then laid down arms hoping that their allies, Aus of Medina, would intercede to save them. True, their friends spoke on their behalf, however, Muhammad made a certain elder the judge of their fate, and he passed death sentence on them.

To carry out his verdict, in the market-place a trench was dug which was intended to be the last dismal resting place of the Jews. About eight hundred Jews in chains walked through the market-place of the city; except only one who renounced his religion to preserve his life, they in successive groups descended alive into their grave, on the periphery of which they were beheaded and thrown into the ditch. Such was the labour of decapitation, that it went on the whole day and extended far into the night as well.

Muhammad with an inflexible eye saw the mass execution of the Jews, and though time and again he had eulogized his God as the compassionate and merciful one, he himself as the prophet of such a God had no feelings towards the agony of the Jews.

The Kaaba was never out of Muhammad's mind, and in 6 A.H. he set out with his followers to Mecca as a pilgrim. But the Quraysh resisted his progress, having no wish to see him in Mecca then. Muhammad had no stomach for war, although he contemptuously said that his opponents had "clothed themselves with the skins of tigers," and turned to negotiation by which a truce of ten years came into effect. He by the treaty of Hudaibia obtained the right to convert heathens to Islam without opposition, and to visit Mecca in the following year to perform religious services. It is said that the treaty was favourable to the infidels, but in reality he won a diplomatic victory so that more people came to his side, in a state of affairs which reflected adversely on the fortunes of the opposite side.

As Muhammad on grounds of security was reducing the Jews around Medina and appropriating their wealth, he could not overlook Khaybar, an opulent town as well as the citadel of Jewish power in Arabia. At the outset, Abu Bakr was in command of the Islamic forces, but it was Ali who showed exceptional abilities in what otherwise was a hazardous enterprise even for him. The Jews decided to give in on condition that their lives would be spared, but their chief was tortured to know the place of his hidden treasure; then, with his cousin, executed. Besides these two, one more to be put to death was a Jewess, her name Zaynab. This unfortunate woman having lost her dear ones in the battle had served Muhammad with a dish of poisoned lamb, and he ate very little suspecting foul play, yet he, with not many years to live, complained to his dying day of its bad effects.

The Muslims accepted in principle the right of the Jews to exist and carry on their occupation, so long as they shared half of what they earned with the conquerors. But the Jews of Khaybar under Caliph Omar were shifted to Syria, and in defence, he alleged that such was the order of his dying master who thought that only one true religion should prevail in Arabia. On the whole, the Muslims at the economic level immensely benefited by the persecution of the Jews. Erasing all the traces of their indigence, they became an affluent class which fact redounded to the fame of Muhammad, so that more Bedouin fighters irresistibly were pulled towards him.

Muhammad next year in conformity with the treaty entered Mecca, went round the Kaaba seven times, and touched with the staff the black stone in customary reverence, while the Meccans kept distance by going to the hills. The exile had achieved a triumph, very much at the expense of the ruling power, that is the Quraysh to whom it was a premonition of worst things to come. Such was the attraction of the prophet, that the renowned general Khalid was seduced into abandoning the cause of paganism.

The Quraysh were weary of their conflict with Muhammad, much more so now as the sacred character of Mecca was upheld by him. It was obvious that they could not match in power their opponents; since in politics the usual tendency is for the strong to do what they have the power to do in relation to the weak to compel obedience, Muhammad, looking for an excuse to resume hostilities, and finding fault with the other side for the breach of the truce, suddenly appeared with a force of ten thousand before Mecca. Abu Sufyan was haughty once, but, now delivering the keys of the city, submitted meekly to the new theocracy of Islam.

Muhammad, terminating his seven years of exile, got no revenge on his most obnoxious enemies, avoided a massacre, pardoned the guilty and brought together the factions of Mecca under the banner of Islam. But all his suppressed anger was reserved for the inanimate objects, and so, while carrying out the purification of Kaaba, about three hundred sixty idols were destroyed.

By this step he satiated his thirst for vengeance, but not for conquests. He had not yet reached the end of the road, and to expand the horizon of his religion he fought at Hunain against the infidels; then besieged Taif, which is about sixty miles to the sough-east of Mecca. After forcing its leading men to make terms with him, he destroyed its temples, in a process that saw Arabia denuded of its pagan gods.

As Muhammad's territorial gains increased, he came into contact with the Arab Christians, whom unlike the Jews he treated well, allowing them to live as they had lived once without forcing religion upon them; however, they must pay tribute in recognition of their inferior condition under the new setup.

Even as far back as in the reign of Trajan there was a Roman province of "Arabia," but after the fall of the Roman empire, the Arabs came under the sphere of influence of its surviving eastern part with Byzantine as its capital. Presently, the Roman emperor of the east was Heraclius; against him, Muhammad led a formidable army in order to forestall a probable attack from that quarter. The Muslims were unwilling to go with him, and put forward excuses particularly the heat of the summer, but retorting, "Hell is much hotter," Muhammad went ahead discovering the kind of loyalty he expected at least in some companions—the foremost among them was Abu Bakr.[47] Much hardship the troops faced on the way, with heat and winds of the desert sucking their vital power, and further distressed by lack of drinking water, they were reduced to the necessity of drawing it from the belly of the camel, a faithful and serviceable animal, on which ten persons mounted by turns on this expedition.

The prophet made no progress beyond Tabuk, fearing perhaps the might of the eastern Roman emperor and his battle hardened soldiers. But Khalid was active building Islam by force of arms, and many cities and tribes as well as the Christian John of Ayla came to terms with Muhammad.

For the last time after going to Mecca as a pilgrim, Muhammad returned to Medina, and planned an expedition to Syrian frontier. But death was fast approaching him, and he was sensible of his impending dissolution. He fell sick owing to fever, and his disease so much worsened that he was not even able to attend the mosque to offer his normal prayers.[48] He breathed his last soon, at the age of sixty-two, but Omar refused to believe that the prophet was gone.

Then Abu Bakr addressed the mob that had gathered hearing the sad news, and asked: "Is it Muhammad, or the God of Muhammad, whom you worship?" He said that the God of Muhammad lives to infinity, but Muhammad like many prophets before him was dead. The city of Medina which once gave him sanctuary from his persecutors was sanctified by the death and burial of the prophet.

Now the future of the empire Muhammad had built for the believers hung on the choice of a successor. Ali, the husband of Fatim and hence the son-in-law of the prophet, thought that he had a better right than anyone else to succeed him. He combined in himself the normally opposing traits of a solider and a saint, however, with all his merits, he was not forward in pressing his claim to the Caliphate on account of which he got the censure of his allies.

Though the spirit of democracy percolates through the teachings of Muhammad, it is said "politically, Islam was not an advance, but retrogression from the traditional freedoms and customary laws of the desert.[49]" Among the believers of Islam, Muhammad inculcated certain social virtues particularly brotherhood and charity. By his own example and his laws he checked the thirst for revenge, and the oppression of the weak. He united the warring tribes under one faith, and turned their energy against the foreign enemies who had used the Arabs for their aggrandisement.

His achievements notwithstanding, he left no political system founded on the principles of democracy. The three elements of Islamic polity are: first, there is God who laid down the law; second, the prophet who enforced the divine law; third, the ruler who governs in accordance with the commandments of God and the *sunnah* or practice of the prophet. Two opinions have gained currency with regard to the question how the rulers obtain power. The Shia view is that the power to rule is vested with the descendants of the prophet through his cousin, the fourth Caliph, Ali. The Sunnis however consider that, after the prophet, the rulers are chosen through a process of *Shura* or mutual consultation as ordained in the divine Book.[50]

Such mutual consultations to elect rulers were thrown to the winds, during the centuries of monarchical system in the Islamic world. But this was not so in regard to the pious Caliphate that emerged after the prophet's death, and the *Shura* was respected as the events leading to the elevation of Abu Bakr points out.

The two foremost contenders for the throne of Muhammad, were related to him by matrimonial ties; but Ali's connection with the prophet was nearer as he was his cousin as well. This advantage, however, was somewhat overbalanced by the sagacity and resolution of Abu Bakr who was well qualified even to guide Muhammad himself in a complex situation.

The elders who had assembled to choose a successor would not countenance the election of Ali; the Quraysh particularly were not reconciled to the preeminence of the line of Hashim. Furthermore, the Ansar or the Helpers' of the prophet at Medina, laid claim to the Caliphate, in opposition to the interest of the once exiled Meccans, with so much vigour that they were ready to see two instead of one in that office in order to harmonise conflicting interests. But even among the Ansar there were two groups, Aus and Khazraj, who never saw eye to eye on most issues. Abu Bakr in order to break the impasse, and to soften their inflexibility addressed them in a conciliatory way: "Gentlemen, I acknowledge your merits and the excellent services rendered by you, but the fact is that the Arabs at large will never accept any Amir except some one from the Qurayshites."[51]

Finally, it was the intervention of Omar, that tilted the balance in favour of Abu Bakr, but Ali sulked at home refusing to accept the new ruler, as long as Fatima was alive. The reign of Abu Bakr was marked by an upsurge of unrest and insubordination, especially the Bedouin taking up arms refused to pay the alms tax. His short rule, besides, witnessed the noble work of prophethood degenerate into a cancer which spread all over the Arabian peninsula. In fact, even earlier a certain false prophet, Musailma, infatuated with power and sovereignty over nations, had dared to write to Muhammad on an equal footing:

> I am a partner in your prophethood. Half the world belongs to me and half to you.

The prophet Muhammad did not fail to give him a suitable reply:

> From Muhammad the Prophet of God to Musailma the liar. Undoubtedly, the whole of this earth belongs to God, and He gives it from among his people to those whom He desires to give and to the pious.[52]

After the demise of the prophet, the monomania for prophethood became to extensive that a woman, Sajah Hartha Tamimi, set herself up as a prophetess with great pomp, and to have wider appeal struck up nuptial relationship with Musailma. The Muslim troops attacked and killed him, after meeting fierce resistance of his followers, but his wife escaped to die at Basra later on.

Abu Bakr, meanwhile, took up the Syrian war which was planned during the time of Muhammad, and could not be put off now although he had other urgent matters on hand. He sent Osama bin Zaid in that direction, who finishing the task assigned to him returned to Medina.

But the man who towered above others was Khalid, who from Iraq crossing the Syrian desert reached Damascus, and in A.D. 634 captured it. Though the Arabs were made to fall back , they two years later beat the Romans so thoroughly, that Heraclius gradually withdrew from all Syria. Much earlier, Khalid had attacked the Persian frontier town of Hira, and in A.D. 637, the Arabs defeated the Persians at Qadisiya, and the whole of Iraq came into their possession. Egypt without much of a resistance passed from the Romans, or more rightly the Greeks, to the Arabs.

Abu Bakr meanwhile had died, and Omar in spite of his mercurial temper on account of which some were prejudiced against him succeeded him.[53] Much of the Arab conquests took place in the reign of Omar, and he went in person to oversee the formal surrender of Jerusalem, then in the ownership of the Christians.

The triumph of the Arabs in the name of one supreme God over their foreign enemies is amazing, but the speed of their conquests, both in the east and west was facilitated by the local population who saw them less as invaders and more as deliverers from the Byzantine tyranny. Their rapid progress, however, was checked as soon as they met with native opposition farther west.

Omar whose violence others feared himself met a violent end at the hands of an assassin; thereafter, the task of choosing a successor devolved upon a council of six members, and it raised Uthman to the Caliphate; while the followers of Ali perceived his right again set aside only because he did not push his claim, and submitted to the jurisdiction of the electors.

Together with the two caliphs who preceded him, and the one that followed him, Uthman was related by marriage to Muhammad. He came from the ruling aristocracy of Mecca, and his nomination dashed the hopes of Medina. The aged Caliph was unable to sustain the weight of the empire; unable to cope with the tide of discontent, and with Koran in his lap, at Medina he submitted to his murder. There followed a few days of anarchy, until the accession of Ali to power.

The discord of his times split Islam into two factions so enduring as to be present in our own days. The fighting energy of Ali so characteristic of him in his youngish days had been subdued by age as well as pious meditation, but he was forced into the battlefield by his enemies. At their head was Aisha, the widow of the prophet, together with two powerful Meccan leaders. Ali worsted them in what is known as the Battle of the Camel, but he had to face one more foe by no means a contemptible one.

Muawiya, once the secretary of the prophet but later nominated to rule Syria by Uthman, was the nephew of the murdered Caliph; so he demanded satisfaction for blood guilt, insinuating, rightly or wrongly it is hard to say, Ali's complicity in that plot. He took the title of Caliph, and Ali to uphold his authority led an army against the rebel. The outcome of the battle was yet undecided but Ali was almost certain of victory, when his foes resorted to subterfuge by fixing the leaves of the Koran on their foremost lances, and so making God a party to the dispute. By this unusual tactics, Ali was deprived of his glory, and forced to yield to a truce as well as arbitration. His weakness, reflected in his approval or rather submission to compromise, so embittered a fanatical party known as the Seceders (*Kharijites*) that they did not support his interest. What is more, his insidious rival Muawiya took Egypt from his control, and beset with troubles Ali was groping in the dark when a *Kharijite* assassinated him; then the usurper became the real Caliph.

By a strange turn of events, the persecutors of Muhammad and worshippers of idols inherited his empire after robbing it from his progenies. Muawiya, the son of Abu Sufyan and his lusty vampire wife Hind who gloating over the victory at Uhud had licked the blood of the prophet's uncle, now took over the Caliphate and ushered in the Umayyad dynasty. Ali's son Hasan gave up his right to the Caliphate, which Muawiya transformed from an elective to a hereditary office, thereby helping his son Yazid to ascend to the throne of Damascus as the successor of the prophet. Husayn, the younger brother of Hasan, rose against Yazid but lost the battle, and his head was sent to Damascus as a war trophy; then was buried together with the body at Karbala, now a holy city of the Shia community. The tenth of

Muharram, the day of the murder, signifies the end of ten days' mourning observed every year by the Shia Muslims. The Shias put their faith in their Imams, who are the descendants of Ali. While among the Sunnis the Caliph is the head, and dispenses justice through the *sharia* or sacred law, the Shias look on the Imam as the divinely nominated ruler, their spiritual guide as well, and the successor to the inheritance of the prophet.

Islam under the rule of the Arabs never got over the land barrier of the Taurus Mountains, so Muawiya launched two sea attacks on Constantinople. The power of the Umayyads in the reign of two Caliphs, Abdul Malik and Walid I, reached its zenith. The Arabs overran Roman Africa, and in 711 having crossed the straits of Gibraltar they conquered Spain. Not appeased by these possessions and desiring to extend the domain of Islam farther, they crossed the Pyrenees and seized all the south of France. Excepting Corsica, all the great islands of the Mediterranean came under the control of Islam. Suleiman, the successor of Walid, laid siege to Constantinople but the Byzantine king Leo against all odds kept his capital, the last bulwark of the Christianized Graeco-Roman culture in the east. The advance of the Muslim troops in the west was stopped by the Frank, Charles Martel, and in 732 at the battle of Poitiers he with much slaughter defeated them. But the siege of Christendom had just begun; the two foes ironically professing monotheistic religion fought each other for another nine hundred years, and the successive Crusades for the recovery of the Christian holy city of Jerusalem reflected the intensity of the struggle for preponderance.

The Umayyads owed their success to the *mawali* or client peoples, who were treated notwithstanding the brotherhood of Islam as an inferior class, and not allowed to marry Arab women. Finally, the dynasty of Abbasids, capitalizing on grievances, overthrew them, and Baghdad became the capital of its empire.

Among the Caliphs of this dynasty, Harun ar-Rashid is well known not only by the reality of his power, but also by the unreality of the romantic world of *Arabian Nights*; so pleasing are its images that they lull the mind to a false sense of grandeur. The Abbasid power at its zenith marked the boom of economic activity; however before long everything was blasted, and dissolved into thin air not unlike the *Arabian Nights'* golden illusion. The Caliph lost Egypt, Persia, Spain,

Tunisia, and Morocco to other rulers; himself turned into a symbolic head, being overshadowed by the energy of upstart rulers. A new rising star which shone brilliantly for a while was the Fatimid dynasty of Egypt, which had an extensive domain, but Saladin destroyed its power. The Mongols in the thirteenth century took Baghdad, and the Caliph was done away with.

In 1453, the portentous event waiting, all these years to happen at last happened. The city of Constantinople, a museum of civilizations, fell to a new Islamic renaissance in the reign of Muhammad II, the Sultan of the Ottoman Turks.

The Ottoman Turkish Empire that lasted till the end of World War I was built by the Osman dynasty, which extended its power gradually farther and farther westward. The domain of the Ottomans incorporated many races held together by the said dynasty, and by the missionary ardour to spread Islam throughout the globe. Turkey of the present day, on the other hand, is made up of the (non-Ottoman) Turkish race which in the past conquered by the Osman dynasty had been a part of its empire. After 1517, the Ottoman Sultan, with his capital at Constantinople (Istanbul), assumed for himself the title of Caliph, the successor of the prophet. Such was the inheritance of the prophet Muhammad, so volatile as the shifting sands of desert.

The hegemonic ambition of the Muslims should follow in the footsteps of the Greeks and the Romans is understandable, but not so the fact that, unlike the two powers mentioned, the sea held no attraction to them. Much had been said about the incompatibility between Islam and the sea which, in fact, was a repelling force to the believers. "The sea," the prophet is thought to have said, "is Hell, and Satan reigns over the waters."[54]

Such antipathy for the sea Omar had already imbibed, when he refused Muawiya, the governor of Syria, permission to build a fleet to attack Cyprus. "The Syrian Sea, I am told, is longer and wider than the desert, and threatens the Lord himself, night and day, trying to swallow him up … no, no, my friend, the safety of my people is more precious than all the treasures of Greece."[55] A harsh view of this kind concerning the sea checked the enterprising spirit of the Muslims, but a few had the foresight to go against the taboo.

Had the Muslims ventured on to the sea, and had they taken part in the transoceanic discoveries of the fifteenth century, the geo-political shape of the present Islamic world would have been different. The Mediterranean is a sea for galleys and coasting; however, on the Atlantic Ocean and the North Sea winds are more prevalent, seas run higher making the sailing ship a necessity. But the Muslims never hazarded their lives by sailing across the Atlantic Ocean, which they perceived as "the sea where no ship sails," the realm of phantom tales. Similarly, lack of Muslim seafaring activities in the inland waterways of continental Eurasia was obvious, despite being under the dominant influence of Islam.

The South Seas were more favourable to the maritime expansion of Islam, but here too the Muslim sailors lagged behind others. Guided by the maritime trade routes leading to the Far East, inherited from the Sassanid dynasty, the Arabs and Persians went as far as China, when the Abbasid Caliphs were in power; however, from the eleventh century their utility substantially diminished. The maritime superiority of Europe in the South Seas was so firmly established, that the Muslims had no strength to unsettle it. The Ottoman Turks after possessing Egypt held sway over the Red Sea, but they could not stop the European intrusion into the Persian Gulf.

After the Arabs' rapid conquests in the Mediterranean Sea, their penetration into Europe was halted, and from the end of the tenth century all the European outposts gained before were lost to Islam. During the Crusading era, having controlled the sea the Christians for almost two centuries bolstered the fortunes of the Latin Kingdom of Palestine. So when Ibn Jubair of Spain began in 1183 his famous pilgrimage, he hired four Christian ships, and met with ten other Christian ships during his voyage.[56]

The Christians were aware of the weakness of the enemy; as early as 1390, regarding the Christian expedition to the coasts of Tunisia, Jean Froissart said: "The Saracens have no strength at sea in the form of galleys or vessels, unlike the Genoese and Venetians. And when the Saracens put to sea they do nothing except plundering and thieving, neither can they catch Christians unless they are right on top of them, for an armed Christian galley could defeat four of Saracens."[57] The Muslims having neglected the sea were quite sensible of their deficiency on the sea.

Hence in 1540, in the meridian period of Turks' maritime influence over the Mediterranean, the Grand Vizier Lutfi Pasha observed that "many Sultans of the past dominated on land, but few ruled the seas. In the organization of naval expeditions, the unbeliever is our superior." Furthermore, the Sultan of Morocco Moulay Ismail, writing to the dispossessed king James II of England, apologized for not coming to his help, because "we are Arabs and unversed in maritime matters."

It would be tempting to impute this state of affairs to the backwardness of the Muslims in marine technology. True, the Europeans put others in the shade by pioneering maritime innovations in the modern era. In fact, the superiority of the iron-clad sailing ships of Europe, over the indigenous boat held together by palm thread was beyond dispute. The gain arising from this forward step, however, was insubstantial, because secrecy in this field of innovations was not possible, and so others too copied them. When the Venetians in the sixteenth century revolutionized the movement of galleys by making all oarsmen on the same bench operate a single oar, the Muslims at Algiers quickly adopted the innovation.

But still the Muslim fleets were inferior, ponderous and slow in comparison with the Christian ships. The Arabs did not lack ingenuity in an earlier age; they were credited with the first use of sailing vessels as warships, and the Byzantines owed to them much for adopting the technology of ships not known to them before. Later, the maximum speed of Muslim ships was a little over four knots, about one know less than the Byzantine ships, which therefore possessed superiority in manoeuvrability, likewise in fighting tactics. Lack of good timber is said to be the reason for the weakness of the Muslim fleets; however, when Nadir Shah wished to build in the 1740s the last great Persian fleet, he got the tree trunks hauled out of the Caspian forest, and over difficult passes to their destination.

Instead of searching for flaw in contrived things, we can fix our attention on the type of people responsible for them, invoking the well known maxim of the ancient Greeks: "Man, know thyself." None of the three ethnic groups—the Arabs, the Turks and the Berbers–that took to the sea under the flag of Islam had a continuous maritime tradition. In such a background, the Muslims who put themselves at the mercy of the sea heavily depended on the help of others. Till the mid-ninth century, the Christian crews manned the first Egyptian fleets that carried Muslim soldiers ready to fight in the event of a battle. Later, the Slavs had a big role in the development of the Fatimid navy.

The omnipresence of the renegades, especially the Venetians and the Greeks, in the Islamic fleet over the centuries underscored its weakness.

The ethnic reason why the Muslims had an abhorrence of the sea is not comprehensive. The Persians by the nineteenth century neglected the sea absolutely, but earlier for several centuries after they embraced Islam had preserved the maritime tradition of the South Seas. The absence of seafaring Muslims was not completely true, and some were so much lured by the sea as to take it as their vocation.

Born at Mecca some ten years before the hegira, Bosr ibn Abi Artat, a companion of the prophet, was the first admiral of the Arab fleets launched against Constantinople. About the great Abbasid voyages of discovery in the east, the description of the journey attributed to the merchant Suleiman testifies good knowledge of the South Seas. More instances of this kind do not belie the fact that the Muslim society as a whole was averse to the sea.

The construction of big fleets notwithstanding, the sea did not matter to the Caliphs as an accessory to power. Their capitals, first at Damascus, and then at Baghdad were continental; similarly, in Egypt the focus shifted from the port city of Alexandria to Cairo when Islam got power. While the Byzantines prided themselves about their sovereignty "over all the Mediterranean and as far as the columns of Hercules," the Caliphs were content with their gains on the land and their laudatory claims make no reference to their power over the sea.

With apathy to the sea uppermost, the Muslim naval policy was capricious, showing a burst of activity followed by lethargy, in a cyclical manner over a period. Almost for three centuries, the Ottoman navy was a power to contend with, but poor maintenance and slack practice ate into its efficiency to such an extent that the Venetian ambassador, Antonio Barbarigo, pictured the ships as "lasting no more than a year, so that when they come back to be decommissioned, it is pitiful to see their state of decline." Such a neglect reflected the inferior status of naval officers in the social hierarchy, and inevitably they found no place in the cream of the military society. What is more, the head of the Islamic navy was not on a level with the commander-in-chief of the army, so that in many instances he got his orders from him.

The sea has decisively influenced the mind of the Christians, but this is not so in regard to the Muslims, of course, with the important exceptions applicable to Malaysia and Islamic Andalusia. Their disregard of the sea is imputed to Islam, which means submission; however, a sailor is a rebel, an individualist so moulded after struggling with the uncongenial surroundings apparent on the water. In fact, with no settled life, he is given over to vagrancy and debauchery, lowering himself in the estimation of society. A well known text by Maqrisi tells that, after Saladin's death and the end of his naval policy, service at sea "had become a shameful thing which was grounds for insult. When one addressed a man in Egypt with the words: 'Hey sailor!' he would become very angry." As there had been always a conflict between the seafaring culture and the normative values of Islam, the sailors, more or less like barbarian hordes or nomadic tribes, were forced to live on the fringes of the society. By this attitude the Muslims were the losers as they were deprived of the gains of maritime business, a trend even now discernable, in the background of a expanding global economy.

The efflorescence of Islamic civilization was followed by its decay, then it went through colonial exploitation by the western powers. At present the Muslim countries are mostly free, and exploitation by others is not a serious issue. But they have to grapple with widespread poverty, economic underdevelopment, sexual inequality and political instability. Giving his views on Islam as it exists now, in his book *Among the Believers: An Islamic Journey,* the Nobel prize winner V.S. Naipaul says: "Islam, going by what I saw of it from the outside, was less metaphysical and more direct than Hinduism. In this religion of fear and reward, oddly compounded with war and worldly grief.... The glories of this religion were in the remote past; it had generated nothing like a Renaissance. Muslim countries, where not colonized, were despotisms and nearly all, before oil, were poor."

The boom period of Islam was gone forever, and what currently exists is a dispirited Muslim world. True, there is a growing demand for a return to Islam; but the religious extremist has to contend with the intellectual man who has emerged from his long hibernation to be a major force in the contemporary world.

The two revealed religions, Christianity and Islam, professing monotheism with universal appeal, since their inception were looking far beyond their confined existence. Their zeal to expand the influence of their faith, or rather to convert the world to their religion brought them into contact with other nations. Especially India which had its attraction, for the polytheism of the masses expressed through idolatry was more conspicuous, than the abstract idea of monotheism rooted in the mind of philosophers and intellectuals.

According to a tradition, the first known contact of Christianity with India occurred in the first century when St. Thomas came to India to preach the Gospel.[58] This was an isolated instance of missionary exuberance, hardly designed to shake the hold of Hindu religion.

In 712, when the Islamic juggernaut was moving forward in triumph, the Arabs seized a chunk of territory on the north-west of India, known as Sind. Their taking of this land, surrounded by vast desert, had no impact on the dynastic power centers of India.

The Sind episode was soon forgotten, with India secure for about three centuries in the absence of invasion from abroad. Then from a different quarter, that is Ghazni in Afghanistan, the peace of India was threatened. At this hour of crisis the Indian defence against the hordes Ghazni sent out was organized not on a national basis, but to preserve fragmented dynastic interest. The success of the invasion opened an era of temple destruction in India, ostensibly to overthrow polytheism but in reality to enrich the conquerors.

About the growth of Islam, those provinces in India near to its birth place, or to central Asia whose vigorous people spread this religion, became more rapidly and more thoroughly Muslim than areas farther south and east; however, Bengal to this rule was an exception, peopled mostly with Muslims who were converts from Buddhism. Somehow, the mountainous land of Nepal was untouched by Islam, which from India made its way to Malaya and to the islands of Sumatra, Java and Borneo.

The Muslim rule in Kashmir began in about 1339 when Shah Mirza, the Muslim prime minister of the former Hindu king, defeated the king's widow who had desired to rule by her own right.[59] First few of his successors tolerated their dominant Hindu subjects, but things changed drastically when Sultan Sikandar reigned over them. At this time Kashmir absorbed large immigrant Muslims, and heartened by their presence the ruler set about overthrowing the idols worshipped by the so-called Hindu infidels. Helped by his minister Suhabhatta, a convert from Hinduism, Sikandar went astray to such as extent that he "forgot his kingly duties and took a delight day and night in breaking images.... There was no city, no town, no village, no wood where Suha the Turushka left the temples of gods unbroken.[60]" Then Ali Shah succeeded him, however, the before mentioned proselyte was still at the helm, obnoxiously harassing the Brahmins as a caste. But the reign of next dynast, the great Zain-ul-Abidin, which beginning in the year 1420 extended over nearly half a century, was distinguished by such a broad outlook that religious persecution ceased, and the Brahmins got back their privileges.

Events of this type, particularly the vicissitudes of luck the Hindus in Kashmir passed through, have parallel with the rest of India under alien despotism. To be sure, a few Muslim rulers cared very much for the good of their Hindu subjects; but some mainly on grounds of religion persecuted them with a vengeance, while others displayed a cold indifference to their fate. It is certain that in areas under direct Muslim rule, the Hindus were suffered to exist as second-class citizens; they palpably had less religious freedom, and had to pay the invidious *jizya* tax. What is more to the disadvantage of the Hindus, their temples and monasteries accustomed to royal patronage from bygone times saw it ended. In the belief that religion was superfluous to the Hindus, the building of new temples and the renovation of old ones were prohibited. Furthermore, there is not much doubt though it is difficult to research in this field, that many temples were dispossessed of some or all the tax free land which once supported them.

True, even before the Muslim conquest, there are ubiquitous references in Indian source history to bitter religious conflict, although the Hindu tradition allowed a wide range of beliefs and practices to co-exist. Asoka the king of Maurya dynasty, despite his inclination to Buddhism, typified this wide outlook, and he preaches the "essential doctrine of all sects" based on "the control of one's speech, so as not to extol one's own sect or disparage another's on unsuitable occasions, or at least to do so only mildly on certain occasions."

But the very diversity of human thought, and the proliferation of new ideas gave room for tension, with the result certain groups were regarded as heretics, either because, like the Buddhists and the Jains, they denied the divine origin of the Vedas, or because, like the various tantric sects, their practices outraged Hindu moral sensibilities.

Mostly, the conflict materialized in the form of sect competition, capped with sophisticated verbal duels and miracle contests between the heads of rival sects. Such events occasionally seemed to have ended in violent confrontations and riots among the partisans of opposing factions.

Of Hindu ascetics who carried an iron lance, there is a mention as early as in Panini, who lived probably in the sixth or fifth century before Christ.[61]

Nevertheless, the early sect competition did not lead to the birth of anything resembling military orders. Such militarization, of course, is obliquely hinted in Madhavacharya's description of the legendary encounter between the great eighth century saint Sankara and his followers, and the tantric Kapalikas led by Krakaca or Nityananda. Probably, the military legions of the Kapalikas are an "anachronism introduced by an author familiar with the military orders of later medieval India."[62]

A potentially more dangerous threat to the existence of religious institutions than sectarian feud was state persecution. Kalhana in his history of Kashmir tells of king Sankaravarman (883-902) who was so filled with avarice, that he resorted to the expediency of taxing and confiscating the wealth of the temples: "He took from the temples the profits arising from the sale of incense, sandal wood, and other (articles of worship), under the pretext that they were the (king's legal) share of the selling price. Then, again, he plundered straightway sixty-four temples, through special officers placed over them under the pretence of (exercising) supervision."[63]

Many more pre-Muslim persecutions of religious institutions in Kashmir show that in post-Gupta times such things were more common than is admitted. The period in question saw alienation of more and more taxable lands, through grants to temples, monasteries and groups of Brahmins, thus paving the way for the growth of the feudal system. Any king desirous of curbing the power of the feudal barons had nowhere to go for funds, except to lay hands on the wealth of the temples.

Though Hindu kings of Kashmir like Jayapida, Sankaravarman and Harsa squeezed the Brahmins and robbed the temples, they did so against their own religious principles, and against public opinion.[64] The Muslim rule, however, gave religious colour to the persecution of Hindu sacred institutions, and confiscation of their wealth especially tax-free lands held by them. In other words, the Muslim rulers had the support of their co-religionist subjects, as well as Muslim law and tradition. The oppression of Brahmins, and the seizure of wealth of Hindu temples seemed to have occurred more frequently, under the reign of the Muslim kings. What is certain is that the coming of Islam did make it possible to openly advocate or threaten such actions to break the spirit of the Hindus.

When the British displaced the Muslim rulers, Hinduism in India instead of being discriminated stood on a level with Islam. With the English, however, Christianity entered India to which religion both the Hindus and Muslims were heathens. At first, the British unsure of their ground were solely guided by profit motive; in which background knowing that Christianity would not be well received by the people, discouraged entry of missionaries. This cautious policy after a time the English abandoned, and since they were in a position to see beyond their trade interest, in other words to civilize India, they let missionaries in.

Furthermore, the nineteenth century was an age of enlightenment, and the principle of reason bequeathed by the French philosophers to Europe strengthened the belief in the superiority of the west over other nations. There was a need for bringing western ideas into India, because the Hindu religion was perceived as superstitious, and besides many questionable practices such as rampant idolatry, widow burning and infanticide flourished in the name of religion. The innovators who moved forward to reform India were the rationalists, and the Evangelical Christians to whom the scepticism of the former especially their atheism was wholly unpalatable. Both however professed humanism which made them work together in India, despite the fact that Christianity sees atheistic humanism as no humanism at all. In our own times Pope John Paul II proceeded along a line of thought propounded by the French theologian Henri de Lubac, that the failure of atheistic humanism lies in its destruction of man's transcendental character, and therefore, his ultimate meaning as a human being. According to John Paul, godless humanism was based on "an inadequate view of man" which deprived him of "an essential dimension of his being, his search for the infinite."[65]

The Christian missionaries had worked in India from the time of Saint Francis Xavier, but under the influence of British power, they from preaching soon entered to teaching, encouraged by the rising demand for English language.[66] As their activities expanded they succeeded in changing the faith of some Indians especially the marginalized persons in the caste-ridden Hindu society, who from a desire for gain or other self-serving motives less to do with religion could not resist the temptation to embrace Christianity.

In the theological controversies of the day the ordinary man was out of his depth, but the Hindu intellectuals, the foremost among them Raja Ram Mohan Roy, knew their ground well and launched a counter-attack on missionary propaganda. Roy gave his attention to those classical Hindu texts which in content came nearest to an ethical monotheism, thereby offering to his fellow Hindus a chance to reform certain aspects of their religion without diminution of respect.[67] The strategic reinterpretation of Hinduism forestalled the impending conversion of many educated Hindus, who like Roy perceived the merits of Christian ethics, but now they could say these were equally a part of their faith. Raja Ram Mohan Roy founded in 1828 the *Brahmo Samaj* or *Divine Society* which since its inception was against idolatry, and stood for the worship of one supreme Being. It was to his credit that he defended Hinduism when it was under siege, and when it despaired of seeing the light. But his religious ideas were too intellectual, too much divorced from Hindu tradition, and greatly indebted to Christianity to have any lasting impression on the people.[68]

Next, reflecting the face of militant Hinduism, the *Arya Samaj*, founded by a Brahmin from Gujarat Dayananda Saraswati, was rooted in the soil and so had better appeal to the middle class. As it symbolized Indian nationalism, as well as resistance to Islamic and Christian expansionist movements, to meet their challenge, in a spirit of competitive rivalry it introduced into Hindu religion proselytization, discountenanced in the past owing to the existence of a tight caste system. But since it put faith in purism, that is in the original Vedas to the exclusion of everything else that Hindu thought later on absorbed and blossomed into maturity, and even rejected idol worship it lacked the ingredients of a mass movement.

The revival movement of Vivekananda, however, got over the above deficiency with regard to narrow outlook in so far as it was grounded firmly in Hindu tradition as a whole. He was the disciple of a mystic saint, Ramakrishna, whom his followers now see as an avatar, that is an incarnation of God Vishnu. This illustrious saint inspired Swami Vivekananda to set up Ramakrishna Mission to revivify Hindu religion; so the aforesaid establishment with its presence all over India, and with its "saffron-robed monks in the place of white missionaries" did much spiritual, medical and educational work, of course, in the footsteps of Christian pioneers. It was not long before Hinduism got transformed from passive realization to an active principle, under the leadership of Mahatma Gandhi.

At the close of the nineteenth century, the Maratha resistance and Hindu militancy found an outstanding leader in B.G. Tilak. He wished to revive the Hindu spirit, by awakening the religious feelings of the common man, and so conjured up the image of Lord Ganesh. In fact, the liberation movement of the Marathas in an earlier age had strong religious overtones; their king Shivaji prided himself on the title "protector of cows and Brahmans," and his contemporaries hailed him for having freed the Hindus from the Muslim domination. The ritual worship of Ganesh, the elephant-headed god of wealth, wisdom and success, was a big annual festival with the Marathas. The palace of their ruler Peshwa had a special hall where the idol of Ganesh was ceremoniously installed, and then for twelve days was worshipped. Then came the immersion in water ceremony of the god, an occasion of much pomp and revelry, as the idol of Ganesh was carried in a palanquin, accompanied by the picked infantry and cavalry units of the Maratha army that marched through the streets.[69]

Further, Tilak's hand in Ganesh festival had undercurrents of political opposition; in fact, nothing he did in the public sphere could be divorced from politics, and he even interpreted the sacred book Gita in such a way as to bolster up the hope of Indian nationalism.

Gandhi was the heir to such a tradition in which religion and politics went hand in hand to build a mass movement. As a party the Congress stood for Hindu revival, and nobody personified that spirit better than Gandhi. He over and above his role in politics was a religious leader of the people, and his title Mahatma was in recognition of his saintly character.

Though Gandhi in his younger days had resisted attempts to convert him to Christianity, his religious ideas agreed with it on many points, and in fact "the Hindu Gandhi is closer to Christ in heart and spirit" than the diluted Christians of the contemporary world. Romain Rolland and Gandhi Correspondence, P. 427. Indeed the Christian society over the years has so much changed that what it honours now is the antithesis of Christ, that is Caesar and his militaristic force.

No less important is the point of difference between Gandhi and the two religious faiths, Christianity and Islam. Both were propelled to the center stage of world religions by missionary activity leading to conversion, but Gandhi, though he entertained profound respect for the two prophetic religions, maintained formally his opposition to conversions, on grounds of elevated principles. For he said: "We must eliminate from us any secret pride which would tell us that our religion is the truest and that the others are less so.... Our attitude towards other religions ought to be absolutely frank and sincere. Our prayer for others ought never to be: 'God, give them the light Thou hast given to me!' but 'Give them all the light and truth they need for their higher development....' If some persons think that they ought to change their religious 'etiquette' by conversion, I cannot deny that they are free to do so, but I am sorry to see it."[70]

At the Christological level, however,, the reason for missionary activity, inspired by the command of Jesus to the eleven apostles to go forth and make all nations his disciples, "is the evangelization and the implanting of the Church among peoples or groups in which it has not yet taken root."[71] This reason is strengthened by the conviction, that the one true religion exists in the Catholic Church. The man responsible for mission work at the top is the Pope, the Supreme Head of the Universal Church, in whom devolved the task Christ had given to St. Peter, the first bishop of Rome, to convert the world so that there would be one flock and one shepherd.

Gandhi, advocating peace and wishing to see the basic elements of harmony in several religions rather than conflict, observes that the forms are many but the Spirit is one, so "the final goal of all religions is to realize this essential oneness." In other words, religions are different roads converging to the same point.

But the great religions are beyond doubt in conflict over the nature of the transcendent, and over man and his fulfillment. In fact they are not different paths to the same goal. Expatiating on this matter Professor Zaehner says: "It is then only too true that the basic principles of Eastern and Western, which in practice means Indian and Semitic, thought are, I will *not* say irreconcilably opposed; they are simply not starting from the same premises. The only common ground is that the function of religion is to provide release: there is no agreement at all as to what it is that man must be released from. The great religions are talking at cross purposes."[72]

The points of divergence coming in the way of synthesis of religions were made obvious, though discreetly, by the Second Vatican Council (1962-5) which issued a declaration on the relation of the Church to non-Christian religions: "The Catholic Church rejects nothing which is true and holy in these religions. She looks with sincere respect upon those ways of conduct and of life, those rules and teachings which, though differing in many particulars from what she holds and sets forth, nevertheless often reflect a ray of that Truth which enlightens all men. Indeed, she proclaims and must ever proclaim Christ, 'the way, the truth, and the life' (John 14:6), in whom men find the fullness of religious life, and in whom God has reconciled all things to Himself (2 Cor. 5:18-19).

The Church therefore has this exhortation for her sons: prudently and lovingly, through dialogue and collaboration with the followers of other religions, and in witness of Christian faith and life, acknowledge, preserve, and promote the spiritual and moral goods found among these men, as well as the values in their society and culture.

The Church has also a high regard for the Muslims. They worship God, who is one, living and subsistent, merciful and almighty, the Creator of heaven and earth, who has also spoken to men. They strive to submit themselves without reserve to the hidden decrees of God, just as Abraham submitted himself to God's plan, to whose faith Muslims eagerly link their own. Although not acknowledging him as God, they worship Jesus as a prophet, his virgin Mother they also honour, and even at times devoutly invoke. Further, they await the day of judgement and the reward of God following the resurrection of the dead. For this reason they highly esteem an upright life and worship God, especially by way of prayer, alms-deeds and fasting."[73]

Exuding fraternal love, the declaration seemed to be not further advanced than the Anglican statement at the Lambeth Conference of 1930, which affirmed: "We gladly acknowledge the truths contained and emphasized in the great religions; but ...each of them is less than the Gospel of the unsearchable riches of Christ. The majesty of God in Islam, the high moral standards and profound truth in other Eastern religions, are approaches to the truth of God revealed in Christ."[74]

Till the colonial period many Christian associations, such as the Mission to Lepers and the Salvation Army, thought it right to combine evangelical and humanitarian aims.[75] Although some such as World Vision still dovetail the two objectives, the mainstream Christian establishments are today opposed to such a policy. In fact, conversion of people who are hungry, sick or otherwise disadvantaged is now denounced as unethical, by the World Council of Churches. The Second Vatican Council announced that the Church has the obligation, and also the sacred right to evangelize; however, it saw the need to "avoid any action which seems to suggest coercion or dishonest or unworthy persuasion especially when dealing with the uneducated or the poor."

The Roman Catholic Church has come a long way from its once humble circumstances, and now it is a big organization, doubtless with vast resources. About 750 million Roman Catholics, the largest religious fraternity, live in our planet. Their head is the pope, known variously as successor to St. Peter, the Supreme Pontiff, Bishop of Rome, and Christ's Vicar on Earth, he reflects three cardinal virtues: Faith, Hope and Charity. When John Paul II assumed office as the head of the Church, the number of the clergy was put at 1,556,754, besides there existed 331,960 parishes, making up some 2,372 ecclesiastical territories.

The Church runs diverse institutions: from newspapers to radio stations, knowing well that means of communication decisively help evangelism; from hospitals to gradational schools whose impact on education is obvious from the existence of its 79,207 primary schools, over 28,000 secondary schools, and universities which at the end of 1977 had 986,000 scholars on the rolls.[76]

In the Middle Ages, the fortunes of the papacy was in the ascendent, and the pope at Rome radiating the power of heavenly court "exercised vicariously the authority of Christ and dispensed justice to monarch as well as their subjects, his decisions ultimately determining every aspect of human behaviour." Heresy leading to schism was one of the potent ills that afflicted Church supremacy, even before Reformation destroyed it.

In its simple form, heresy beginning with the nature of Christ, questioned the truth of a doctrine fundamental to Christian faith and asserted that the Second Person of the Trinity, God the Son, is not really God in the sense in which the Father is God. So "if God the Son was not really divine then Jesus Christ was no more than a creature."[77]

Such theological arguments that baffled and divided Christianity were alien to the nature of Islam, since its inception. The Muslim have not succumbed to "the temptation of reducing the object of their faith and devotion to a level with the senses and imagination of man."[78] What they always profess without change is: "I believe in one God, and Muhammad the apostle of God," and the honours they bestow on Muhammad have never gone beyond the finite virtue of man.

The schism between the Eastern and Western Church was rooted in the separatist tendencies of the former. The Eastern part of the Church, under the influence of the Patriarch of Constantinople, desired to have its own way in regard to administrative and liturgical matters. Their antagonism came to a head in 1054, and afterwards the Eastern Orthodox Chrches gradually ended connection with the Holy See. Hence, the Orthodox Churches do not accept the Pope as their supreme head, and indeed some anti-Catholic Orthodox priests have regarded him as their arch-enemy, though papacy has spared no efforts in order to achieve one flock one shepherd objective.

The Greek Orthodox Church inherited the historical antipathies against everything Western, and harboured suspicion about its minority Catholic population connected with the Roman See. Till 1833 the Greek Orthodox Church came under the jurisdiction of the Patriarch of Constantinople, but Greece which obtained freedom in 1827 put less faith in it unless religion too was made free of external control, and in the sequel was born Greek State Church, divorced from the influence of Constantinople.

Again the fear of getting submerged by alien influences made the Greek parliament to discuss laws by which Catholics would be forbidden to proselytize among the Orthodox. Mixed marriages conducted in a Catholic Church were declared by the state as invalid, while the Orthodox Church opposed the presence of a Latin rite Catholic Archbishop in Athens.

The law against proselytizing was published in 1938, and it was defined in the first draft as an effort to influence, in any manner, the conscience of a member of any religious group in order to bring a change in his religion.[79] Every type of religious propaganda was prohibited. The second draft saw proselytizing merely in the light of such propaganda that was carried on illicitly with a promise of material help to those who were the target of the aforesaid propaganda, and with the purpose of deceiving and of exploiting the ignorance, faith, poverty, or mental weakness of others. Further, proselytizing in schools, centers of learning or charitable institutions attracted harsh penalties, and besides restrictions were put on the publication and sale of Catholic literature.

Later, the Greek Catholic episcopate protested, and other countries too raised objection, so that the law was modified. The Greek resentment against foreign religious interference was fed by nationalism, and likewise in India, when nationalism in conjunction with religious fundamentalism made certain state governments pass anti-conversion laws, Pope John Paul II thinking how to defend freedom of religion from state interference was far from easy. The Second Vatican Council had observed that "it is wrong for a public authority to compel its citizens by force or fear or any other means to profess or repudiate any religion or to prevent anyone from joining or leaving a religious body."

At the height of anti-Muslim fury in the aftermath of India's freedom, violence against the Roman Catholics too broke out in a place close to Delhi. When Gandhi heard about persecution of the Christians, he called it a plague, and noted that it was spreading over India, and made it clear that the Christians should enjoy the freedom to practise their religion without molestation.[80]

There is one remarkable thing common to Muhammad, Gandhi, and Pope John Paul. They all perceive the dehumanizing effects of civilization. Indeed Pope John Paul II echoed the views of Gandhi, when speaking in defence of spiritual and moral values against the assaults of materialism and licence, he asked the Irish Catholics what use political freedom was if they became prisoners of their own material selfishness.

Pope John Paul shares Gandhi's pessimism bordering on dread with regard to a civilization based on consumerism. While gloomily reflecting on the advancement of the West, he believes that "progress, which has been brought about by generations of men with such labour, with the waste of so much energy and at such a cost, contains in its complexity a powerful element of death.[81]" Why? Because the consumer's world is merely the other side of the coin of nuclear weapons.

Looking at the world in the secular environment, this much becomes clear: Man who makes God die, finds himself without restraint against killing man too. Gandhi on a level with Jesus as "a teacher of truth and a servant of love" would have agreed with the views of Paul concerning the wrong track on which the civilization is moving towards its destruction. Much more so with the perception of Paul, that violence is the antithesis of love.

The relationship between God and man lies at the root of Christianity, as well as Hinduism. On the subject man, the dynamic thinking of John Paul bares certain simple truths: Man needs God because he knows well that the withdrawal of God presages his own self-assassination; yet, in the background of his love-hate relationship, he carried away by pride and audacity feels impelled to challenge God, in conformity with the words in the Old Testament: "I will not serve, *Non serviam.*"[82]

Gandhi was aware of the ruin caused by pride which tempts people to turn away from God, and his complex exercises revolving around self-restraint and chastity were aimed at reducing himself to zero.

Christ was mercy incarnate, and his mission on earth was to dispense mercy. The secular thinker, however, conceives mercy as a unilateral act, and so prefers justice. Hence the preference for impersonal and reciprocal social welfare systems based on justice, without the humanizing touch of mercy. This explains why Pope John Paul lacks faith in secular Utopias, and as a dispenser of mercy his Church transcends secular concept. It is obvious to him that "the equality brought by justice is limited to the realm of objective and extrinsic goods, while love and mercy enable people to meet one another on the plane of humanity, with a dignity proper to man's estate."

It is mercy that made Gandhi the Mahatma, a kind of mercy which discovered proximity to God through service to people.

The belief of John Paul, that dedication for service means becoming "a man for others," that the heart of the priest in order that it may be available for service must be free, and celibacy is a sign of that freedom, is in agreement with Gandhi's view. By his experience in South Africa Gandhi learnt the hard truth, that indulgence in sex and public service do not go together.

Praise of celibacy is the core of Gandhi's ideology. He by a precocious marriage knew at a too young age the obsession with carnal desire, so that to liberate the soul took steps to embrace *Brahmacharya,* the law of absolute chastity. True, John Paul, upholding the moral standards in a world where the sacral nature of inter-personal relationship is disappearing, thinks that a man who lusted after his wife in his heart committed adultery, and the degradation of the wife into an object of lust annuls the moral value of marriage.[83] Such views were consistent with the thoughts of Gandhi, and in this respect his lapses in his boyish days, which he himself confessed, were extenuated by the purity of his subsequent life.

With so many points of convergence notwithstanding, Gandhi sees proselytization an obstacle to peace. As all the great religions are fundamentally equal, he reasons that each must respect other religions on a par with his own. It is noteworthy that Gandhi's ties with Hindu religion were so strong that he once said he would not give his daughter (had he one) in marriage to a Muslim for anything in the world, even to the one he most highly esteemed.[84]

NOTES & REFERENCES

1. The Shape of Things to Come, V. 1, H.G. Wells, p. 51.
2. The Decline and Fall of the Roman Empire, Britannia edition, V. 1, Edward Gibbon, p. 187.
3. The Republic, Plato, B. Jowett, p. 170.
4. A Study of History, Arnold J. Toynbee, laural edition, p. 574.
5. Journal of the American Oriental Society, 98.1 (1978), Warrior Ascetics in Indian History, David N. Lorenzen, p. 72.
6. Pope John Paul II and the Catholic Restoration, Paul Johnson, p. 122.
7. The Peloponnesian War, Thucydides, p. 122 (Penguin Classics).
8. Women and Islam, Fatima Mernissi, p. 146
9. The Jerome Biblical Commentary, V. 2, Raymond E. Brown, p. 33
10. The Quest of the Historical Jesus, Albert Schweitzer, p. 258.
11. *Ibid.*, p. 319.
12. *Ibid.*, p. 95.
13. *Ibid.*, p. 152.
14. *Ibid.*, pp. 54-55.

15. Augustus to Constantine, Robert M. Grant, p. 124.
16. The Jerome Biblical Commentary, *op. cit.*, p. 804.
17. A Popular History of the Catholic Church, Philip Hughes, p. 21.
18. *Ibid.*, p. 27
19. Edward Gibbon, V. 1, p. 328.
20. *Ibid.*, p. 329.
21. Journal of the American Oriental Society 95:2 (1975), Medieval Muslim Views of Indian Religions, Y. Friedmann, p. 219.
22. *Ibid.*, p. 221.
23. *Ibid.*, p. 211.
24. Islam, Alfred Guillaume, p. 14.
25. A Popular History of the Catholic Church, Philip Hughes, p. 72.
26. The Koran, Sura 9:29.
27. *Ibid.*, Sura 5:51.
28. Edward Gibbon, V. 2, p. 234.
29. Encyclopaedic History of World Civilization, Arthur Gilman, Islam, pp. 132-133.
30. The Koran, sura: 93.
31. Interpreting Islam, Edited by Hastings Donnan, Ideological Dimensions of Islam, Ilyas Ba-Yunus, p. 103.
32. The Koran, Sura: 33: 32; 33.
33. Interpreting Islam, op cit., p.103.
34. Edward Gibbon, v. 2, p. 246.
35. Abu Bakar Siddique, Shah Moinuddin Nadvi, pp. 16-17.
36. Islam, Alfred Guillaume, p. 9.
37. The Koran, Sura 17: 49 and 6:29.
38. Edward Gibbon, v. 2, pp. 236-237.
39. Abu Bakar Siddique, Shah Moinuddin Nadvi, p. 28.
40. Interpreting Islam, *op cit.*, Organized Charity in the Arab-Islamic World, Jonathan Benthall, p. 150.
41. Interpreting Islam, op cit, Ilyas Ba-Yunus, p. 102.
42. Islam, Alfred Guillaume, p. 40.
43. *Ibid.*, p. 12.
44. Edward Gibbon, v. 2, p. 238.

45. Islam, Alfred Guillaume, p. 43.
46. The Koran, Sura 3:134ff.
47. Edward Gibbon, V. 2, 243.
48. Abu Bakar Siddique, Shah Moinuddin Nadvi, p. 40.
49. The Outline of History, H.G. Wells, p. 622.
50. Interpreting Islam, Edited by Hastings Donnan, Ideological Dimensions of Islam, Ilyas Ba-Yunus, p. 105.
51. Abu Bakar Siddique, Shah Moinuddin Nadvi, p. 45.
52. *Ibid.,* p. 52.
53. *Ibid.,* p. 67.
54. Interpreting Islam, *op cit.*, Islam and the Sea, Xavier de Planhol, p. 144.
55. *Ibid.,* p. 143.
56. *Ibid.*, p. 130.
57. *Ibid.*, p. 134.
58. Advanced History of India, K.A. Nilakanta Sastri and G. Srinivasachari, p. 309; A History of India, v. 1, Romila Thapar, p. 134.
59. Journal of the American Oriental Society, 98.1 (1978), Warrior Ascetics in Indian History, David N. Lorenzen p. 67.
60. *Ibid.*, pp. 67-68.
61. *Ibid.*, p. 64, and Advanced History of India, op cit, p. 85.
62. Journal of the American Oriental Society, *op cit*, p. 65.
63. *Ibid.*, p. 66.
64. *Ibid.*, p. 68.
65. Pope John Paul II and the Catholic Restoration, Paul Johnson, p. 95.
66. The Oxford History of India, Vincent A. Smith, p. 724.
67. Sources of Indian Tradition, Wm. Theodore de Bary, p. 572.
68. A Survey of Indian History, K.M. Panikkar, P. 267.
69. Journal of the American Oriental Society, 1985, v. 105, Extracts from the Religious Complex in Eighteenth-century Poona, Balkrishna Govind Gokhale.
70. Romain Rolland and Gandhi Correspondence, p. 427,
71. Vatican Council II, Editor Austin Flannery, O.P., p. 736.
72. Christ and the World Religions, Charles Davis, p. 51.
73. Vatican Council II, *op. cit,* p. 668.
74. Christ and the World Religions, *op cit.*, p. 48.

75. Interpreting Islam, Edited by Hastings Donnan, Organized Charity in the Arab-Islamic World, Jonathan Benthall, pp. 160-61.
76. Pope John Paul II, Paul Johnson, p. 57.
77. A Popular History of the Catholic Church, Philip Hughes, p. 25.
78. Edward Gibbon, V. 2, p. 252.
79. Pope John XXIII, Zsolt Aradi, p. 179.
80. Delhi Diary, M.K. Gandhi, pp. 195-197.
81. Pope John Paul II, Paul Johnson, p. 106.
82. *Ibid.*, p. 107.
83. *Ibid.*, p. 113.
84. Romain Rolland and Gandhi Correspondence, p. 5.

2

GANDHI'S CRUCIAL YEARS

The Gandhi's who belonged to the Vaisya caste•seemed to have been originally grocers.[1] In Hindu society, the value of a person from bygone ages was measured by the caste, and the social importance of the Vaisyas was neither too high nor too low, with the result the wealth they had accumulated as traders did not help them much to improve their status. Gandhi's ancestors, however, had been prime ministers in several Kathiawad States, and his father too, Karamchand Gandhi, otherwise known as Kaba Gandhi, belonged to this ruling class. Kaba in another respect stood out from others, by going through matrimony four times altogether.[2] His first marriage brought him into the state of a widower, and his other successive wedlocks were the result of his attempt to escape such a forlorn existence. His last wife Putlibai was fated to outlive him, after she gave birth to a daughter and three sons, the youngest among them was Mohandas Karamchand Gandhi, born on 2nd October 1869 in Porbandar, a coastal town facing the Arabian Sea. Kaba Gandhi was known for his incorruptible nature, and lacked the desire to accumulate wealth, the chief preoccupation of his caste people, and his wife named above was a pious woman. No wonder their progeny, Gandhi, should inherit their traits. But without that lust which distinguished his father in conjugal life, and Gandhi's backwardness to indulge in sexual gratification in his middle years could be attributed to an incident which happened in the following way.

In a society where the son had to submit to the will of the patriarch, more so the daughter, Gandhi when still a child had been forced into marriage. His wife Kasturbai he loved to the point of infatuation, and this did not come in the way of his showing too much affection for his father. Once his father fell sick, so that Gandhi divided his time between going to school and looking after him. On a particular day when he was tending his father, his uncle came to relieve him. Gandhi walked away happily, thinking of the attraction of a warm bed and its pleasures, though his wife had grown in size with child. He got into the bedroom, soon there was a knock on the door, and then Gandhi received the news of his father's demise. Gandhi was filled with grief, reflecting that had he stayed beside his father to help him at his last moments doubtless he would have died in his arms, thereby depriving his uncle of that privilege[3]. He carried throughout his life his guilt complex, born out of the fact that sexual act intended for procreation was misused in favour of too much sensual delight.

While pursuing college studies, Gandhi, although capable professors taught him, being aware of his limitations was ill at ease in his new academic environment. But his disquiet was removed before long in this way. His mother was enlightened about his chances of getting into the ministerial position his father had held, by a certain Dave, a man well versed in worldly matters. He let her know that if Gandhi completed his graduate course he would obtain a middle level position, with moderate remuneration, but the eminence achieved by his forebears would be beyond his reach. He expressed the opinion that Gandhi could get over his deficiency, if he went to England to study law in order to become a barrister. He then turning his face towards Gandhi asked him: "Would you not rather go to England than study here?"[4] Gandhi was pleased with the suggestion, and, having made up his mind to go abroad at any cost, nerved himself to overcome opposition to such an adventurous enterprise. "I am not sure," his uncle said, "whether it is possible for one to stay in England without prejudice to one's religion."[5] But he had no wish to stand in the way of Gandhi's soaring hopes, and was ready to give his consent provided his mother Putlibai too did so.

Gandhi coaxed his mother into obeying him, but getting the approval of the caste order as it existed in its degenerate condition at this period was a different matter. It represented the rigid and unthinking mind of the community, evident from the fact that the caste leader told Gandhi, in the assembly called to deal with him, that he should not cross the seas because nobody in his caste had done so; he tried to persuade him to give up his overseas ambition, and Gandhi reasoned with him to break his resistance, both failed, in the sequel Gandhi was expelled from the caste.[6] This would have been a calamity for a person in earlier times, but now the fact that caste order was on the decline cushioned the harm of such a blow.

Gandhi went to London in 1888 after an uneventful voyage, and was admitted to the Inner Temple.[7] It was not so much his scholastic labour as the difficulty of adapting to his alien surroundings that worried Gandhi. He was not even fluent in English, so that he had to go through a lot of mental exertion to build the pattern of a sentence before he could speak with anyone[8]. He had acquired a belief in so many taboos in his sheltered existence back at home, and now encumbered with them Gandhi forlorn of hope in his urban jungle of London searched with the instinct of an explorer, until at last his efforts paid rich dividends. The sight which thrilled him with joy was nothing more than a vegetarian restaurant, then as scarce in London as an oasis in the Arabian desert. Over and above the problem of adjusting to the life of English society, Gandhi took seriously his intellectual pursuits. He mastered the intricacies of law, that is Common Law and Roman Law, and passed the final examination without much ado. Before long he was called to the bar, and in less than three years his overseas education being over he was back at home to engage in law practice, which posed more problems than he had expected. For it demanded high level of competence, and survival instinct in a cutthroat competitive world. This was more so in Bombay where Gandhi failed to impress as a lawyer, and burdened with financial commitments not balanced by earnings he for his own comfort moved out; that is to Rajkot, where his brother was a pettifogger, and consequently under his patronage he was sure to get some business at least in the shape of drafting petitions.[9]

About this time Gandhi had firsthand experience with the arrogant power display of a British officer, who ordered his peon to eject him from the office and his command was literally carried out.[10] The importunity of his brother, who was under a cloud for not having properly discharged his official duties, had forced Gandhi much against his better sense to put in a word at the official level to clear the prejudice against the said person; however, the officer or rather Political Agent as he was styled, known to him in England, not only said his brother was an intriguer but dealt in a harsh manner with Gandhi, who could not for a while get over his discomfiture.

On the whole Gandhi was in a dismal condition, since the great expectation he had entertained concerning his legal profession, notwithstanding the glamour of his foreign qualifications, had come to nothing. He was troubled by the uncertainty of his future, just then relief came when Dada Abdulla and Company involved in a legal dispute with another firm over outstanding dues wished to send him to South Africa in order to make use of his professional acumen. The assignment, for the duration of not more than a year, was attractive to Gandhi, as the Company was ready to pay first class fare both ways, his expenses in that country treating him rather like a guest than a servant, and besides one hundred five pounds compensation to him.[11] Gandhi set sail for South Africa, and in about thirteen days the ship put in at Lamu; meanwhile he and the Captain had developed intimacy which gave room for undesirable consequences as the sequel illustrates. The next port of call was Mombasa, and then Zanzibar, which in its wealth of trees and in its vast carpet of green fields somewhat resembled the State of Kerala in India. The Captain was itching to go out of his floating prison, in order to have sex with a woman, and he besides an English friend took Gandhi with him, after virtually concealing his real intention from him.[12] They took a boat, crossed the waters and then landed on shore, from where as they moved further a pimp guided them to a bawdy house.[13] Here each was directed to a room; till now Gandhi had kept up the illusion that he and the Captain were of like mind, because his false sense of shame weakened his resolve to show himself what he really was. But once he got into the room he was true to himself, kept his distance from the woman, and escaped from temptation by having recourse to passivity. In the sequel Gandhi blamed his weakness, overlooking his inner strength, which later played so much havoc with the British power, and which had helped him in front of the woman not to lose his head.

After a halt at Mozambique, at last Gandhi arrived in Durban where his employer and merchant prince Abdulla received him, in the sequel confirming his guest status.[14] It did not take much penetration for Gandhi to see the wide divide between the subject people and the ruling class. The arrogance of the latter he felt when a magistrate taking offence at his turban told him to be off with it.[15] Far from obliging him Gandhi got away from the court, in the spirit of a nonconformist rebel. Later, when he was traveling by rail, at Maritzburg, the capital of Natal, the colour prejudice went against him, and on his refusal to quit the compartment to add to the ease of white passengers, a constable pushed him out. At every step in South Africa he suffered discrimination; while traveling by train he had been harassed, then he shifted to a stagecoach where he was told to sit on the footboard, and when he protested he was dealt with roughly. The Indian settlers lived under a harsh regime which administered laws palpably unjust; consequently, they had no franchise, had to pay a poll-tax of three pounds sterling for entering into the Transvaal, could not own land wherever they wished to do so, and could not freely move in the night after a particular time. What is more, the public footpath instead of being a safe ground was hostile territory for them; how much it was so Gandhi learnt to his dismay when a policeman put him in the right place by kicking him out of the reserved ground.[16]

About the case for which he had been hired, Gandhi at the inceptive stage itself had told his employer that he would try for a out of court settlement. He presumed this would be a more sensible course than court wrangling, especially because the opposing parties were related to each other. He later convinced both the parties that it was to their advantage to go in accordance with his plan, and so an arbitrator was appointed who upheld Abdulla's claim to about thirty-seven thousand pounds sterling with costs. But the trouble of Gandhi did not end with this verdict, since he who should pay was not in a position to discharge his obligation, the fear of bankruptcy hung over him. Gandhi, therefore, again used his persuasive talent and extracted such favourable terms from his employer that the defaulter could pay over a long period by installments. Now both the parties were happy and Gandhi more so, because, instead of taking part in a court strife in the spirit of an unfriendly opponent, he had learnt how to enter into people's heart and how to unite parties divided by mistrust. This set the pattern of Gandhi's life, and the way of peace won for him later millions of adherents who saw in him the qualities of a great leader.

Gandhi, meanwhile, was in the forefront of agitations aimed at redressing the grievances of the Indians. At first, in the choppy waters of politics, he went by the path of least resistance, and so he submitted a big petition endorsed by ten thousand signatures to Lord Ripon, the head of colonial affairs; this monster petition as it was called made so much noise that it even reached India. Then in order to fight for the franchise, and against the poll-tax, feeling the need of a permanent organization, Gandhi, in 1894, set up the Natal Indian Congress, which at the outset of its existence agitated for the benefit of indentured Indians, especially to remove their tax burden.[18] His activities to promote the good of the exploited class, while it increased his reputation, brought him the ill will of powerful vested interests. Hence, when he returned after a brief stay in India, a hot reception awaited him; indeed he ploughed his way through a hostile crowd which beat him; then the house was blockaded where he had taken sanctuary, but from where he made good his escape in disguise.[19]

About this time Gandhi was taken with the idea of celibacy. "It became my conviction," Gandhi said, "that procreation and the consequent care of children were inconsistent with public service."[20] He had ploughed and had raised a crop of children, but now he had to deal with the question how to take his thoughts away from such routine preoccupation, and towards platonic love. At first although they bedded keeping distance from each other, his self-control did not mean much as he himself to himself was unfaithful, with the result he sought her company to partake with her in carnal pleasures. However after 1906, with his wife's co-operation, not a small thing in a matter of this kind, he succeeded in keeping sexual temptation at bay.

Gandhi later was in India to get what help he could from the Indian Congress, which was to meet at Calcutta in 1901 under the leadership of Dinshaw Wacha. At this time, the reign of Lord Curzon symbolized the high tide of imperialism, and one Pherozeshah Mehta had so much influence in Bombay that he was pompously styled its uncrowned king. Indeed his personal life did not lack ostentation, and he had engaged a special saloon for his exclusive use while traveling by rail to Calcutta to attend the Congress meeting. But when he talked with Gandhi, who was also in the same train to go to the same party meeting, his words belied his importance as the uncrowned king. For he said: "Gandhi, it seems nothing can be done for you. Of course we will pass the resolution you want. But what rights have we in our own country? I believe that, so long as we have no power in our own land, you cannot fare better in the colonies."[21]

Later the Transvaal government tried to abridge the rights of the Indians further, and wanted them to register and to give fingerprints, demanded only from the criminals. Gandhi started his passive resistance, otherwise known as *satyagraha,* which instead of being passive was an active struggle. The upshot of his open defiance of law was he was tried in the very court where he had appeared as a lawyer, and then he was sent to Johannesburg prison. Assuming the role of an intermediary, the police chief of Johannesburg in January 1908 took Gandhi to Pretoria for parleying with a leader of the ruling clique, General Smuts, who told him that he had consulted General Botha, and that he would repeal the law in question, if the Indians went through voluntary registration.[22] Nothing having come out of this talk Gandhi again and again went to prison, and once at Pretoria he was confined in a solitary prison intended for dangerous persons. His day in jail commenced after a lamp was lighted up at half past five in the morning in order to wake up the prisoners, to help them roll up their beds, and to prepare them for prison routine.[23]

Afterwards, Gandhi went to England, where the situation was somewhat complicated by the assassination of Curzon Wyllie, a high officer of Indian affairs. Later, on a festival day sacred to the Hindus, Gandhi in England shared the platform with one Savarkar, who delivered an emotional speech reflecting his nationalist ardour.[24] This man Savarkar gave a nickel-plated revolver to Madanlal Dhingra, who like a robot obeyed him, did the murder of Wyllie, and in turn was quickly executed about this time, but his prompter escaped for lack of evidence.[25] Gandhi told Lord Ampthill, former Governor of Madras, that his resistance movement in South Africa had nothing to do with Indian terrorist violence, which he found it hard to accept on any moral grounds. Ampthill influenced by what he heard wrote to Smuts, that Gandhi was contending for a principle which he was not likely to abandon, and that "it is impossible not to admire the man, for it is evident that he recognizes no court of appeal except that of his own conscience.[26]" Even the head of the colonies, Lord Crewe, seemed to have been impressed by the fact that Indians "have always enjoyed the right of entry, at any rate in theory, in every part of the Empire until they were deprived of it in the Transvaal.[27]"

Gandhi, in South Africa, to get the better of his opponents, relied on his ability to create friction at the border, taking advantage of the fact that without a permit entry into the Transvaal from Natal, as well as in the reverse direction, was not allowed. Some women followers of his crossed the border without permit, and went to Newcastle coal mines to stir up disaffection, particularly among the Indian labourers. Gandhi after he came to know that workers were on strike rushed to Newcastle to assume leadership over them.[28] About five thousand in strength, this army of the proletariat during the strike lived under the open sky, since Gandhi was unable to provide them with any sort of accommodation. He did not let them idle away their time, and, seeing his opportunity at the head of the masses, desired to advance towards the Transvaal border, thirty-six miles away, that too on foot. The great march of the unarmed army started on 28th October 1913, and when it was close to Johannesburg, Gandhi was arrested, and the strike crushed. But this did not help matters in the least, in the background of widespread discontent, and before long Smuts made peace with Gandhi on terms favourable to the working class.

NOTES AND REFERENCES

1. An Autobiography, M.K. Gandhi, p.1.
2. *Ibid.*
3. *Ibid,* p. 26.
4. *Ibid*, p. 31.
5. *Ibid*, p. 32.
6. *Ibid*, p. 34 & 35.
7. Mahatma Gandhi, A Chronology, K.P. Goswami, P. 2.
8. Autobiograpy, p. 36.
9. *Ibid*, p. 80.
10. *Ibid*, p. 82.
11. *Ibid*, p. 85.
12. *Ibid*, p. 87.
13. *Ibid.*
14. *Ibid*, p. 88.
15. *Ibid*, p. 89,
16. *Ibid*, p. 108.
17. *Ibid*, p. 112.

18. Satyagraha in South Africa, M.K. Gandhi, p. 42.
19. *Ibid*, p. 54, 55 & 56.
20. Autobiography, p. 172.
21. *Ibid*, p. 186.
22. Satyagraha, p. 144.
23. Collected Works of Mahatma Gandhi, V. 9, p. 215.
24. *Ibid*, p. 499.
25. Veer Savarkar, Dhananjay Keer, p. 53.
26. Collected Works, V. 9, p. 583.
27. *Ibid*, p. 588, Lord Ampthill's letter to Gandhi.
28. Satyagraha, p. 260.

3

THE OLD GUARD BANISHED

Gandhi returned to India in 1915, and had to his credit reputation on account of his foreign exploits, as well as experience in mass agitation. No doubt, under the compulsion of Gandhi-Smuts agreement, the tax on indentured emigrants to Natal was done away with for ever. But Gandhi wanted to stop the flow of indentured labour from India as it was reminiscent of slavery; however, before he could start an agitation towards that end the indentured system was abolished. At the foot of the Himalayan mountains was Champaran, close to Nepal, and here the farmers were forced to grow indigo to serve the interest of their landlords. Once to meet an aggrieved farmer Gandhi rode on the back of an elephant, which was a normal conveyance here as bullock-cart elsewhere.[1] By Gandhi's intervention the farmers got relief; so ended the popular belief that the stain of indigo could never be washed out. Further his peace diplomacy helped to terminate the conflict between the mill owners and workers at Ahmedabad. His agitation in Kheda, Gujarat, was to compel officers to give tax concessions to farmers facing hardship due to crop failure.[2] Gandhi in the face of parsimonious officials here did not flatter himself with complete victory. He after attending the war conference held in Delhi by the Viceroy recruited people for military service, but soon the war itself came to an end.

Whatever relief this gave to Gandhi did not last long. For the government by formulating what is known as Rowlatt Bill made it evident that wartime restraint on individual liberties would not be removed. Before contributing his energies to the war effort, Gandhi had made it clear to the Viceroy, Lord Chelmsford, that the desire for home rule had widely penetrated to the Indian masses, and that arbitrary power of the bureaucrats would not be tolerated, an assertion which he backed up with a veiled threat, "I shall resist organized tyranny to the uttermost.[3]" He in having recourse to the execution of this threat was compelled to abandon amity towards the British. To him always habituated to see the good aspects of British regime the revelation of its dark side opened up a new sphere for action.

Shortly afterwards the bill got the sanctity of law and yet Gandhi had not made up his mind in what way to offer civil disobedience against it. Meanwhile, having traveled to the South he stayed with Rajagopalacharia at Madras as his guest. At night, revolving in his mind the matter in hand he fell to sleep. After a while he woke up, then all of a sudden what he was looking for broke into his mind which at that moment hovered in the misty zone between sleep and consciousness. "The idea came to me last night in a dream," he reported to his host, "that he should call upon the country to observe a general hartal.[4]" It was fixed on 30th March 1919, but then it was decided the event should take place some days later.

A hartal in the sense of total cessation of all economic activities conjures up the idea of a tumultuous and disorderly mob. Why one should be followed by the other leading to destruction of life and property is hard to understand, except in terms of social background which puts a premium on conflict. The leaders ability to manipulate the rabble to an extent unknown before was the inevitable fall-out of organized political parties opposed to each other. To these parties circumstances were favourable; besides the national spirit the world itself on account of a revolution in transport and communication had so shrunk that the battlefield was as large as the nation, the ideas as good as weapons, and the masses as powerful as the warriors of old in settling the issues of the day.

In the absence of these tendencies, especially of warring political parties, the nature of a hartal in the social setting of the old order would be revealing. Such an event one account in fact describes as it happened at the beginning of the nineteenth century, when the British power was not yet imposed upon all parts of the country and the caste order had still enormous influence over the people. The place was Benaras, the year was 1810, and the cause for resentment culminating in a boycott was the house tax. "Between twenty and thirty thousand of the inhabitants of that city," Writes J.R. Erskine," consisting of all ranks and descriptions relinquished their occupations, abandoned their dwellings, and assembled in the open fields."[5]

Like their discipline with which they moved in a body their city as well, in conformity with the traditional pattern of living, reflected order and coherence. Into several wards Benaras was divided and each harboured a particular caste people; what is more, these wards had gates which could be shut at night, either for protection or to safeguard the insularity of caste dominated life. To revert to our story, in the open ground each caste was under the supervision of a leader, who invariably punished instances of misconduct and disobedience. "This state of things continued for more than a month; and whilst the authority of the British Government was, in a manner, suspended," the power of the caste headman was so large as to maintain order and peace.[6]

In contrast, the present hartal not only touched India as a whole but also was spoiled by violence. This was especially so at Amritsar and Delhi but fortunately Bombay under the overseeing care of Gandhi did not meet with any kind of trouble. He thought it was incumbent upon him to go there, in order to relieve the people in distress. So he set out for Delhi but the police at a certain point intercepted him, kept him for a while under duress, and then put him in a train moving towards Bombay, however, without letting him out of their custody, because he refused to give them any undertaking that if he was set at liberty he would abandon his original tour programme. Meanwhile, the people at Bombay getting to know of his detention were thrown into such a mood of excitement that crowds formed in the streets. After he was allowed to go free by the police he hurried away to be in their midst in order to pacify them. No doubt the masses were delirious with joy after seeing him, but he was not able to control them as their leader and was virtually a prisoner of the mob. While they were determined to push on to the Fort, the commercial hub of Bombay, the police would not let them go there as that would result in chaos. As they moved forward, Gandhi saw the police on horseback with lances bristling in the air gallop close by him, and then fall upon the massed ranks of his followers. For a while there was total confusion, and later the mob ran pell-mell leaving a field of desolation.

After this setback, Gandhi, in the wider context of the boycott he had launched with so much forethought, tried to understand why it did not go the way he expected. He laid the blame partly on the intellectual poverty of the masses to take up in the right spirit disobedience movement, and partly on himself for not for seeing their weakness. In fact, not everyone was qualified through civil resistance to break the laws, and this privilege was reserved only for those who had obeyed the laws of society for a long while, rather from honourable motives than fear of punishment. After they had such a training in citizenship, they know how to distinguish good law from the bad one which alone should be opposed. His mistake, or rather blunder, he knew was of a Himalayan magnitude. As a result he later set up an institution to train pure-minded volunteers, wedded to the concept of non-violence, and gave them the task of guiding the people during mass civil disobedience. By eternal vigilance they were expected to keep the people on the right path, and their performance did not belie his faith in them.

The disturbances in Bombay were nothing in comparison with the unrest in Amritsar, which is in the Punjab. This region even prior to the Sikhs was known for warriors, and was the route of most foreign invaders, except the English of course. So much force the rulers resorted to in Amritsar that a massacre ensued, which electrified the mood of the whole country. On 13th April many had come to a meeting at Jallianwala Bagh, without knowing the proclamation of British General Dyer restricting their movements on the streets.[7] Cooped up in this ground with buildings around and with narrow exit points, they were for all purpose sitting ducks for Dyer's well armed police, who turned their rifles towards them. About four hundred people according to official estimate, but Gandhi believed thrice as many, died on account of firing. Neither was he much convinced when the British enquiring into the conduct of Dyer found him guilty of error of judgement. "General Dyer," in the view of the government, "acted beyond the necessity of the case, beyond what any reasonable man could have thought to be necessary, and that he did not act with as much humanity as the case permitted.[8]"

Gandhi to widen the base of his popular resistance did not spare any effort to win the favour of the Muslims. As he was always in close touch with them, he knew by experience that they and the Hindus did not mix well upon the foundation of true affection; that the task of uniting both would therefore be a severe trial on his principle of non-violence. At the moment, however, he did not face obstacles mainly because the Muslims needed him more than he needed them. For they got worried that the Caliph, the temporal ruler in Turkey and the religious head of the Muslims in general, for having taken the side of Germany in the war would be made to pay heavily through loss of his power. To relieve him and to put pressure upon the British, they commenced in India the Khilafat movement for which they solicited the help of Gandhi.

Never he was backward in aiding them, but those who had gathered in Delhi to talk on matters connected with the issue of Caliph imagining efforts were needed to win him over, made it known to him that cow protection would also be a subject for discussion, by way of concession to his sensibilities.[9] He was not pleased because he did not want his support weighed just like a commodity for what it was worth to them; then bargained for and exchanged for a return benefit. On the other hand, if the Muslims out of a generous impulse abstained from cow slaughter to show their concern for the religious feelings of the Hindus, he welcomed it. His appeal that the two issues should be kept apart went home and the assembled Muslims gave way to him evidently because they saw the difficulty of opposing him at the moral level. He had close intimacy with two Muslim brothers, Shaukat Ali and Mahomed Ali, about this time, and did think highly of this connection, in the hope that it would open the way for better understanding between the two communities. But the two brothers did not have as much faith in non-violence as he had.

Another leader on the national scene was Mohammed Ali Jinnah, but did not get much attention of Gandhi, though both often met on the same platform. Born into a wealthy family and in the year 1876, Jinnah was the eldest son of a Karachi merchant; he went to England when he was a tall thin boy, studied law at Lincoln's Inn, and before long was called to the bar.[10] Soon he fell under the influence of Gokhale, who perceived his gifted mind void of prejudices, and therefore could not help bestowing encomium on him. Others too considered him as the leader destined to strengthen Hindu-Muslim unity. His family had gone through financial ruin, but not daunted by this Jinnah by his perseverance and courage made himself an outstanding leader.

For a while, Jinnah acted as private secretary to Dadabhai Naoroji and helped him, in the 1906 session of the Congress held in Calcutta, to project the idea of self-government for India.[11] To realize this religious concord was essential, and young Jinnah, with this head filled with visionary ideas and his heart warmed by his experience at having worked on a broad secular platform, left Calcutta determined to turn his energies towards that goal. Since he was desirous of taking on the mantle of Gokhale and Naoroji, and of reaching the heights of power to guide the future of India, he set a high value on his national outlook. In the aforesaid year was born in Decca the All India Muslim League, whose leaders perceived things somewhat differently. Its Chairman, the venerable Nawab Viqar-ul-Mulk, before a large gathering spoke about the suspicion of the Muslims thus: "When even now that a powerful British administration is protecting its subjects, we the Musalmans have to face most serious difficulties in safeguarding our interests from the grasping hands of our neighbours, instances of which are not rare in any province or district, then woe betide the time when we become the subjects of our neighbours, and answer to them for the sins, real and imaginary, of Aurangzeb, who lived and died two centuries ago, and other Musalman conquerors and rulers who went before him."

In spite of religious differences which reached a high point in the era of Aurangzeb, both in a spirit of live and let live carried on everyday activities as neighbours. So the Hindus entered into the service of Muslim potentates and the Muslims too followed the same example; hence there was nothing unusual for a Hindu army, moving towards the battlefield to fight against the Muslim enemy, to have been composed of a large number of Muslim captains as well as soldiers.[12]

Both had lost much of their self-esteem when their empire melted away owing to British expansion; their effort to regain it in 1857 proved abortive. However the bad consequences of a lost empire were felt more by the Muslims than the Hindus for the simple reason that they did not adapt themselves to the new situation. Persian was no longer the language of administration, but the Muslims were slow to accept and learn English, the language of the conquerors.[13] Moreover, although both had a share in the Mutiny, in the eyes of the British the Muslims were far more culpable for having rebelled in order to oust them from power.[14] The credit for delivering them from their unenviable situation must go largely to Sir Sayyid Ahmad Khan; for he did much to remove the prejudices of the British and to assure them of Muslim loyalty to existing dispensation.[15] He besides stood in opposition to the national freedom movement on the ground that the Muslims required time to consolidate their strength.[16]

He was favourably disposed to the British, but less so towards the Hindus, looking at them in the sense of competitors; he decided to keep his distance from the Indian National Congress for the reason a democratic government meant majority rule, which was equivalent to Hindu domination. After so long trying to curry favour with the British, the Muslims were rewarded when the Indian Councils Act of 1909 gave them separate electorate. In view of their wider objectives, the Congress leaders were not inclined to agree with the idea that the Muslims needed to be in this way bolstered up. Jinnah, as yet "free from the egoism of sect and narrowness of bigotry", was on their side.[17] But his feeling that he belonged to a separate religion was heightened, and his nationalist colleagues with "raised eyebrows" watched his move to enlarge his reputation, when he stood for election from the Bombay Muslim constituency which sent him to the Central Legislative Council.[18] His liberal views, however, did not forsake him, and in the 1910 Allahabad session of the Congress, Jinnah, three years before he joined the Muslim League, with no less gusto than he was formerly accustomed in putting forward his national ideals, denounced the extension of separate electorate to local bodies.[19]

About this devilish principle that Muslims could only be elected by separate Muslim electorates Jawaharlal Nehru says: "A political barrier was created round them isolating them from the rest of India and reversing the unifying and amalgamating process which had been going on for centuries, and which was inevitably being speeded up by technological developments"[20] The mischief caused by it right now was so little as to be imperceptible, but later with every extension of the franchise it engendered so much ill feeling and mutual suspicion that public life got divided into two warring camps. There came into existence separate Muslim trade unions, students' organizations and merchants' chambers, all created from above artificially.

Overlooking the opposition of some the Muslim League attempted to get closer to the Congress, with the result both the parties in1915 held their annual sessions in Bombay, in fact, within walking distance of each other. "It is said that our object," argued the President Mazhar-ul-Haque before the delegates, "in holding the League contemporaneously with the Congress in the same city is to deal a blow at the independence of the League, and to merge its individuality with that of the Congress. Nothing could be further from the truth."[21]

Such an assertion notwithstanding, he and his compeers had brought in Congress leaders to the meeting, had in an expansive mood cheered them, and had passed a resolution noting the sense of loss at the death of Gokhale in order to please them.[22] While carrying on the business of the meeting in English, Haque to establish closer affinity with everyone claimed that he was "a man of ordinary intelligence," but the dissenters as well as religious fundamentalists present there were not taken in, by his professed humility, and knew to what extent he deviated from the philosophy of the founding fathers of the party. Among the dissenters foremost was Hasrat Mohani, and his motion for adjournment followed by disturbances made it difficult for Haque to maintain his authority, so that invoking the Koran he told them "to put faith in His words if they were Mohammedans." But his own words were turned against him when a dissenter vehemently spoke thus: "If you are a Mohammedan, you ought to appear like a Mohammedan. The Holy Koran asks you to dress like a Mohammedan. You must speak the Mohammedan tongue. You pose to be a Mohammedan leader, but you can never be a Mohammedan leader.[23]" While Haque was intellectually incapacitated by the hot words shot at him by his enemies, Jinnah got away looking for help; however, much to his disappointment the Commissioner of Police Edwardes present at the meeting was ready if the situation called for it to clear everyone off the ground.

At the next meeting of the League held on 1st January 1916 in the aristocratic Taj Mahal Hotel, Haque after giving a start to the interrupted business took an opportunity to eulogize the service rendered by his friend Jinnah to the party.

Forever concerned with the problem how to unite the Hindus and Muslims on a national platform; how to protect the Muslims from being swept away by the tide of Hindu nationalism, Jinnah came up with an ingenious solution; by which the Muslims would be assured of a fixed number of seats in various councils and in the Central Legislative Council their weight would be as high as one-third of the elected Indian members.[24] In the Muslim League meeting of 1916 held in Lucknow, President Jinnah spoke at length about the common destiny of the Indian people.[25]

The difference between Gandhi and Jinnah came to light at the time of Delhi war conference; unlike Gandhi's soft-line approach, he wanted the British to trust the Indians as their partners, and to take steps towards self-government. Jinnah belonged to the old school of politics, that was made respectable by Annie Besant, into which Gandhi however by forcing values founded upon the power of the masses was intent upon taking the party in a pathbreaking direction.

The Amritsar session of 1919 marked Gandhi's real entry into the Congress; he accepted the reforms styled Dyarchy, though Tilak of Maharashtra and Chittaranjan Das of Bengal disagreed with him, but later changed his stand. He reasoned that the British power could not be imposed on people, but existed by their co-operation, so the way to be rid of that power was by denial of co-operation.[26] For which the Muslims keeping in mind the Khilafat agitation gave support; then to get into the favour of Gandhi, they said Islam did not prohibit its adherents from following non-violence as a policy, and one respected Muslim assured him that the great prophet himself had made use of non-co-operation.[27] Whether it was so or not, the burden of Gandhi's talk was that sword could not be depended upon, especially against the powerful British, who could however be brought to their knees by denial of their primacy.

With the unity of both communities to his credit, Gandhi made it known to the government of his intention to start on 1st August 1920 non-co-operation. Such a policy was based on boycott of, in order to bring the government to a standstill, educational institutions, law-courts, legislative councils and foreign goods. More than this, to harm the reputation of the ruling class the concerned people would resign from government posts, and from military service; besides would refuse to pay tax. "But whilst I pursue the policy of non-co-operation in so far as I can carry the people with me," Gandhi wrote to the Viceroy, "I shall not lose hope that you will yet see your way to do justice."[28]

Many to whom the boycott of the preceding year, the orgy of violence it unleashed, and the matching reprisals of the government were all fresh in the memory feared to see a repeat performance now.[29] What was uppermost in their mind was the mob, its frenzy, and its potential for violence. Though Gandhi believed that no great movement could be stopped because some people go wrong, he had no illusions about the risks. "It is easier to oust a government that has rendered itself unfit to govern," said he, "than it is to cure unknown people in a mob of their madness."[30] On the supposition that no general worth the name gave up a battle because he had suffered reverses, Gandhi moved forward wishing to profit by his mistakes.

On the 1st inaugurating the movement Gandhi in Bombay fraternized with the Muslim leaders, and reminded everyone of the sacrifice needed to make it a success. Into several stages he had divided what he expected to be a long struggle, and he thought that the British would feel the pinch in the later stages after being reduced to worthless rulers.

There was in the Congress no small opposition to Gandhi's policy, which represented a deviation from the constitutional and traditional ways: in fact, the elder leader Pandit Malaviya advised Gandhi to suspend his movement until a special party session approved of it; but he could not drop something he had taken up in so high spirit without making the Muslims feel let down.[31] Hence he ignored some of these dinosaurs, too ponderous and slow-witted to adjust to the changing situations. The older leaders brought up in a quiescent tradition were out of their elements having failed to reconcile themselves to the upsurge of the masses.

Who should hold power in the Congress and how that power should be turned against the British were the issues to be settled at the Calcutta extraordinary session of the party; for which large contingents from several provinces had assembled in a spirit of rivalry. Gandhi spoke to the gathered delegates, pleading support for his resolution to non-cooperate, in the background of the fact that the party lacked unanimity. "I am aware that a large number of our leaders who have given the time and attention to the affairs of my motherland, which I have not been able to give," said he, "are ranged against me."[32] Though he was not explicit there was no doubt who they were: Annie Besant, Jinnah, Malaviya, Bipin Chandra Pal, C. Das, and the editor of the newspaper "The Hindu" Kasturi Ranga Iyengar. "I have been told," continued he echoing their views for the benefit of the audience, "that I have been doing nothing but wreckage and that by bringing forward the resolution I am breaking up the political life of the country."[33] Large differences manifested in regard to the policy of rejecting the councils, with Gandhi in favour of it but others against it. For him, no flexibility was possible on this matter, but under pressure he agreed to so broaden the objectives of resistance as to include the demand for self-government.

Jinnah held the view that the programme of Gandhi was not realistic. Between his old loyalties and the new challenges made obvious by Gandhi, he knew the choice was not a easy one. At ease in the august surroundings of law-courts and the parliament, he lacked confidence in his ability to cope up with the task of resistance which aimed at their ruin. He lived in hopes, was indecisive, and made no efforts to conceal his antipathy to Gandhi, all evident from this. "Yet I would ask the Government not to drive the people of India to desperation, or else there is no other course left open to the people except to inaugurate the policy of non-co-operation, though not necessarily the programme of Mr. Gandhi."[34]

The climax to the party deliberations came when the non-co-operation resolution was put to a vote; by a large majority Gandhi carried the day, thus establishing his full preponderance over the party.[35] Yet his opponents could not reconcile themselves to the new realities, and so they put up a last ditch fight at the next session of the party, although it was a foregone conclusion who wins and who loses.

Before that Gandhi and Jinnah again encountered face to face to renew the conflict in Bombay, where on October 3rd a meeting of the Home Rule League was held.[36] Its President Annie Besant long before had resigned to make way for Gandhi; his followers later did not let her speak before an audience, and he had to intervene begging with folded hands to check their spite against her.[37] Now presiding over the meeting he did not wish to see any sort of opposition to his policies. On the other hand, Jinnah argued for self-government within the British Commonwealth and for the adoption of constitutional methods to achieve that. Gandhi opined that anyone who did not fall in with the views of the majority was free to submit resignation.[38] Jinnah and his adherents from the meeting sallied out; realizing his and Gandhi's ways were different he along with his nineteen colleagues resigned from Swaraj Sabha, a new name Gandhi had given to the same League.[39] Gandhi then asked him to reconsider whether he had not acted hastily in severing connection with a body which he had till now nursed with affection, to take his "share in the new life that has opened up before the country" and to benefit it by his experience and guidance.[40] Gandhi's letter was couched in such a manner as to entice him back; yet failed to undo the harm already done; so Jinnah replied thus: "If by "new life" you mean your methods and your programme, I am afraid I cannot accept them, for I am fully convinced that it must lead to disaster." After charging that his methods had caused split and division in almost every institution he had approached hitherto, Jinnah said: "People generally are desperate all over the country and your extreme programme has for the moment struck the imagination mostly of the inexperienced youth and the ignorant and the illiterate. All this means complete disorganization and chaos. What the consequence of this may be, I shudder to contemplate."[41]

A similar warning was issued by Annie Besant who said that Gandhi's victory would be his defeat, because "the spirit of indiscipline and lawlessness, resulting in loss of respect of law which he was inculcating through civil disobedience would react against the Indian government and people would disobey authority on the lines taught to them."[42]

While they assessed the cost of his activities in a bad light, Gandhi more than anyone else understood the cost of his inactivity, which would result, on the one hand, in the perpetuation of foreign rule and the evils associated with it, and, on the other hand, in the escalation of violent acts in order to overthrow the government by force.

Another powerful critic C.Das shifted his loyalty to Gandhi, at the Nagpur session of the party held at the close of the year;[43] here about twenty thousand delegates had come together to give final assent to what Gandhi stood for. It was a measure of Gandhi's popularity that the substantial opposition evident in the last session to non-co-operation now vanished to such an extent that only two stood against him.[44] Of this one was Jinnah who did not lack courage, vehemence, and reason to push his case before that large audience. He believed that the religious frenzy which pervaded every sphere of life would result in confusion, and in more harm than good.[45] A debonair Jinnah moved up the platform to speak his mind, but once there he was at the mercy of Gandhi's followers whom he had no reason to like for reflecting their well known plebeian manners. Not minding their uproar he went on thus: "At the moment the destinies of the country are in the hands of two men and one of them is Gandhi. Therefore, standing on this platform, knowing as I do that he commands the majority in this assembly, I appeal to him to pause, to cry halt before it is too late.[46]" The audience broke out in a noisy disapproval, some jeered, others hissed at him, finally driving him off the Nagpur stage in a humiliating manner. Since he was no more wanted by the Congress than by the Muslim League which was in the pocket of Gandhi, Jinnah was in the political wilderness, and his dream of national leadership in the footsteps of Gokhale was gone.

It was believed, in the background of western influence dominating over his life, that he did not fit in with his surroundings. He was by nature a solitary man with few intimate friendships, besides he could not merge with the crowd like the two Ali brothers in order to excite its enthusiasm; however, as later events proved, the folly of those who consigned him to oblivion was as great as his confidence in his ability to return to the centre stage of politics.

About this time Gandhi met the new Viceroy, Lord Reading, who referring to him in a letter to his son observed: "His religious views are, I believe, genuinely held, and he is convinced to a point, almost bordering on fanaticism, that non-violence and love will give India its independence and enable it to withstand the British Government."[47] It was a matter of prestige for Lord Reading, in the midst of a popular movement against him, that the goodwill visit of Prince of Wales, later King Edward VIII, should evoke wide interest, but Gandhi for reasons of policy wanted to frustrate his purpose. While the Prince having thought about the perplexing question: "How would Mahatma Gandhi and his radical Congress party react to my visit? Would he try to spoil my show?" resigned himself to the inevitable, those overseeing his tour worried that he might be greeted "with empty streets, insulting placards and perhaps even incidents of violence."[48] He went through the streets in a horse-drawn carriage with a gold-embroidered umbrella held over him, but elsewhere trouble broke out in consequence of which the police had to fire on the mobs.

Gandhi who was in Bombay guiding the boycott of royal visit had not expected so much rioting, violence and bloodshed; meanwhile, opposition to the government caused by his movement was in evidence everywhere, with the students abandoning the classes, lawyers boycotting courts, officials resigning from posts, people giving up titles and burning foreign clothes in the streets. The rulers took harsh steps by arresting large number of people including very prominent leaders, while Gandhi said that no talk with the opposite side was possible till all the prisoners as well as Shaukat Ali and Mahomed Ali were released.

Choosing a place where his movement would hit with the force of earthquake, Gandhi wrote to the Viceroy about his plan to start in Bardoli mass disobedience. Lord Reading in reply issued a statement for public consumption as follows: "The issue is no longer between this or that programme of political advance but between lawlessness with all its dangerous consequences on the one hand, and on the other, the maintenance of those principles which lie at the root of all civilized governments. Mass civil disobedience is fraught with such dangers to the State that it must be met with sternness and severity."[49]

He was on the eve of inaugurating the first step towards throwing out the government in that limited area by a no tax campaign; however, all of a sudden an avalanche of violence fell upon his movement and extinguished the fire within him. For a excited crowd attacked a police station at Chauri Chaura in the United Provinces on 4th February 1922, and left a trail of destruction in which twenty-one people mostly constables died.[50] The sequence of events began with a procession moving on quietly, but when taunted and abused by the police cried out for help to the main body ahead which in consequence turned back. At which crowd the police opened fire until the ammunition was exhausted, then fell back into the station and closed the door. But the mob seized with frenzy set fire to the station and when those within sallied out cut them to pieces which it threw into the inferno.[51]

Gandhi immediately sent a confidential note to the Congress making this much obvious: "The whole conception of civil disobedience is based upon the assumption that it works in and through its completely non-violent character."[52] Although his followers told him not to take seriously this particular violence, Gandhi was fixed upon his resolve not to launch mass disobedience movement.

He then got back to the Ashram from where he sent a message to his friend Jamnalal Bajaj about the thick rumour of his impending arrest.[53] To be sure the Viceroy decided to put him in prison, ostensibly for writing seditious articles, and on 10th March the police officer who came to effect this purpose was so affable that he did not make his way into the Ashram but waited for him on the public road where he gave himself up[54]. He was later brought to the court at Ahmedabad and was charged for being a rebel as well an agitator.

Instead of contradicting, Gandhi most willingly supported the accusation, himself speaking against himself, in what is undoubtedly a strange case in legal history. Against him, the advocate-general had leveled certain charges which Gandhi echoed in the court in such a manner as to stress his own fallibility. "He is quite right when he says," said Gandhi, "that as a man of responsibility, a man having received a fair share of education, having had a fair share of experience of this world, I should have known the consequences of every one of my acts."[55]

Then Gandhi let the judge know the dilemma he was confronted with, as well the ethical basis of his opposition to law. " I had either to submit to a system which I considered had done an irreparable harm to my country, or incur the risk of the mad fury of my people bursting forth when they understood the truth from my lips."[56] He now stood before the face of law, not asking for mercy, not pleading any extenuating circumstances, but only looking for maximum punishment.

"Mr. Gandhi," said justice Broomfield delivering the verdict, "you have made my task easy in one way by pleading guilty to the charge. Nevertheless, what remains, namely, the determination of a just sentence, is perhaps as difficult a proposition as a judge in this country could have to face. The law is no respector of persons. Nevertheless it will be impossible to ignore the fact that you are in a different category from any person I have ever tried or am likely to have to try. It would be impossible to ignore the fact that in the eyes of millions of your countrymen, you are a great patriot and a great leader. Even those who differ from you in politics look upon you as a man of high ideals and of noble and of even saintly life."[57]

After noting the fact in favour of Gandhi that he had constantly preached against violence, the justice thought it right to pass a sentence of six years' prison life upon him, but said that "no one will be better pleased than I" if the government reduced the period of confinement on account of favourable events.[58]

NOTES AND REFERENCES

1. An Autobiography, M.K. Gandhi, p. 342.
2. *Ibid*, p. 362.
3. *Ibid*, p. 373 & 374.
4. *Ibid*, p. 383.
5. Journal of the American Oriental Society, V. 82, No. 3, 1962, Political Systems in Eighteenth Century India, Bernard S. Cohn, p. 319.
6. *Ibid.*
7. Collected Works of Mahatma Gandhi, V. 18, p. 311.
8. History of British India, P.E. Roberts, p. 593.
9. Autobiography, p. 398.
10. Mohomed Ali Jinnah, His Speeches and Writings (1912-17), Sarojini Naidu, p. 3
11. *Ibid*, p. 5.
12. A Survey of Indian History, K.M. Panikkar, p. 280.
13. *Ibid*, p. 281 & 282.
14. The Aftermath of Revolt, Thomas R. Metcalf, p. 298.
15. *Ibid*, p. 302.
16. Panikkar, p. 284.
17. Naidu, p. 48.
18. *Ibid*, p. 6.
19. Jinnah, Sharif Al Mujahid, p. 9.
20. The Discovery of India, Jawaharlal Nehru, p. 354.
21. Foundations of Pakistan, S.S. Pirzada, V. 1, p. 330 & 331.
22. *Ibid*, p. 348 & 351.
23. *Ibid*, p. 350.
24. The Political Study of Mohammad Ali Jinnah, M.H. Saiyid, V. 2, p. 894 & 895.
25. Foundations, Pirzada, V. 1, p, 376.
26. C.W. M.G., V. 18, p. 172.
27. *Ibid*, p. 185 & 186; Autobiography, M.K. Gandhi, p. 414.
28. *Ibid*, v. 18, p. 105.
29. *Ibid*, p. 92.
30. *Ibid.*

31. *Ibid*, p. 123.
32. *Ibid*, p. 245.
33. *Ibid*, p. 246.
34. Foundations, Pirzada, V. 1, p. 544.
35. C.W. M.G., V. 18, p. 260.
36. Saiyid, V.1, p. 261.
37. C.W.M.G., V. 18, p. 224.
38. Jinnah of Pakistan, Stanley Wolpert, p. 70.
39. Collected Works, op cit., p. 370.
40. *Ibid*, p. 372.
41. Saiyid, p. 264 & 265.
42. Mujahid, p. 51.
43. Autobiograpy, M.K. Gandhi, p. 416.
44. Sardar Vallabhbhai Patel, Narhari D. Parikh, V. 1, p. 120.
45. Saiyid, p. 267.
46. Wolpert, p. 72.
47. Mahatma, D.G. Tendulkar, V. 2, p. 57.
48. A King's Story, The Memoirs of H.R.H. the Duke of Windsor K.G. p. 165 & 166.
49. C.W.M.G., V. 22, p. 515.
50. Mahatma Gandhi, a Chronology, K. P. Goswami, p. 91.
51. Parikh, V. 1, p. 162.
52. Collected Works, op cit, p. 350 & 351,
53. Seven Months with Mahatma Gandhi, Krishnadas, p. 258.
54. *Ibid*, p. 260.
55. Terndulkar, V. 2, p. 129.
56. *Ibid*.
57. *Ibid*, p. 134.
58. *Ibid*.

4

EXILED FROM POLITICS

As Gandhi had shied away from battle after building up his forces, the Viceroy Lord Reading wrote him off as a political adversary; in fact, his own partymen including Das and Motilal Nehru for similar reasons reflected on the weakness of his leadership. The British doled out reforms in order to consolidate their power, knowing this truth Gandhi had no faith in the legislatures whose functioning, doubtless, would weaken his movement. Das however was too fond of power, so he wanted to gain entry to the council through elections and then destroy its strength by means of well planned tactics. His policy seemed to resemble Gandhi's lack of faith in the British experiment in democracy, but the Congress refused to support him, so he launched the Swaraj Party into which Motilal Nehru entered as his partner. With elections not far away, the main party was split into factions on the basis whether loyalty to Gandhi existed or not among its followers.

The disunited Congress leaders with suspicion rooted in their mind, just before the elections, came together in 1923 at Delhi to take stock of the situation. This extraordinary session, presided over by Mohammed Ali, made a shift in ground so that participation in the elections was not seen as an invidious step. So Das after causing so much hubbub in the party triumphed over his opponents, but this came about because Vallabhbhai Patel and his followers not wishing to exacerbate tempers did not vote against him.[1]

Das with the help of Motilal was able to turn the new party into an efficient organization. So in the elections the Swaraj Party met with success in Bengal, in the Central Provinces and elsewhere, so that Das had the good fortune to become the mass leader of a party.[2] About this time Gandhi's routine of prison life was disturbed by illness; so he got away to a hospital in Poona, had to undergo an operation for appendicitis, and in February 1924 was released from prison.[3] Since a big chunk of his party had got into the legislature, where to the rulers it was less difficult to manage than on the streets, he himself, before the Viceroy took such a step in his favour, might have appeared not capable of overturning the government.[4] To be sure defection from the party had so weakened his position especially his determination to fight, that none expected him to frighten the government into submission through non-co-operation.

Gandhi wanted to deal harshly with the turncoats, by denying them the right to hold office in the party;[5] but at the same time he desired to forestall a power struggle as well as a split, keeping in mind that the party had already gone through that process once when Annie Besant and her followers parted company with him. To achieve unity now he was ready to keep his distance from politics, and to work for the good of the people outside the Congress; so he sent to Motilal Nehru a confidential letter in which he said "I was prepared to facilitate your securing the Congress machinery, actually assisting you to do so."[6] Finally, Gandhi went to Calcutta and with Das and Nehru entered into a treaty, by which the non-co-operation movement was kept in cold storage; the new party of Das was treated as a part of the Congress.[7] Although he thought that it was a prudent step to give the rebel party as much freedom as it desired, those who had stood by him when he was in prison and upheld his principles were downhearted on account of the treaty, which they saw as a capitulation on his part without consulting their interest.[8] He was scarcely in a position to dispute their point, especially when it appeared to everyone that Das and Nehru had taken over the centre stage of politics by driving Gandhi into exile.[9]

However Das in 1925 died leaving the burden of carrying the struggle through the new party on the shoulders of Motilal Nehru. As for Congress a great depression had overtaken it which lasted pretty long till the appointment of Simon Commission in 1927, after which event it recovered enough spirit to adopt a fighting posture. Likewise a change was taking place in Motilal Nehru whose fascination with the council began to diminish with the passage of time. Finally, he was unwilling to spend his energy in a sham parliament, and desired to work out of it in the midst of the revolutionary enthusiasm of the masses, thus paving the way for the return of the penitent to the ground he before held.

Gandhi, meanwhile, having moved away from politics on account of rebel activities, kept himself engaged by plying the portable spinning wheel, through which he wanted to encourage constructive activities in others too. But those who were overactive in politics often showed correspondingly less interest in spinning the wheel and producing home made cloth.

More than the intractability of his followers what concerned him was the increasing acrimony in the relation between Hindus and Muslims. That which held them together lost its value when Kemal Pasha in Turkey ushered in a secular state by taking away the power of the caliphate. So the Indian Muslims were left high and dry; "no mass movement among the Muslims was so great a success as the Khilafat, though in the home of the Caliph the people cared not a straw for him."[10] In this situation in order to promote unity by inducing a change of feeling towards peace, Gandhi for twenty one days fasted.

A perpetual source of friction between them was the cow; while the Hindus venerated it the Muslims slaughtered it. How dear was cow to Gandhi became evident when he said "the cow to me means the entire sub-human world. Man through the cow is enjoined to realize his identity with all that lives."[11] On the other hand, the Muslims got angry when a Hindu religious procession accompanied by the sound of music and the beating of the drums went past their mosque disturbing their prayer. These two issues were often so difficult to manage that they had resulted in street brawls and bloodshed. Of course Gandhi knew that violence would not end cow slaughter and that his own method of working through the heart had a better chance of success.

At the bottom of this violence were deeply rooted differences which engendered intolerance in each against the other. Islam believes in one god in contrast with Hinduism which puts faith in scores of gods who through many beautiful myths and romantic tales surrounding them have made their way into the heart of worshippers.[12] Further, those who preach Koran throw open wide the door of conversion with equality of rights to everyone, thereby making Islam an expansive religion.[13] But no such equality exists under Hinduism even in theory, nor is it fond of conversion, the chief obstacle to that is caste, into which Hindus are born, and by which their status is fixed eternally in such a way that inequality is the cornerstone of society.[14]

Notwithstanding this divergence a few Muslim kings stand high in the estimation of posterity for showing a laudable moderation; on the other hand, several have displayed a blamable want of toleration. Because of them, the Hindu agitators say that the Muslim kings of bygone times revive unpleasant memories.[15] In spite of their religious zeal, and in spite of their hold for a long time over the country, these kings only dominated over the physical body of, but never did influence the soul of the Hindus.[16]

In one respect the Hindus and Muslims are alike in so far as they live for the sake of religion which is to them the very ambrosia to sweeten life. The Mogul king Akbar knew this well; therefore, he aimed at joining them together by a policy of religious toleration. The last great king of that dynasty Aurangzeb too was aware of this; however, he thought of bringing them together by religious intolerance and forcible conversion, wrecking his empire in the sequel on the rock of religion.

Now seeing the broken temples of long antiquity, in the precincts of which were built the mosques in sacred places like Mathura, Benares and Ayodhya, the Hindus suffer from anguish.[17]

This legacy from the past undid much of the efforts of Gandhi towards conciliation; neither his close friend Mohammed Ali Jinnah made things any way easy for him, when to circumvent the attack of the Muslims for his proximity to Gandhi he said: "As a follower of Islam I am bound to regard the creed of Islam as superior to that professed by the followers of any non-Islamic religion. And in this sense the creed of even a fallen and degraded Musalman is entitled to a higher place than that of any other non-Muslim irrespective of his high character, even though the person in question be Mahatma Gandhi himself."[18]

True, this was something well known, rather too stale for anybody to know as news, but the fact that it was reiterated by an outstanding leader gave it the effect of a deadly missile shot at the Hindus. Gandhi quickly intervened to put down bad feelings between the two sides; he said that he found nothing wrong in what his ally had asserted, and that besides "thousands of Christians certainly hold that a righteous man without belief in Jesus Christ is less than an adulterous Christian.[19] He then asked whether an orthodox Hindu fared any better than others. No. The observant scholar Alberuni long back noted: "The Hindus believe that their no country but theirs, no nation like theirs, no kings like theirs, no religion like theirs, no science like theirs."[20]

What is more they did "not desire that a thing which has once been polluted should be purified and thus recovered."[21] Now however to meet the challenge posed by competitive spirit in religion the Hindus under one Swami Shraddhanand had started a purification movement to attract the lost sheep to the flock. Gandhi had no interest in conversion, especially when it was encouraged with a view to get the better of one's opponent.[22] But the Swami, a friend of Gandhi, was so much committed to his movement that he continued his activities, though the Muslims after having greatly maligned him held out threat to his existence.

At the Aligarh Muslim League session held in 1925 President Abdur Rahim dwelt at length upon the Hindu revivalist movements led by Lajpat Rai and the aforesaid Swami, underscoring the threat posed by purification whose object was to convert Muslims "in millions" to Hinduism.[23] He said that the Muslims regard these movements "as the most serious challenge to their religion that they ever had to meet—not even excepting the Christian crusades, whose objective mainly was to wrest back from the Muslims some places sacred to both.[24]

Gandhi was on way to Gauhati at the close of 1926 to attend the party meeting when he got the tragic news concerning the Swami which perturbed him.[25] Owing to illness the Swami had been confined to bed; however a Muslim almost forced his way into the house allegedly in order to engage in a religious dialogue, contrived a means to make the sick man more helpless by sending off the attendant to fetch drinking water, then pulled off a revolver and murdered him in the bed itself.[26]

While telling the Hindus not to avenge this deed Gandhi knew that neither trust nor love existed between the two adversaries; but rather each saw the other with fear and suspicion. So Gandhi's role as a mediator was quite difficult, especially because some accused him of being partial to the Muslims. It was even said that he in supporting the Muslims over the Caliphate issue rather promoted the cause of Islam than the unity of India.[27] This from the mouth of no ordinary mortal but from the poet and Nobel prize winner Rabindranath Tagore.

NOTES AND REFERENCES

1. Sardar Vallabhbhai Patel, Narhari D. Parikh, V. 1, p. 190.
2. Life & Times of C.R. Das, P.C. Ray, p. 192.
3. Parikh, p. 265.
4. *Ibid*, p. 269 & 270.
5. *Ibid*, p. 270.
6. Collected Works of Mahatma Gandhi, V. 24, p. 536.
7. *Ibid*, V. 25, p. 288 & 289.
8. Young India, 20th November 1924, p.382.
9. Jawaharlal Nehru, An Autobiography, p. 128.
10. India in the Crucible, C.S. Ranga Iyer, p. 298.
11. The Gandhi Reader, Homer A. Jack, p. 170.
12. Foundataions of Pakistan, S.S. Pirzada, V. 1, p. 43.
13. *Ibid.*
14. *Ibid.*
15. Ranga Iyer, p. 295.
16. Pirzada, *op cit.* p. 44.
17. Ranga Iyer, p. 295.
18. Young India, 10th April 1924, p. 121.
19. *Ibid*,p. 120.
20. A Survey of Indian History, K.M. Panikkar, p. 129 & 130.
21. *Ibid*, p. 130.
22. Collected Works. V. 32, p. 515.
23. Pirzada, V. 2, p. 42
24. *Ibid.*
25. Collected Works, V. 32, p. 451.
26. *Ibid*, p. 452 & 453.
27. Roman Rolland and Gandhi Correspondence, p. 61.

5

THE PEACEMAKERS

While he was touring the south to advertise the virtues of home made cloth popularly known as Khadi, Gandhi got a message from the new Viceroy Lord Irwin to see him on urgent matters. He set out from Mangalore covering part of the distance upon the sea and part upon the land, and was in Delhi on Ist November 1927, a day before he was to meet on official business the Viceroy.[1] It would be right to say that Gandhi traveled more than a thousand miles on the wings of soaring expectations, but was brought to earthly reality of things in the presence of Irwin. For he took delivery of a piece of paper by which act came to an end the purpose of his meeting him, and the paper gave the news about the intent of Britain to dole out more freedom by the appointment of the Simon Commission[2].

He set always a high value on the performance of duties in a direct way, so that he would exhort his adherents even to think audibly, but setting up the Commission implied a roundabout way of doing things, a charade to buy time, or rather a flanking movement of the enemy to defeat his purpose. It further implied that heat was slowly up in British politics on account of approaching general elections. So the Conservatives who held power desired to score a point against the other party in their battle to retain imperial heritage; but oddly enough the opposite side too welcomed the Commission with an eye to future advantage.

For it is well known that party leaders out of power often indulge in loose talk, and get away with it just because they are not running the show; but in power are brought to their sense of responsibility especially when the words they had uttered before catch them, in which situation the subterfuge of Commission and conferences helps to secure them from the charge of inconsistency.

Unrepresentative of Indian opinion the Commission for that reason was boycotted by most of the parties who besides organized countrywide hartal against it. The presence of John Simon in the country therefore brought about that unity which had eluded so far; by keeping out of the mind animosity against each other and remembering only their present interest orthodox Hindu leader Malaviya and his counterpart among the Muslims Jinnah saw eye to eye on policy matters. Moreover, the Hindus and Muslims got together day after day in the house of Congress President Dr. M.A. Ansari to devise ways to root out differences.[3] Even moderate leaders opposed to Gandhi shifted ground; at the height of the non-co-operation movement they had supported the British in order to fill up the prison with Congress agitators. "I take the full share of my responsibility," said Tej Bahadur Sapru with pride, "for the condemnation of Mr. Gandhi."[4] Nobody however stood now more vehemently for the condemnation of the British than him. This is because even he, along with his fellow leaders who had made common cause with the British in unleashing repression, was considered as not good enough to sit beside the British Simon Commission members on a basis of equality.

As the British were playing up Indian disunity in which they too had a hand, Motilal Nehru came forward to draw up a constitution acceptable to all which would serve as an alternative to Simon report. To achieve results in this field he had to come to grips with the demands of the Muslims. Not only Muslim leaders were eager to hold talks with the Congress about their interest in a future constitution but they were prepared to give up separate electorate for compensatory benefits. "Some say the separate electorate," said Wahid Hussain in the League Calcutta deliberations which started at the close of 1927 "is our Magna Charta. I deny that."[5] They to arrive at settlement with the opposite side had put up at a conference held in Delhi on 20th March 1927 certain proposals which Jinnah praised saying that they "are the outcome of many heads" and that "so far as the spirit of the proposals is concerned it is undoubtedly just and fair to both communities."[6]

Formulated by Jinnah in concert with twenty nine Muslim leaders, the Delhi Muslim proposals asked for one-third representation to

Muslims in the central legislature, in the Punjab and Bengal legislative presence in accordance with their population, uncoupling of Sind from Bombay Presidency, and besides in North West Frontier Province as well as Baluchistan democratic reforms, which the British till now had kept in abeyance in order to have a firm grip on the restive tribes.[7] "By the Lucknow Pact," said Maulana Abul Kalam Azad before the League session, "they had sold away their interests." However the current proposals, asserted he, safeguarded their rights by giving them five provinces (all mentioned above) in opposition to nine Hindu provinces, so that whatever treatment they got from the other side they would reciprocate it in their sphere of influence. Was not this a big gain? Did not the Muslims get a new weapon for the assertion of their rights?[8]

Nehru in August 1928 came up with his constitutional report which conceded Muslim demand in respect of Sind and Frontier Province; besides it recommended Dominion status for the country, exit of separate electorate and reservation in the legislatures for only ten years to the Muslims.[9] A federation was approved; although this tallied with Muslim desire, his object in putting it forward was to decoy the princes into accepting the new robe of democracy he himself had cut and fashioned by expending so much labour in the process.[10]

And yet his report contrived to appeal to the national sentiments was seen by Jinnah as nothing more than Hindu counter proposals to what the Muslims had offered.[11] As the Hindu Mahasabha by adopting a hard posture stood in the way of granting favour to the Muslims, Jinnah diverted his attention towards creating a strong League without factions.

At a conference of parties which met to patch up differences Jinnah put forward his proposals. The legal pundit Sapru, formerly a member of the Viceroy's Council got up to throw his weight behind Jinnah. "If you examine the figures," said he, "you will find that, including nominated members, Muslim representation in the Central Legislature is 27 per cent." But remembering Jinnah demanded 33 per cent Sapru told the assembled delegates to "give him what he wants and be finished with it."[12]

The Hindu Mahasabha leader M.R. Jayakar, however, was not willing to let Jinnah get away with what he desired; he not only undervalued tempered him as a man who spoke for "a small minority of Muslims" but pointed out that the Hindu Mahasabha in its present aggressive mood was sure to turn down Nehru report if it was tampered with.[13]

Even in the Congress opposition to Nehru report came from younger leaders who had set their heart on getting complete freedom and anything short of it was not good to them. So the 1928 Congress meeting at Calcuta witnessed between the father and son the unusual contention as who should get the better of whom; the elder Nehru spoke in favour of dominion status because his own constitutional plan begot that, while the younger Nehru advocated severance of British connection and independence, because his constitution hot and impulsive by nature would not reconcile to anything less.[14] Now Gandhi was hard put to it to effect a compromise, especially when he himself was a party to the dispute after having sided with Motilal Nehru and having opined his report was a sacred document.[15]

The dissension in the party assumed so dangerous proportion that he had to appease his radical followers. Therefore, he ordained that Nehru report was a sacred document up to the end of 1929; thereafter not so if Britain did not honour it meanwhile and the Congress in retaliation would disown it likewise, by going for independence as a better alternative and civil disobedience as the only course open to it to overthrow the British power.[16]

Gandhi had goaded his followers into action in the disobedience movement started about ten years back; however they now led him by the nose into a situation which was certain to bring in a period of conflict. His position was weak, very obvious from the fact that he feared a split in the party, to avoid which he tried to appease those who clamoured for hard steps against the rulers. But with the help of Vallabhbhai Patel, he had won a limited victory in Bardoli so that the reputation of the government to a certain extent was harmed. Here well disciplined peasants fought against increased land tax non-violently, despite the efforts of the officers to put them down by coercive measures.[17] When Gandhi here planned the disobedience movement which he could no begin for reasons already explained, he wanted to undermine the power of the Viceroy. The present successful Bardoli struggle had not such wider objective, and yet Irwin and Viceroy could not ignore it especially after he was subjected to uncharitable attacks for his inability to crush it. But he wished to avoid a clash with Gandhi, in the background of the hot reception people gave to Simon, and to keep the door open for reconciliation, hoping that peace through a conference was attainable.[18]

His optimism was encouraged when in May 1929 the Labour Party in Britain got power, and Ramsay MacDonald was installed in office as the Prime Minister. He was open to suggestions, and Jinnah whose mass based influence had gone into temporary eclipse thought that this was the right time to take initiative. So he wrote to MacDoland briefing him about the situation in India, and telling him with candour what a dismal view people entertained in regard to Simon's task. "I may tell you without exaggeration," he continued, "that the movement for independence is gaining ground, as it is supported by the Indian National Congress."[19] Consequently, he desired that MacDonald would forestall the agitation for independence by making clear at the official level his strong commitment to Dominion Status.

To be sure Lord Irwin had seized initiative thinking how to bring about a settlement, and had gone to England to be in touch with policy makers. He took with him the feelings, the anxieties, and the aspirations of those who despaired of getting what they longed for, and faithfully gave an account of their expectations, to several party leaders there. In the sequel, after he returned to his seat of power he made a public declaration on 31st October which contained the "blessed words" Dominion Status, and an assurance of its realization through a conference.[20] Gandhi was "less enthusiastic, more cautious" but on the whole took an optimistic view of things.[21] The very next day after Irwin spoke, the leaders of different parties met in the house of a colleague of theirs in Delhi, and Gandhi was also in the capital. Gandhi as well as the two Nehrus, Sapru, Annie Besant, Malaviya, Vallabhbhai Patel besides others appreciated in a statement the sincerity underlying Irwin's words, but indulged in wishful thinking, when they observed that the proposed conference was to meet to draw up a Dominion Constitution, and not to discuss when to establish it.[22] All of a sudden, to the great annoyance of Jawaharlal Nehru, the balance of power in the Congress changed in favour of the older leaders by Irwin's diplomatic move. "To give up the demand for Independence," Nehru pondered, "even in theory and even for a short while, was wrong and dangerous."[23] Yet he did not want to push his opposition too far, and to wreck the Congress on the eve of the contemplated mass action against the ruling autocrats. Therefore, under the decisive influence of Gandhi, he allowed himself "to be talked into signing" the manifesto of leaders. But he knew that if the opposite side refused to accept the conditions laid down, he would be in a good position.

In Lord Irwin, Gandhi perceived a sincerity of intention; however, this view was moderated by the fact that the Viceroy's spoken words on the last day of October were so ingeniously contrived as to "mean much or very little." Hence Gandhi did not wish to make a move, until the Viceroy took certain practical steps in order to break the ice; however, in a situation when nothing could be expected when nothing was done, some party leaders taking initiative wished to do something. Consequently, Jinnah, Vallabhbhai Patel, and his brother Vithalbhai Patel went to Sabarmati Ashram, and on 30th November saw Gandhi in his austere surroundings; the upshot of their conversation was if they could procure an interview with Irwin they would be able to discuss the issues in such a way as to arrive at a better understanding.[24] Further, they agreed if they received an invitation from Irwin they should meet in Delhi on a day already fixed, however without Vallabhbhai Patel in the company and with Motilal Nehru as well as Sapru added to it.[25] When this matter reached the ear of Lord Irwin, he was "very pleased" to ask them to wait on him in the afternoon of 23rd December at his residence in the capital.

Not many days were left for the deadline set by Gandhi for Dominion to expire; when that happened, the Congress after meeting in Lahore under Jawaharlal Nehru as the President was certain to declare independence unilaterally, and start hostilities to subvert the British regime.

Irwin, conscious of the future possibilities either in the direction of peace or its opposite, was returning by rail to Delhi to keep the appointment with the party leaders when a bomb exploded under the train, but he came to no harm. Obviously, there were some who wanted to overthrow the British government by force, had no faith in the methods of Gandhi, and would have been happy if the Viceroy had not been able to see him.[26]

By his affable nature and sweet disposition, Irwin at the conference gave enough indications about his concern to reach an agreement.[27] Sapru and Jinnah were impressed, saw the good intention of the Labour government in his eyes, and entertained hope in regard to the ultimate result of the meeting to convene which they had taken much pains. "Where shall we begin?" asked the Viceroy, and left to himself he would have initiated the business of the day with that topic which "would easily lend itself to a tangible proof of goodwill."[28] He was prevented, however, from going his own way by Gandhi who drew his attention to the matter worrying him, Dominion constitution, of which he wanted an assurance. When the Viceroy let him know of his inability to give any more promises than what he had already made in his public address, a chill descended upon the conference.

He realized that Gandhi under the influence of hostile parliamentary discussion back at home was adopting an inflexible attitude.[29] In fact, the Conservatives prompted by the former Secretary of State Lord Birkenhead were spitting fire at the government over the Dominion issue, since they presumed that the authority of the Simon Commission had been undermined, and that the Viceroy was made to give in under the threat of civil disobedience.[30] Aside from polemics, the truth is neither of the parties in Britain wished to see India slip away into freedom, ostensibly because of Hindu-Muslim discord, of the princely states tied to Britain by treaties, and the weakness of the Indian army about this time.[31]

About Irwin's professed faith in Dominion status Gandhi was not much impressed; because he talked on the pertinent issues with the Viceroy and wanted to probe into the truth of the matter, he got the blame when the conference failed on the supposition that another in his place would not have been so captious, although the matter he talked had been discussed by different party leaders shortly before, and was in conformity with the views expressed by them.[32]

From the conference Gandhi together with Motilal Nehru went to Lahore in order to put into execution the threat of open declaration of independence, and of civil disobedience to back it up. So a bitter conflict to test the mutual strength of Gandhi and Irwin was imminent, but this development was not expected in the background of a lot of similarity between them. Their upbringing as well as their experience in life was such that both were alive to the idea of sin, and besides were very sensitive to external signs of poverty and social injustice. The stress Gandhi put upon character at the expense of intellect was something Irwin could appreciate as he himself was brought up in that environment. Both, the pious Hindu and the devout Christian, spurred by conscience had chosen the path of self-denial which pointed to the stoic way of life.[33] Gandhi saw in Irwin the three gifts of sincerity, simplicity and humility, and believed that he could trust him.

At the party meeting Gandhi's attitude so hardened that he allowed the young leaders more initiative, and he thought that it was "a crime against man and God" to submit any longer to British domination. In spite of mass feelings against the establishment, he assessed the situation with so much realism as to reject the advice of Subash Chandra Bose to set up a parallel government.[34]

His adherents knew well how strongly he was predisposed to non-violent methods, and naturally worried that he might call off the movement after it was started at the first signs of violence as he had done previously. Soon their fears were removed because Gandhi gave hints that he was unlikely to be influenced by isolated acts of violence if they were not in any way part of his movement.[35] He lipped the word "suffering" as if it was possessed of charm, and thought that under its influence his followers would raise to the level of sacrifice expected of them.

His adherents got an insight into his mind when the news spread that salt laws were to be broken, if not with impunity, at least with the satisfaction of having delivered a blow to the edifice upholding British power. The abolition of salt tax was one of the eleven demands Gandhi had placed before the Viceroy, and if he obtained satisfaction in respect of them he promised the other not to trouble him with civil disobedience.[36] Irwin was told to surrender those powers without which he would hardly pass for a viceroy; therefore, he had no relish to bargain with him Gandhi himself knew too well but he published his demands not so much to see their acceptance as to close the ranks of the people behind him. Gandhi, however, refuted Shaukat Ali's charge that his present movement was not towards emancipation, but to set up Hindu Raj in opposition to the interest of the Muslims.

Gandhi set out on 12th March 1930 from his Ashram at Ahmedabad, at the head of seventy-eight ascetic disciples whose strength before long increased as others joined them, and his destination was Dandi, a deserted village towards the south about two hundred miles away, and on the coast skirting the Arabian Sea. At his age of sixty-one years he as a divine man usually found quiet in life by listening to the melody of hymns under whose inspiration he humbled himself before the inscrutable one; but now a new spirit burned in him, a new role was assigned to him, so that encumbered with a noble task he was transfigured into a zealot, somewhat like the warrior popes of bygone times, in order to set right the wrongs of an invidious era. As he pushed on, part of the winding dusty road under the hot sun was made somewhat easy to walk on, by the people who sprinkled with water and cushioned it with green leaves, so that he was not deprived of a modicum of comfort.

The audacity of his march to defy law drew the attention of the country as a whole and everyone knew that the significance of his act went beyond taking a handful of salt. Though the developing threat to the government was very obvious, and though Irwin owned vast powers and besides was assured of support from the home authority, he did not do anything to interrupt the progress of Gandhi. Now he did not wish to haul him to prison, especially when Gandhi was at the summit of popular veneration, and so by necessity adopted a posture of lofty indifference to the situation.

Gandhi leaving behind Surat moved on with so much determination that he said, "Either I shall return with what I want or my dead body will float in the ocean."[37] At last on 5th April he reached Dandi, then moved towards the sea, and on its shore as people gathered about him he scooped with his hands a lump of salt, in the process broke the law; was instantly hailed as the deliverer. Next a popular uprising broke out along the coast, as people trying to imitate him waded through the sea to take salt in defiance of law.

It is true that Gandhi was the Mahatma, and Irwin who stood against him passed for a saint, but this did not in anyway help matters. Such of those who carried out his orders testified "that his religious convictions seemed to reinforce the very ruthlessness of his policy" aimed at rooting out opposition to him[38]. In fact, to put down resistance, this allegedly "weak" viceroy filled the jails with no less than sixty thousand political offenders.

Among the political heavyweights, Jawaharlal Nehru was imprisoned, but his father Motilal Nehru filled the void by taking over the party. In the face of repression, the younger Nehru writes that the Congress was reluctantly compelled to adopt a sort of dictatorship.[39] So the President owned larger powers than in normal times; was authorized to act on behalf of his Working Committee if it could not meet owing to unusual situations, to fill up the place of those members taken to prison, and, with an eye to the future, to nominate a successor to himself presuming that he too at any moment might find his place in prison.

Mass civil disobedience, especially the illicit production of salt, went on with so much vigour that the police took harsh steps to uphold the sanctity of law. True, the leaders of repute were treated considerately, but the rank and file of the party were dealt with in a savage manner.[40] The wrath of Irwin fell on those who were in the movement, yet had no faith in Gandhi's non-violence, and openly spoke of their willingness to embrace violence if such a course was expedient.

After Gandhi embellished Yeravda prison, there was complete hartal all over India, and in Bombay, which was in the front rank of resistance, the textile mills and railway works were deserted.[41] The great economic depression impinged on the peasants, and in certain areas especially in Gujarat they refused to pay land tax. So they were beaten, their property including livestock was seized, and their confiscated lands worth a lot in terms of productive capacity were often disposed of for a song mainly because revenge on enemies is sweeter than anything else in times of political strife.

At the head of an impressive force of volunteers, the poetess Sarojini Naidu and Manilal Gandhi (the son of Mahatma) continued the anti-government agitation. "You will be beaten," she told them echoing the views of Gandhi, "but you must not resist; you must not even raise a hand to ward off blows."[42] Later, some efforts were made by third parties to bring in a measure of understanding between the Congress and the government.[43] The tribe of Liberal leaders, well known for opportunist politics, was not held in esteem by the people in consequence; Jayakar and Sapru were an exception to this rule however. They with the approval of Irwin saw in the prison Gandhi, who was assisted in the negotiations by Congress leaders especially Jawaharlal Nehru.

Obviously, Irwin was tired of Gandhi, and searched for grounds to make peace with him, but knowing how much he stooped to his prisoner the chief spokesman of the Conservatives Winston Churchill was outraged. The conference in the prison made no headway as Gandhi over and above his recent eleven demands put forward now one more demand hard for Irwin to swallow, that is the right to secede from the empire.[44] In spite of pressure for hard action by those close to him, Irwin was aware of the spiritual force propelling the civil disobedience movement, and he found a way to come to terms with it by setting free in January 1931 Gandhi.[45]

Though his movement was not ended Gandhi made it clear that he was after peace, and would do everything to obtain it in a honourable way. A decisive stage in Gandhi's life had arrived, when he needed the advice of a statesman right now but he was robbed of that benefit by the death of Motilal Nehru. Later, the two Liberal leaders before mentioned together with another of the same tribe, Srinivasa Sastri, persuaded Gandhi to write to the Viceroy seeking an interview for a "heart to heart" talk.[46] When he did so, Irwin favourably responded to his letter with alacrity. In accordance with Gandhi-Irwin Pact, signed on 4th March, Gandhi agreed that civil disobedience should be discontinued; that Congress should attend the Round Table Conference at London to draw up a federal constitution on the basis of self-government with "safeguards in the interests of India for such matters as, for instance, defence; external affairs; the position of minorities; the financial credit of India, and the discharge of obligations."[47] By this clause Irwin got a victory as the Congress settled for something less than complete independence; however, Gandhi said that both sides had won as a result of the pact.

NOTES AND REFERENCES

1. Mahatma Gandhi, A Chronology, K.P. Goswami, p. 28.
2. Mahatma Gandhi, H. S. L, Polak, p. 166.
3. India in the Crucible, C.S. Ranga Iyer, p. 135.
4. *Ibid*, p. 77.
5. Foundation of Pakistan, S.S. Pirzada, V. 2, p. 122.
6. *Ibid*, p. 123.
7. *Ibid*, p. 119.
8. *Ibid*, p. 122.
9. Gandhi and Modern India, P. Moon, 128 & 129.
10. *Ibid*, p. 129.
11. The Indian Quarterly Register, 1929, V. 1, Mitra, p. 364.
12. The Political Study of Mohammad Ali Jinnah, V. 1, M.H. Saiyid, p. 426.

13. *Ibid*, p. 430.
14. IQR, op cit., 1928, p. 32 & 38.
15. Collected Works of Mahatma Gandhi, V. 38, p. 291.
16. Sardar Vallabhbhai Patel, V. 1, p. 384 & 385.
17. The Story of Bardoli, Mahadev Desai, p. 78.
18. Viscount Halifax, Alan Campbell Johnson,p. 246.
19. Saiyid, p. 456.
20. Collected Works, V. 42, p. 514 & 515.
21. *Ibid*, p. 520.
22. *Ibid*, p. 80 & 81.
23. Jawaharlal Nehru, An Autobiography, p. 197.
24. Collected Works, V. 42, p. 224.
25. *Ibid.*
26. *Ibid*, p. 361.
27. *Ibid*, p. 324.
28. The History of the Indian National Congress, B.P. Sitaramayya, p. 354.
29. Fulness of Days, the Earl of Halifax, p. 146.
30. Indian Quarterly Register, 1929, V. 2, p. 443.
31. As It Happened, C.R. Attlee, p. 67.
32. Collected Works, V. 42, p. 422.
33. Viscount Halifax, Alan Campbell Johnson, p. 295.
34. Collected Works, V. 42, p. 351.
35. Jawaharlal Nehru, An Autobiography, p. 210.
36. Collected Works, V. 42, p. 434.
37. Mahatma, D.G. Tendulkar, V. 3, p. 38.
38. Viscount Halifax, Alan Campbell Johnson, p. 255.
39. Jawaharlal Nehru, An Autobiography, p. 210 & 211.
40. Tendulkar, V. 3, p. 45.
41. Mahatma Gandhi, H.N. Brailsford, p. 177.
42. *Ibid.*
43. Collected Works, V. 44, p. 81.
44. *Ibid*, p. 83.
45. Indian Problems, Speeches by Lord Irwin, p. 110.
46. Gandhi and Modern India, Penderel Moon, p. 153.
47. Speeches and Writings of Mahatma Gandhi, p. 772.

6

THE PARIAH'S ALLY

After attending the conference in London and touring certain continental states, Gandhi returned to India to see things falling apart owing to irreconcilable differences. The new Viceroy Lord Willingdon, perceiving that the control over the affairs of the State had been relaxed during the reign of Irwin, had taken steps to establish his authority. Gandhi came to know of the arrest of Nehru besides other leaders, and he who "is fundamentally a force for peace" now found himself in No Man's Land between a Congress which was prepared for an immediate resumption of civil disobedience and a government which was ready to put it down with an iron hand.[1] As there was a breach in their alliance, and as the two sides were already engaged in skirmishes, Gandhi was under pressure not to do anything towards restoration of peace because he would run the risk of demoralizing his side at a time when action against the rulers was urgently needed.[2]

Nevertheless, he wrote a conciliatory letter to the Viceroy to know whether good relations between them were at an end, or "you expect me still to see you and receive guidance from you as to the course I am to pursue in advising the Congress."[3] He, however, sensing the danger inherent in Gandhi's claim to talk on equal terms and relying on the support of the Muslims, other minorities as well as the princes decided to strike at his chief opponent. So once again Gandhi went to Yeravda prison where he was lucky enough to get the company of another prisoner, Vallabhbhai Patel, both chatted for long to enliven what was otherwise a dismal existence.[4] Lending his help to Gandhi, the poet Tagore asked the people to uphold the eternal moral values of the nation in the face of damnable behaviour of the government, "which is only a passing accident."[5] Indeed the rank and file of the party courted arrest; but without direction, without funds, and without enthusiasm they "entered unwillingly to battle" and before long the fighting power of the Congress was gone.[6]

So far as Gandhi was concerned, however, he would even in prison create more difficulties than the government could deal with. On August 17th 1932 Ramsay MacDonald came up with a scheme of minority representation in the legislatures, and to be sure the Depressed Classes, otherwise known as untouchables or more respectfully as Harijans (God's people) got separate electorate.[7] Gandhi had expected that the other would not meddle with the delicate subject of caste, knowing that such voting privilege was contrived to drive a wedge between the Hindu castes and had vast potential for mischief. Now the plan to deliver a blow to Hinduism was put into effect, Gandhi was seized with horror and besides he could not reconcile himself to the fact that Christian Irwin was involved in this nefarious purpose.[8] When so much was at stake he could not passively look at the situation, but made known his resolution to fast himself to death.[9] He fixed the date for starting it, September 20th refused to put off the date when his companions asked for it in the hope of patching up the quarrel, and made it evident that his contemplated step was guided by god's will; that he counted his life as a thing of no consequence.

The Pariahs for whose sake so much noise was made were treated in the past with cold indifference, and were condemned to the humiliation of living at the margin of the society. A measure of their degradation could be understood by this: the Hindus often used bad and foul language in their quarrels but this exchange of defamatory words did not prevent them later from going through normal social relations; however, if one should say to another that he was a man without caste (like the Pariahs) the "insult would never be forgiven or forgotten."[10] In fact, the Hindus were so fond of caste that if one were to ask a man born to the caste of *Kullars*, with whom robbing was a hereditary occupation, to what people he belonged he would with a cool head say, "I am a robber!," thereby disassociating himself from the invidiousness attached to that profession because it was both a duty and a right handed over by his forbears with the approval of tradition.[11]

While caste brought in respect to the individual, the deprivation of its protection caused a lot of miseries. Gandhi knew what it was to lose the status of caste irrespective of the fact whether it was high or low when he was declared an outcaste, but his moderate policy towards the caste elders together with the fact that the sunny days of Hindu orthodoxy had passed over saved him from bitter experience.

It is fashionable nowadays to denounce caste because it does not match well with the values of materialistic society. However Gandhi, as well as the nineteenth century missionary traveler Abbe Dubois, from whom I have borrowed heavily to add colour to this chapter, with their deep insight into the workings of Hindu society had nothing but praise for caste division of society. "I do not consider caste to be free from many great drawbacks," says Dubois, "but I believe that the resulting advantages, in the case of a nation constituted like the Hindus, more than outweigh the resulting evils."[12] To guard against the dangers of political innovation and to create a right atmosphere for human endeavour, the ancient lawgivers set out from the cardinal principle that to the State nobody should be thought of as useless. But people were indolent and careless by nature; this circumstance was aggravated by the climate, so that the lawgivers cameup with a remedy through caste, without which society would not have held together, and by which each person got a profession rigidly imposed upon him.

Likewise, upon the basis of occupation people in ancient Egypt were divided into castes; "these are, the priests, the warriors, the cowherds, the swineherds, the tradesmen, the interpreters, and the boatmen."[13] And what is more "the warrior class in Egypt had certain special privileges in which none of the rest of the Egyptians participated except the priests."[14] This arrangement was somewhat like the Kshatriya-Brahmin axis which set them above the rest of the Hindus; yet the difference between the two countries was fundamental. While in Egypt all the castes were held in respect, among the Hindus so much prejudice is entertained even now against certain types of work considered as menial in nature that those who are unfortunate enough to do them scarcely get the respect of their contemporaries.[15]

From very early times the Pariahs existed and in the sacred books they are referred to; they were at first made up of disreputable people who because of several offences against the norms of the society lost their right to associate with respectable citizens. So they lived as a separate class within the society, and gave themselves up to their natural inclination towards vice and excess.[16] Over and above their lack of attention to cleanliness they were too fond of boozing, a vice abhorrent to the rest of the Hindus.[17]

The Pariahs often indulged in the pleasure of communal feasts, but these invariably degenerated into orgies. According to the usage of their caste* they gulp so much liquor of the palm tree as to get themselves inebriated. And the guests forewarned about the type of company they met with there and of the risk they faced in attending the wild debauch would come well prepared with hefty sticks to the festivities. Such a precaution did credit to their sagacity because the party rarely ended without the guests coming to blows, and without spilling over of blood.[18]

Both in towns and villages each caste people tended to live in separate quarters, but the Pariahs some distance away from them.[19] The Chinese traveler Fa Hian has observed that Pariahs and Chandalas (a far more bad appellation to describe everything that is evil) had to live out of the city walls; but if they walked in, they had to strike a gong in order to make known their undesirable presence and to warn passers-by not to touch them.[20] Further, the Brahmins entertained fear of pollution by approach; indeed the stock of their purity was made to go up by adding impurities to the outcaste people.[21] Whatever they did, to justify their behaviour, they could always fall back upon the authority of a certain Manu whose legal code written about the beginning of Christian era was favourable to them.

And yet nobody questioned the preponderance of caste, least of all the Pariahs whose spirit anyway had been broken, and besides a set of people living on the edge of society could not be expected either to weaken or to overthrow the then existing order, which it was the foremost duty of the king to uphold with all the power at his disposal. The values of the present day look upon the good of the individual as the end of life, but the Hindu ideal sanctioned by tradition and propagated by sacred books covered the whole society.[22] In such a background caste was a mighty engine for orderly progress as it eliminated conflict between master and servant, landlord and tenant, capital and labour, above all between the State and citizen.[23]

---

* The casteless later became a caste.

Whatever the Pariahs suffered was somewhat mitigated by the fact that the notion of high and low did not matter much in the past, especially when the projection of self, and the display of individual power through wealth were both not valued. The forces at work in the old order balanced against each other with the result a body lacked strategic advantage to dominate over others. The king as the head of the ruling caste was in the pocket of the Brahmins who in spite of vast influence owned least material wealth or habitually looked at it with indifference. Furthermore, the Vaisya trading caste people on account of their large wealth should have counted much in society, but they were ranked below the rulers, and the Brahmins, to whom they customarily showed high reverence. All these must have contributed to explain why class war between the possessed and the dispossessed in the Indian context either was conspicuous by its absence or at least did not emerge in so ferocious manner as some countries in Europe had to pass through.

However everyone stood on a level with each other concerning the satisfaction of spiritual wants which mattered very much then.[24] Among the Pariahs existed a class that maintained exclusiveness, and looked after the spiritual needs of the community; since those who belonged to this class were held in respect they were called the Brahmins of the Pariahs in mockery.[25] The Brahmins were careful not to let others carry on their functions, but still instances were not lacking when their prerogatives were exercised by others. "At one of the most famous temples of Mysore, called Melkota, during the great festival which is there celebrated annually, the Pariahs are the first to enter the sanctuary and to offer sacrifices to the idol, and it is only after they have finished that the Brahmins begin their sacrifices."[26]

The miserable situation of the Pariahs became evident when the new order founded upon proprietary rights and self aggrandizement through material riches started to dominate life. For these despised wretches hardly anywhere were allowed to cultivate the soil for their own benefit, but were obliged to hire themselves out to others who made good use of them by paying the least.[27] Their master at pleasure beat them and yet they never so much as raised their voice to complain of at their humiliation. They acquiesced in their bad lot and never entertained the idea of joining hands to compel the other castes to treat them with that common respect and natural humanity which one person expects from another. Apart from farm labour, they as village scavengers cleaned public latrines, swept the streets and removed all the rubbish lying there. Further, as servants to the European rulers they did such menial work that no other caste people would condescend to do.[28]

Even before Gandhi went on a fast, Malaviya presided over a conference of Hindu leaders which included Pariah spokesmen too; they arrived at the opinion that at any cost Gandhi's life must be preserved, and that steps should be taken to remove the vile practice of untouchability in order to keep up their unity.[29] In fact, what Gandhi aimed at by his fast was to prick Hindu conscience in reference to the Pariahs; now things began to move in that direction if the buzz and noise occasioned by his fast was any indication.

At last the day for taking action arrived; as usual Gandhi went through the ritual of morning prayer, breakfasted on milk and fruit, and then at noon launched his fast not alone. For millions of people all over the country did like him, but on that particular day only. Keeping in mind his advanced age people close to him got worried about his health, especially because his body lost strength quickly. "A shadow is darkening today over India," said the poet Tagore, "like a shadow cast by an eclipsed sun."[30] Soon he was shifted to a more congenial place where he lay on a white iron cot right under the shady branches of a low mango tree, within the prison ground.[31] Both Vallabhbhai Patel and Mahadev Desai were by his side; he would now and then take water mixed with soda bicarbonate and salt.

Now the leader of the Pariahs, Ambedkar, drew everybody's attention because his words had great weight in any endeavour to rescue Gandhi. Although he was educated abroad and was a lawyer by profession, his achievements did not bring him that respect which was his due; for his caste background was held against him in order to undervalue him. Finally, it was Sapru who by taxing his brilliant legal mind came up with a formula, which could bring together people at variance. So the number of seats reserved for Harijans in the provincial legislatures would be doubled, but they should be filled through primary and secondary elections, with separate electorate coming into the picture only at the first stage.[32] By this arrangement, the Depressed Class voters would elect a panel of four candidates for each seat from whom a choice would be made by all the Hindus.[33]

Nobody knew how Gandhi would respond to this proposal, but Ambedkar was favourably disposed towards it in the hope of getting for his caste a larger representation.[34] An extraordinary meeting of political leaders took place in the jail, one day after Gandhi started his fast, presided over by himself.[35] Sapru put forward his scheme to which Gandhi offered no resistance, seeing that Ramsay MacDonald's dagger thrust of separate electorate very much blunted by a ingenious device.

Further, on the following day, Gandhi held conversation with Ambedkar who was outspoken in airing his views.

Ambedkar: But I have only one quarrel with you, that is, you work for the so-called national welfare and not for our interests alone. If you devoted yourself entirely to the welfare of the Depressed Classes, you would then become our hero.

Gandhi: Very sweet of you to say so.

Ambedkar: I want political power for my community. That is indispensable for our survival. The basis of the agreement therefore should be: I should get what is due to me. I wish to tell the Hindus that I should be assured of my compensation.[36]

He pushed on his demands fighting every inch of the ground even though Gandhi had no inclination to haggle and was prepared to be magnanimous. In and out of the prison the negotiations still went on, without effecting a breakthrough, while physical exhaustion having set in Gandhi's condition turned to worst. So his adherents rushed through an agreement on matters which did not cause friction. Concerning the number of seats for the Harijans in the provincial legislatures, the Prime Minister had awarded 71, Ambedkar's demand was for 197 which finally settled at 147 in conformity with the present agreement[37]. And eighteen per cent of the general electorate seats in the Central Legislature was reserved for them. With considerable urgency this accord was sent to the British Prime Minister, and it was only after he gave his assent to the compromise Gandhi on the 26th broke his fast. Hardly the British understood the reason for his fast and its subsequent termination; it seemed strange to them that the life and death of Gandhi should hang on a small modification of an electoral formula.

NOTES AND REFERENCES

1. Lord Lothian, J.R.M. Butler, p. 180.
2. Roman Rolland and Gandhi Correspondence, p. 550.

3. Mahatma, D.G. Tendulkar, V. 3, p. 187.
4. Sardar Vallabhbhai Patel, N.D. Parikh, V. 2, p. 91.
5. Romain Rolland, *op cit*, p. 558.
6. Gandhi and Modern India, P. Moon, p. 171.
7. Tendulkar, *op cit*, p. 197.
8. Collected Works of Mahatma Gandhi, V. 50, p. 469.
9. Tendulkar, *op cit*, p. 200.
10. Hindu Manners, Customs and Ceremonies, Abbe J.A. Dubois, V. 1, p. 41.
11. *Ibid*, p. 18.
12. *Ibid*, p. 29.
13. The Persian Wars, Herodotus, Translated by G. Rawlinson, p. 200.
14. *Ibid*, p. 201.
15. Dubois, V. 1, p. 31 & 32.
16. *Ibid*, p. 53.
17. *Ibid*, p. 17.
18. *Ibid*, p. 281.
19. A History of South India, K.A. Nilakanta Sastri, p. 319.
20. A Concise History of the Indian People, H. G. Rawlinson, p. 65.
21. A History of India, Romila Thapar, V.1, p. 153.
22. The Legacy of India, G. T. Garratt, Caste and the Structure of Society by R.P. Masani, p. 150.
23. *Ibid*, p. 133.
24. The Discovery of India, Jawaharlal Nehru, p. 252.
25. Dubois, V. 1, p. 62.
26. *Ibid*, V. 2, p. 591.
27. *Ibid*, V. 1, p. 50 & 51.
28. *Ibid*, p. 54.
29. Tendulkar, V. 3, p. 204.
30. *Ibid*, p. 206.
31. The Gandhi Reader, Homer A. Jack, The Epic Fast by Pyarelal, p. 283.
32. P. Moon, op cit, p. 173.
33. *Ibid.*
34. Tendulkar, p. 207.
35. *Ibid.*
36. C.W. M.G, V. 51, p. 458 & 459.
37. Tendulkar, p. 210.

7

THE KNIGHT OF THE TEMPLE

In his crusade for the rights of the Pariahs, Gandhi's strength lay in the fact that he was temperamentally a conservative, or rather an orthodox Hindu who venerated tradition and looked upon scriptures as revelation. "I believe Brahminism," said Gandhi, "to be unadulterated wisdom."[1] Such a view, however, did not help him to live on good terms either with the leader of the Harijans or with the Hindus more orthodox than himself. For Ambedkar let him know that "there is no hope for the Harijans unless you get rid of caste altogether."[2] This opinion Gandhi was not ready to take in, because he stood for purging caste of untouchability and restoring to it that virginity which confined it to specialization in several professions without distinction in status.[3]

The stubbornness with which the caste Hindus stuck to their beliefs was not to be wondered since their prejudices got the better of their reason. These often draw attention and claim respectability by passing off as wisdom of the past. Through the mouth of one Gyges, Herodotus says: "Our fathers, in time past, distinguished right and wrong plainly enough, and it is our wisdom to submit to be taught by them." [4]Although more than two millennia had gone by since this was uttered, there are many orthodox Hindus who even now speak in a similar manner as the sequel illustrates.

Gandhi partly in prison and partly out of it carried out propaganda to undo Harijan wrongs. Once when he was traveling in the south he fell in with a company of orthodox Hindus, who put a garland of flowers around his neck to show their respect for him. Afterwards, their leader "quite courteously but equally firmly" reflecting the strength of his convictions told Gandhi that nowadays they were not putting restrictions on the Harijans about the type of dress they should wear, except on certain festival days. Still this was too much for Gandhi who asked him:

"But what right you have to dictate their dress for any day at all?"

"It is the custom handed down by our forefathers," replied the caste leader.

"Supposing someone regulated your dress?" said Gandhi.

"Why not?" came the reply pat. "We have to submit to many things that the higher castes prescribe for us, and the Harijans have to submit to us."

"You need not submit to anybody's dictation. There is no higher and no lower," opined Gandhi.

'How can that be?" asked the other. "The Harijans cannot be allowed to cross the limits prescribed by custom."

"But, surely, you won't adhere to a custom which is manifestly bad," remonstrated Gandhi.

"Who is to judge what is bad for me?" said he. "All custom must be good, because it comes from our forefathers."[5]

The Hindu sacred text Rigveda alludes to the idea of high and low embedded in the caste system. For it called the primeval man's mouth the Brahmin and said that from the feet the Sudra got into existence.[6] Hence it came to pass that the purest of the profession was that of the Brahmin and the most impure was that of the Pariah scavenger. A concern for purity begot a desire for exclusiveness, so that the Brahmins kept distance from the lower castes; so that they imagined not only the touch of the Pariah defiled them but even his shadow falling upon their path had the same effect and called for ritual atonement.[7]

Such an attitude brought down the status of the Pariahs and damned their existence forever. According to the precept of the Brahmins the kings should belong to the warrior caste, but in reality this was not always so in bygone times. The dynasty of Nandas was of Sudra origin, and likewise the Mauryas were of low birth and the Yavanas who carried in them Greek blood were definitely Sudras according to Manu, the ultimate judge in such matters[8]. Through the pious guile of the Brahmins, in many instances people of low birth got respectable pedigree, maintained the pretence of having belonged to the Kshatriya caste, and enjoyed its privileges above others. But only the Pariah could not move up because once an outcaste was always an outcaste.

Besides the caste one more pillar upholding the edifice of Hindu life was the temple; in India so numerous were the buildings dedicated to religious worship that nobody could count them with any degree of exactness. In fact there were few villages or hamlets not distinguished by a temple; few mountains not surmounted with a temple provided water was available there.[9] That which catches the eye of a passer-by from a long distance is the lofty tower over the gateway of the temple. It is no small engineering feat to raise a single block of stone measuring in one instance about twenty-five feet square and weighing over eighty tons to the summit of the tower.[10] Unlike the pyramid which outwardly to the eye gives a bald appearance, the tower is a wonderful piece of architecture and besides scenes from traditional life are colourfully as well as aesthetically sculptured there.

It was the saints of the Tamil country who made popular singing religious hymns and playing music in the temples; where dancers too having mastered the stylistic aspects of *Bharata natyam* exhibited their talents[11]. Larger temples recruited hundreds of servants and their revenue from the gifts of devotees and the largess of kings was so high that they profitably invested in trading guilds, or lent money with interest to village bodies. On the whole the management of the temple was a hard task and an old record mentions about a strike of the employees even in that consecrated ground on account of a dispute.[12]

The Hindu temples from time immemorial had kept out of their precincts certain professionals like the tanners and potters, because they were looked upon as unclean.[13] For the same reason the outcastes were prohibited from entering the sacred ground of a temple. Once Gandhi made it clear that temples must change for the better, they were engulfed in controversy. Scholars versed in ancient texts being an influential lot their moderate views helped Gandhi to go against the Hindu orthodoxy. They thought that public temples should keep the doors open to everyone, and looking at the existing state of affairs with a sympathetic mind believed "that there is no such thing as untouchability attaching to birth and incapable of being cured by any penance or purification."[14] To such a view opposition without doubt existed, and a certain researcher dug up facts on the strength of which he asserted: "If an untouchable enters a temple, pollution is caused to idol and purificatory rites should be done to remove it."[15] Gandhi laid the blame for the miserable condition of the Pariahs on the caste Hindus, but they rejected his contention that they had committed a sin in this regard. For in conformity with the theory of *karma* the bad situation of the outcaste people was the result of their action in past life. If this was so, and if it was preordained that they should live in poverty. Gandhi asked: "Why should other people suffering from distress be helped?"[16] He made it obvious to the caste Hindus that they were exploiting the weakness of the Pariahs.

At the height of the controversy Gandhi in his prison room received with courtesy several Pundits, who entered into a long talk with him. Some of the untouchables whom the Hindus in the past had looked down with utter disgust were those begotten as a result of a Sudra man lying with a Brahmin woman. It was agreed by the Pundits that the present day Harijans absolutely did not suffer from this disability. Their other shortcomings including their dirty habits and external manifestation of uncleanness, the Pundits opined, did not belong to them alone, and caste Hindus too shared them. In short their talks with him ended without discord, and Gandhi received their approval concerning the right of the Harijans to enter temples.[17] But even he was reconciled to the fact that they should not make their way into the room where sacred deities were kept and only those well versed in the scriptures could be seen there.[18]

A little off a temple proper usually a well-chiseled stone pillar is set perpendicularly. Now it was said that the untouchables desirous of getting into temples should take this pillar as the boundary and should not move any farther; however, Gandhi could not entertain this proposal since it destroyed the spirit of his temple entry programme, which was treating all as equals.[19]

As Gandhi was not ready to bargain in a give and take spirit it was alleged that he was adopting an uncompromising attitude. Against him, therefore, the ire of the so-called pure Hindus was up, and it was the Zamorin of Calicut who made a stand in their favour. Indeed the resistance for letting untouchables enter temples was greater in Kerala than anywhere else. The reason for this was that Kerala, owing to its geographical position on the southern tip of the Indian peninsula, "has generally escaped the invasions and revolutions which have so often devastated the rest of India, and has thus managed to preserve unaltered many ancient institutions, which in other parts have fallen into disuse."[20].

The Zamorin had with him the key of a well known temple and he refused to open its doors to the untouchables on the ground it was a private one. However it was a public temple and under Gandhi's initiative a referendum was held to know the temple users opinion, which turned out to be against restrictive entry. This satisfied Gandhi's conscience so that he renewed pressure upon the Zamorin for his unreasonable stand. He was a big landlord, and owned a lot of prestige as well as influence; besides the conservatives and the diehards opposed to Gandhi rallied behind him bolstering up his hopes. In a letter to Gandhi, he maintained that "the untouchables have no right to enter the temple on any day.[21]" But the evidence on hand indicated that while the upper castes had all through the year the right of entry, and of way leading, into his temple, likewise the untouchables possessed the twin rights but only on a particular festival day.[22] The Zamorin, however, would not take this into consideration, and made it known that on the festival day so large a jostling crowd pushed its way into the temple that it was uncertain whether the untouchables gained entry or not.

But this denial of entry into the place of worship was just the tip of the iceberg; in fact, they had no right to get into restaurants, barbershops, public schools, and even public latrines for cleaning which however their service was made use of. They had no right to ride a horse; to carry the dead along the highway if there was a temple close by, but were made to cut through crops, dirt and mire of the countryside. Most of the villages were not provided with running tap water, and had to depend upon wells and tanks, but the untouchables were denied access to them. Their inferior status was made very clear by this custom: If an untouchable was taking rest in front of his house, and if a caste Hindu passed by, then in order to pay deference to him he should get up and make a congee.[23]

When the agreement made with Ambedkar and his party during his fast was breached by his side, Gandhi felt it would be a betrayal of trust reposed in him by the voiceless millions if he did nothing.[24] He began to revolve in his mind what sacrifice was needed to blot out the taint got from the days of old, and subsequently his heart was torn by conflicting passions. He then fell asleep, was disturbed by a unknown thing, and heard a mysterious voice telling him to go on fast. He made up his mind then and there to obey the voice; later he told his companions that he would from 8th May 1933 fast up to the duration of twenty one days.[25] Though it was not directed against anyone, and though it was an exercise in spiritual purification, the cause of the untouchables had prompted him towards it; so their interest was dominant in his thoughts. "I want to live for the cause" said Gandhi concerning the fast, "although I hope I am equally prepared to die for it."[26] His decision was not taken well by his followers and they tried to persuade him to desist from such a hazardous undertaking. Nobody could shake his will however, and on the day previously fixed he started his abstinence, but was quickly let out of prison. Not pleased with this he hurried away in a car to Poona, called off the disobedience movement for some days, and asked the Viceroy to set free civil resisters and to revoke emergency powers. His peace overture to the Viceroy met with no result, while his colleague Subhas Chandra Bose denounced his shift in ground saying: "the latest act of Mahatma Gandhi in suspending civil disobedience is a confession of failure."[27] His popularity was not dented by this attack; on the contrary it had gone up on account of his penitential fast. "We are with you," said Romain Rolland from abroad, "in these grave days when again your life is at stake."[28] Without any danger to his life the fast proceeded smoothly however, and on May 29th about twelve in the noon he ended it.[29]

Since Gandhi was completely preoccupied with the interest of the Pariahs, the rank and file of the party did not know whether to follow in his ways or to carry on the disobedience movement. So the leaders of the party approached Gandhi with contrary views; some wished to give up the movement altogether while others desired its vigorous prosecution. Gandhi caught on the horns of a dilemma found a way out by seeking an interview with the Viceroy.

But Willingdon saw no reason why he should make a climb down from his position of superiority to receive him. So it was decided that the struggle must go on, but those who wished to participate in it must do so at the individual level, without help from the party. Among them Gandhi himself was in the front rank; to show his determination, like a general who burns the bridge in order to concentrate on what lay ahead, he wound up his Sabarmati Ashram, set out on August 1st to spread the message of civil resistance, but was taken to the prison along with thirty of his Ashram disciples. In the jail Gandhi proved a difficult customer; on the ground that he was denied facilities to do work relating to the untouchables, he commenced a fast to be ended with his death. His health less than a week after his fast turned to worst, his will to live was gone, and his martyrdom seemed to be at hand.[30] Some said that he would love nothing so much as to die in prison and to put the blame upon the government for that.[31] But the Viceroy made a shrewd move so that he was set free unconditionally.

Thereupon Gandhi set off on a journey which took him all over India, and its main purpose was not to build up resistance against the government, but to redress the wrongs of the Pariahs. Of which wrongs lack of justice and fair play in the temples preoccupied his mind. When it had been suggested to him that untouchables should enforce a sort of blockade of the temples so as to prevent the caste Hindus from getting in Gandhi had unhesitatingly dismissed the idea because it was violence in disguise.[32]

But those who opposed him now had no such scruples, especially because they imagined that he was acting like an atheist. They discovered in a certain Pandit Lalnath a man of their choice since he was as zealous as Gandhi but to prevent the untouchables from entering the temples. What is more, he and his followers pretended to be following Gandhi's non-violence, so that they would threaten to oppose his programme either by lying prostrate in front of the temple or by falling before his car to check his progress.[33] Like a predator which after lying in ambush would fall upon its unwary victim, Lalnath and his company would from nowhere descend on Gandhi, who was at a loss how to deal with them.

On November 18th, at Akola they came in a body to the place where Gandhi was lodged with a view to prevent him from going out to a public meeting. Using the moral weapon of satyagraha as a stick to beat his opponents in the crudest way imaginable, Lalnath had the audacity to tell Gandhi to his face that he was paid back in his own coin. Gandhi however was not impressed, and plainly told him that he was adopting sham tactics which had no resemblance to his own methods. His travel across the country to relieve the hardship of the Harijans came to an end in the sacred city of Benares, where as if to commemorate that event a burlesque was played by the orthodox Hindus with Pandit Lalnath at their head. When Gandhi was about to leave for a public meeting he was served with a warrant, which demanded his presence before the deity of Benares so that he could be put on trial for heresy.

Who gave you the warrant? asked the Mahatma.

The Lord prompted me to serve the warrant and arrest you, replied the messenger.

Then, why does not the Lord prompt me to obey this warrant?

Because you are a sinner, said the messenger.[34]

Then Lalnath himself popped up in order to ask Gandhi his portrait which for obvious reasons he failed to obtain, but his hot blooded followers got it from elsewhere and burnt it in the view of everyone. Gandhi had escaped an attempt on his life at Poona shortly before, and now his life was again in danger as the so-called pure Hindus vowed vengeance against him for introducing religious innovations, which they imagined would undermine the strength of the Hindu faith.

NOTES AND REFERENCES

1. Mahatma Gandhi, H.N. Brailsford (one among the three authors), p. 202.
2. *Ibid.*
3. Hindu Dharma, M.K. Gandhi, p.322 & 374.
4. The Persian Wars, Herodotus, translated by G. Rawlinson, p. 7.
5. Collected Works of Mahatma Gandhi, V. 57, p. 135.
6. The Past and Prejudice, Romila Thapar, p. 296.
7. A History of India, Romila Thapar, V. 1, p. 252.
8. The Past and Prejudice, op cit, p. 31.
9. Hindu Manners, Customs, and Ceremonies, J.A. Dubois, V. 2, p. 585 & 586.
10. A Concise History of the Indian People, H. G. Rawlinson, p. 116.
11. Romila Thapar, V. 1, p. 189.
12. The Past and Prejudice, p. 39.
13. Romila Thapar, V. 1, p. 189.
14. C.W.M.G., V. 52, p. 199.

15. *Ibid*, p. 276.
16. *Ibid*, p. 277.
17. *Ibid*, p. 349.
18. *Ibid*, p. 31.
19. *Ibid*, p. 211.
20. Dubois, V. 1, p. 57.
21. C.W.M.G. V. 52, p. 328.
22. *Ibid*.
23. C.W.M.G., V. 57, p. 260.
24. *Ibid*, V. 52, p. 307.
25. Mahatma, D.G. Tendulkar, V. 3, p. 243.
26. *Ibid*, p. 244.
27. *Ibid*, p. 252.
28. Romain Rolland and Gandhi Correspondence, p. 274.
29. Tendulkar, op cit, p. 254.
30. *Ibid*, p. 264.
31. C.W.M.G. V. 55, p. 455.
32. Harijan, April 15th 1933, p. 8.
33. Tendulkar, op cit, p. 276.
34. *Ibid*, p. 341.

8

THE PARTY INTRIGUES

"I think I can claim," said Lord Willingdon on the verge of retiring from the office, "that the country is more peaceful today than it has been for a good many years."[1] Shortly after he assumed the Viceroy's power he saw the restarting of the civil disobedience movement, "which had caused such terrible trouble and distress during the period of my predecessor." He fought against it, and got success in his efforts to restore British authority. Since the new Reforms Act had come into existence, he thought that the heat of election contests and the lure of offices under the British would keep the people away from Gandhi's resistance.

In fact, enthusiasm for civil disobedience as well as for revolutionary terrorism had disappeared.[2] In their talks with Gandhi, those who had expressed a desire to abandon his popular movement were the ones very eager to occupy positions in the legislature. The fashionable word was socialism, which got a leader in Jaya Prakash Narayan, and the extremists rallied behind him. An ideological rift threatened to destroy the unity of the Congress, because the socialists looked at Nehru for guidance and the conservatives in opposition to them came under the influence of Vallabhbhai Patel and Rajendra Prasad. Nehru for a while lost faith in the methods of Gandhi especially his non-violence, so that he said: "In any event, some form of coercion seems to be inevitable, for people who hold power and privilege do not give them up till they are forced to do so, or till conditions are created which make it more harmful to them to keep these privileges than to give them up."[3]

The British thought that a little more responsibility to the people would help to manage them better, and Gandhi adopted the same policy to keep in check the wayward inclinations of Nehru. Hence, for the year 1936 and the one that followed Nehru became the head of the party. And yet when he spoke hot words to give vent to his socialistic ardour Gandhi made it plain: "But I do not accept practically any of his methods. I would strain every nerve to prevent a class war."[4] However, Nehru before long tempered his enthusiasm, and did not take side in the factional conflict, so that unity in the party was maintained. Moreover, election in accordance with the new reforms was not far away; so the time was not appropriate to start any sort of wrangling in the party.

The Muslim League made up its mind to contest in the elections at the national level, although it was ill equipped to face the older as well as the better organized Congress party. But its prime asset was Jinnah; his enormous confidence in himself, his incorruptible nature, and his unwavering mental powers founded upon his resolution to achieve his purpose were things to be reckoned with by his adversaries.[5] His ego got the better of the finer personal qualities however, and he hankered after power because it was the only way for self-aggrandizement, and for enlarged vision of splendour.[6]

While expending his tireless energy to attract friends and influential people in the Muslim majority provinces, Jinnah got to know the insular nature of leaders there.[7] They were forever influenced by provincial issues; forever quarreling among themselves. His strategy to conquer Bengal for the League met with resistance, since in this province under the domination of Hindu culture no party could resort to Islam alone for success. To establish the influence of the League, Jinnah needed "advice, information, and agents" and one man somewhat fit for discharging this function was M.A.H. Ispahani. Always zealous to promote his mentor's objectives, he vainly tried to lift Muslim politics from the provincial to the national level.[8] Jinnah on 17th August 1936 went to Bengal, and his policy aimed at patching up the quarrel of party lords was so successful that heavyweight leaders like H.S. Suhrawardy and Khwaja Nazimuddin came over to his side. But another prize catch eluded Jinnah's grasp; for Fazlul Haq refused to leave his provincial moorings.[9] No less ambitious than Jinnah he could not subordinate himself to promote the interest of the other.

Though mainly Muslim in complexion the Unionist party in the Punjab represented the interest of Hindu Jats as well as the Sikhs. There was no room for overplaying religion here; so the party leaders, Sikandar Hayat Khan and his successor Khizar, put up resistance with a desire to contain the influence of the League in their sphere of activities. And Ghaffar Khan pursued a similar policy in the Frontier Province although the Muslims constituted the overwhelming majority there.

The Congress in February 1937 elections won five provinces; besides in Bombay it could form a ministry with the help of fellow-travellers, and in the Frontier province its ally Ghaffar Khan triumphed. Out of a total 1585 seats it won 716, but it elected only 26 Muslims, so that its claim to represent them proved wrong.[10] The Unionist party in the Punjab got a majority, and in Bengal a Muslim coalition ministry under Fazlul Haq reflected the election result.

Not giving way to despair Jinnah said before the League audiences: "In each and every province where a League Parliamentary Board was established and League parties were constituted, we carried away about 60 to 70 per cent of the seats that were contested."[11] In short, the League won 109 seats out of a total 482 reserved for Muslims, but it did not contest all the seats on account of its organizational weakness.[12]

When the time arrived for taking over power, Gandhi, who reposed least faith in the new constitution, opined that the Congress should get into office only if the Governor gave an assurance that he would honour the advice of his ministry. This was a tactical move of the Congress to dilute the powers of the Governor which were seen as excessive; but the British thought that the Congress was putting forward an excuse to decline office in which it lacked interest because it wanted to preserve the rebellious spirit in the party.[13] So the new Viceroy Lord Linlithgow was called upon to deal with the crisis in such a way that the new constitution was not undone.

It was suggested that Gandhi and the Viceroy should hold talks in order to break the impasse. But in this Linlithgow saw a well prepared trap, and was averse to do anything that would enlarge the influence of Gandhi; that would add to the stature of his party. However, the Secretary of State Lord Zetland expected the Viceroy to adopt a sympathetic attitude, and to take initiative to remove the deadlock;

which, it was said in the House of Lords, mostly persisted owing to a clash in temperament.[14]

Again Linlithgow reflected on the advantage of parleying with Gandhi. Again he dismissed that idea from his mind and he was backed in that step by his advisers. He knew too well that if his conversation with Gandhi ended in failure its repercussions would be bad indeed. In and out of the government his allies, as well as the princes, were all closely observing his moves; and the chances were that they would form a less flattering opinion of him, even if they did not get alienated from him. Therefore, he did not want to accept the claim of the Congress to be an authority parallel to the government, and entitled to negotiate on matters touching the whole of India, especially such important issues as provincial autonomy and safeguards for the minorities.[15]

It was a well known practice that when the Governor and his ministry disagreed, the latter must either resign or be dismissed. The normal constitutional practice leaned heavily to the side of resignation; but Gandhi under pressure from the extremists in the party wished dismissal, so that the blame for the fall of a ministry could be put upon the other side.[16] If this proposal could not be entertained, the Congress view was that the Governor should at least ask the ministry to resign.

Linlithgow on 21st June broadcasted his message to the nation; he made light of the fears of the Congress, that the Governor would interfere in the running of the ministry, by telling plainly that they had no foundation in facts. About the dismissal versus resignation controversy, he said that there was no law by which the Governor's option could be used "to force the Minister's option."[17] Soon, Lord Zetland perceiving that the stalemate had continued for a long time intervened; he informed the Viceroy that Gandhi would be satisfied if they agreed that the Governor should dismiss the ministry only when the disagreement was of a serious nature. In such a background, he let him know that it might be possible for the British to consider meeting Gandhi's demands.[18]

Linlithgow did not at any stage contemplate that one who he thought supported him completely would thus stab him in the back, when he expected it least. At once he sent off a message to the effect that he would resign if he was ordered to yield.[19]

During the close of June the United Provinces Muslim League leaders, Khaliquzzaman and Nawab Ismail Khan, got in touch with the Congress; their move was related to the business of ministry formation.[20]

At the height of the election campaign it was true both the parties were rivals, and sparing no efforts to malign the opposite side they had often indulged in loose talk. Nehru declared that the two parties that counted in India were the Congress and the British, and others should line up on each side.[21] Jinnah countered him saying "I refuse to line up with the Congress" and made it clear that "there is a third party in this country."[22] Not pleased with this especially because Jinnah talked about Muslim India, Nehru joined issue with him by speaking thus: "What does the Muslim League stand for? Does it stand for the independence of India, for anti-imperlism? I believe not. It represents a group of Muslims, no doubt highly estimable persons, but functioning in the higher regions of the upper middle classes and having no contacts with the Muslim masses and few even with the Muslim lower middle class."[23]

After the elections were over, Jinnah as a practical statesman was ready to co-operate with the opposite party, thinking that there was no big differences between the two sides. Giddy with success in the elections Nehru, however, spoke disparagingly of the League, and believed any sort of partnership with it was dangerous. So Jinnah sensing the mood of his opponents, knowing that his allies in the United Provinces were those "who are in and out of the Congress and in and out of the League", and fearing treachery from Khaliquzzaman warned the concerned politician towards the end of April about the futility of a clandestine deal.[24] Later, Khaliquzzaman however gained the favour of Jinnah, so that he was allowed to continue his talks with the opposite party.

About the time Linlithgow sent the message venting his resentment the Congress Working Committee met at Wardha, and on 7th July decided to get into office without pre-conditions. Thus Linlithgow emerged from the crisis a victor on account of his perseverance. At the committee meeting, Gandhi was reported to have accepted the force of the argument that the Congress should make use of the ministries in order to build up strength in the masses, so that when the final showdown came the party would be in a better position to deal with the British rulers.[25]

It was at the meeting Nehru came to know in a vague manner the backstage manoeuvres of Khaliquzzaman; with whom to hold exploratory talks Abul Kalam Azad traveled from Wardha to Lucknow in order to boost the prospect of the Congress.[26] The confidant of Jinnah was ready to do anything provided he, and likewise his colleague before mentioned were accommodated in the Congress ministry. Azad looked at the offer with habitual suspicion, but felt attracted by the possibility of the League ceasing to exist after getting absorbed into his party.[27] So he made a journey to Allahabad and held prolonged discussion with Nehru on this matter. Obviously, the prospective defectors wished to be partakers in the spoils of election victory, although they belonged to the defeated side. But this would raise the anger of Congress loyalists including the Muslims on their side, because they had a better claim to anything the party would offer. Yet Nehru, like his compatriot Azad, was carried away by the pleasurable idea of seeing the liquidation of Muslim League.[28] After lengthy talks, during which two Congress leaders of United Provinces Kripalani and Narendra Deva participated, they agreed that they should go through the deal if the other side gave assent to their conditions. Of these the most important were that "the Muslim League group will be wound up" including its parliamentary board in that province, that its legislators would enter into the Congress, and that it would not consequently put up separate candidates for bye-elections.[29]

Azad came back to Lucknow, and took up the thread of his previous conversation with Khaliquzzaman, who agreed to all the conditions except two: the winding up of the parliamentary board, and not putting forward separate candidates in bye-elections; he said "that he personally would agree but he had no authority to do so."[30] Later, he made another approach with the suggestion that he would call an emergent meeting of his party executive to consider the question of the bye-elections, if the Congress gave him more time to arrive at understanding, but for such a move he received no encouragement.[31]

This policy of absorption not only awoke Jinnah to the realities but also enhanced his influence in the Punjab and Bengal. For the Muslims suspected that the objective of the Congress when it got power at the Centre was to do away with the League as a party. The Muslim League meeting at Lucknow in October 1937 provided enough evidence of its growing strength as many leaders from the Punjab,

Bengal, Frontier Province, Sind, Madras, Assam and Central Provinces joined it[32]. In his address to the members Jinnah attacked the Congress for alienating the Muslims from the mainstream; then went on to explain his ideology of power based on superior strength. He said that "offers of peace by the weaker party always mean a confession of weakness, and an invitation to aggression." With the result "politics means power and not relying on cries of justice or fair play or goodwill."[33] Further, settlements with the opposite party had no value unless they were backed up by power.

Not long afterwards Gandhi held conversation with him, and endeavoured to revive the national spirit of Jinnah, but met with a rebuff. He saw Gandhi as the spokesman of the Hindus, and himself as the representative of all the Muslims, so there was no ground for agreement. In fact, Jinnah's harsh remarks against the Congress were designed to widen the breach between the two parties. In order to popularize his belief that Congress was exclusively a Hindu body he in front of a Muslim audience asked several questions, knowing beforehand how it would respond, and was satisfied with the negative answers he got: Did the Congress represent the Christians? Did it speak for about sixty million untouchables? Did it represent the non-Brahmins? The last one made it clear that Congress had no authority to talk on behalf of all the Hindus, but Jinnah had sense enough to recognize that it was the largest single party in the country before that same audience. He was certain that there were four forces at play in shaping the destiny of India: the British rulers, the native princes as well as their subjects, the Hindus, and the Muslims. In opposition to Nehru and many others, the Muslims allegedly did not find anything lofty in the idea of socialism, mainly because the socialists "had a materialistic view of life, and considered religion a superfluity." Furthermore, the Muslim rejected the federal part of the new constitution on account of their fears that it would lead to Hindu Raj at the central level.

NOTES AND REFERENCES

1. Speeches by the Earl of Willingdon, p. 206.
2. Netaji Collected Works, V. 2, p. 363.
3. Jawaharlal Nehru, An Autobiography, p. 551.

4. Nehru, Dorothy Norman, V. 1, p. 453.
5. Roses in December, An Autobiogrphy, M.C. Chagla, p. 80.
6. *Ibid*, p. 107.
7. M.A. Jinnah and Ispahani Correspondence, p.2 & 16.
8. *Ibid*, p. 17.
9. The Partition of India, C.H. Philips & M.D. Wainwright, Aspects of Muslim League Policy, Z.H. Zaidi, p. 248.
10. *Ibid*, p. 253.
11. Foundation of Pakistan, S.S. Pirzada, V. 2, p. 266.
12. Zaidi, *op cit*, p. 253.
13. The Viceroy at Bay, John Glendevon, p. 50.
14. *Ibid*, p. 57.
15. *Ibid*, p. 58.
16. *Ibid*, p. 62.
17. Collected Works of Mahatma Gandhi, V. 65, p. 470.
18. The Viceroy at Bay, p. 65.
19. *Ibid.*
20. Selected Works of Jawaharlal Nehru, V. 8, p.168.
21. The Political Study of Mohammad Ali Jinnah, V. 2, p. 557.
22. Zaidi, p. 255.
23. Jawaharlal Nehru, J.S. Bright, p. 108.
24. Zaidi, p. 257.
25. C.W.M.G., V. 65, p. 372.
26. Selected Works of Jawaharlal Nehru, V. 8, p. 168.
27. *Ibid.*
28. *Ibid*, p. 169.
29. *Ibid.*
30. *Ibid*, p. 170.
31. *Ibid.*
32. Zaidi, p. 259.
33. Foundations of Pakistan, V. 2, p. 269.

9

UNSTABLE LOYALTIES

Gandhi had appreciated in value suddenly, in the eyes of Lord Linlithgow, owing to the fact that a day before he met him on 4th September 1939 at his invitation Britain had entered the war.[1] While the Viceroy was looking for a higher level of support from the people, Gandhi made clear his pro-British sympathies; however, in regard to giving substantial help he told him that he spoke for himself, and had no authority to talk for the party.[2]

What troubled Gandhi was not so much the expansionist designs of Germany as the challenge the war posed to his non-violence. It seemed that his non-violence was almost impotent, but then he persuaded himself that it was not so; that it was the people who because of their weakness could not raise to the level of his faith.[3]

Though it was a useless exercise, Gandhi for the sake of humanity sent off a letter before the war expanded to Adolf Hitler that ran as follows: "It is quite clear that you are today the one person in the world who can prevent a war which may reduce humanity to the savage state. Must you pay that price for an object however worthy it may appear to you to be? Will you listen to the appeal of one who has deliberately shunned the method of war not without considerable success? Anyway I anticipate your forgiveness, if I have erred in writing to you."[4]

Gandhi said that it was likely "a Jewish Gandhi in Germany, should one arise, could function for about five minutes and would be promptly taken to the guillotine."[5] In fact, he knew that Hitler worshipped the god of war, and that he would listen to nothing except the boom of the big guns. About this time how the mind of Hitler workcd concerning the situation in India, and what respect he had for Gandhi and his faith he himself revealed to Lord Halifax. "Shoot Gandhi," he said in his staccato voice, "and if that does not suffice to reduce them to submission, shoot a dozen leading members of Congress; and if that does not suffice, shoot 200 and so on until order is established. You will see how quickly they will collapse as soon as you make it clear that you mean business."[6] Lord Halifax, talking with such a person predisposed to violence, indicated his disagreement but prudently avoided an argument.

The brutality of force, Gandhi maintained, did not prove his faith in non-violence to be wrong; indeed saw the he necessity for the death of hundreds, "if not thousands, to appease the hunger of dictators who have no belief in ahimsa."[7] Furthermore, he said that the method of violence was no more safe than that of non-violence, whose votaries in spite of their sufferings might fail to "see the result during their lifetime."[8] But still the success of his faith for which many were prepared to die at any given point of time was a certainty. Well, the triumph of Christianity after battling with violence over the centuries proves to some extent the truth of his assertion.

It is widely accepted that the age produced in Gandhi the greatest exponent of ahimsa;[9] however, the seeds of his doctrine are to be traced in Jain religion under whose influence he came long back in his home state of Gujarat. It is difficult to practise this faith scrupulously, but the Jain monks are an exception, who, about their religious practices, could speak of a tradition going back to more than two thousand years. It is a normal thing even now to see Jain monks walking briskly in the streets with complete intellectual detachment to their surroundings; these monks are so perfect in the observance of non-violence that they habitually cover their mouth as well as nose with a piece of cloth, with the intention of preventing the ingress of even the minutest insects.

Gandhi however applied non-violence to the benefit of whole society; if the Jain monks were not so forward in this respect it was because they were fully preoccupied in their spiritual attainments. The essential aspects of Gandhi's life such as "to manage with the minimum necessities of life, to bear no ill will towards anyone, to take recourse to fasting for self-purification, and to undertake long tours on foot to make contact with the people" were all more or less influenced by the simple life of Jain monks.[10] For Jain religion had its stronghold in Gujarat, and "its influence was felt everywhere and on all occasions."[11]

All the strict rules of behaviour were intended for the houseless monks, and the layman was not expected to observe them.[12] So the kings having embraced a religion which put the greatest stress on non-violence still continued with their occupation of war, without doing outrage to their beliefs. Other kings however, Chandragupta Maurya especially, are said to have given up power, and under the influence of Jain monks did away with themselves by means of starvation.[13]

Likewise Hindu religion did not believe that the use of force was immoral in all circumstances; this matter is made clear by the Hindu sacred book Gita, while expatiating upon the duties of the warrior to the nation.[14] And yet far more important than politics and war are prudence and love. Hence, only when the instinct to kill is purged out of the people could they put up a claim to be known as civilized.[15] Such was the powerful influence of religion on the people that most respectable among them, before the coming of the British, took to vegetarian food.[16] As observed already, non-violence whichever religion preached it did not hinder the kings from warring; but Gandhi reinterpreted non-violence in such a way that it could not be mated with wars; which, in fact, have become very dangerous for the existence of life to be looked upon as continuation of a tradition as old as man himself.

Now the war was fought for the preservation of liberty, and yet neither Linlithgow nor Winston Churchill in his capacity later as the head of the British government were prepared to say that India after the war would become free.[17] Had they done so, Gandhi without caring for interim arrangements would have reconciled himself to British presence. To them Congress support was really not needed to mobilize resources of India for war; but still they expected it would abstain from active opposition, for which gain they were not ready to give much away.[18]

Gandhi's lack of trust in the Viceroy culminated in the withdrawal of Congress from the provincial governments, thus putting an end abruptly to a short period of friendship with the British. Of this step

Linlithgow could not understand what benefit accrued to the Congress, and Gandhi's opinion that it was a necessity did not throw light on the matter. "I am convinced," says Rajendra Prasad, "we did the right thing."[19] Already, the provincial governments had limited powers which came down further by war time ordinances; in such circumstances the continuation of the ministries without any power to do good to the people would have only served the purpose of the rulers. So forced to choose between losing power in the provinces and losing prestige among the people, the Congress made the choice it did in order to keep its popular reputation.[20]

After the provinces fell into the hands of the Governors, Linlithgow, thinking that he was under no necessity to flatter the Congress, altered his posture towards it.[21] He depended upon the Muslim League for support and gave Jinnah for all purposes a veto on further constitutional progress.[22] The accession of Jinnah to the heights of power satisfied him so much that in order to make his position enduringly strong he tried to get into the favour of the Viceroy, and to keep Congress in the background. On the whole, the situation that developed was to the advantage of the British; for, while the Congress moved forward to turn the people against the foreign dispensation, Jinnah bent his energies to turn the Muslims against it.

The Muslim League met on 22nd March 1940 at Lahore, amidst scenes reminiscent of the pomp and splendour of the bygone Moguls, and later passed the well known Pakistan resolution.[23] This put forward the demand that the Muslim majority areas in the west and east of North India should be detached to form separate autonomous and sovereign states. The League justified this step on the ground that Hinduism and Islam were two different religions as well as societies; hence India was made up of two nations.[24] Such a view put the Muslims into difficulties by exposing them to the ill will of the people in Hindu dominated areas.[25]

Gandhi refused to accept the two-nation theory, especially because most of the Muslims not only had lived for long in the environment of India but were converts to Islam.[26] "Those whom God has made one," Gandhi thought, "man will never be able to divide."[27] Yet in conformity with his moderation he said: "I know no non-violent method of compelling the obedience of eight crores of Muslims to the will of the rest of India, however powerful a majority the rest may reprsent."[28]

However, the Muslims generally, perhaps including Jinnah notwithstanding his bombast from the Muslim League platform, were not yet committed to partition, but the danger was there of events moving in that direction.

The allied forces during that summer turned tail unable to face the onslaught of Germany; in consequence, Norway, Denmark, Holland, and Belgium fell to the invading armies. Then it was the turn of France to be attacked by the gargantuan war machine of Hitler, and later Marshal Petain asked the Germans for an armistice, although General Charles de Gaulle was broadcasting appeals for the continuance of French resistance.[30] However, Great Britain disappointed Hitler by fighting on, and so he ordered a plan for invasion; as the danger of Nazi conquest hung over England, there was panic in India so that Gandhi called for discipline. His heart was touched by the enormous proportion of the tragedy, and so his dislike for Britain having considerably abated he said: "We do not seek our independence out of British ruin."[31] Likewise Nehru fell in with Gandhi's views, and despite his antipathy for imperialism said: "I think it would be wrong for us at this particular moment, when Britain is in peril, to take advantage of her distress and rush at her throat."[32] Some Congress leaders saw that, if Britain was beaten in the war, and if the empire broke down in consequence, they might be called on to impose their hegemony on the country by taking up the remnants of power.[33]

To prepare themselves for that eventuality, they wished to take part in the war efforts and to help in the setting up of a national government.[34] But how could they explore the prospect of striking a deal with Britain when Gandhi's non-violence stood in the way! The anti-Gandhi movement which succeeded in putting an end to his influence on the party for a while was spearheaded by Rajagopalacharia. A haughty Brahmin from Madras in South India, he owned a powerful mind which he put at the disposal of the party in order to tide over the war crisis.

In alliance with him was Nehru, who turned a critic of Gandhi, concerning whom he said: "In recent years I have found a certain hardness creeping into him, a lessening of the adaptability that he possessed."[35] Both found fault with Gandhi on the score of his non-violence, which to them was not an abiding faith but a strategy to capture power. He was divested of his right to preside over the party, and was made free to pursue his ideal in his own way.[36] Gandhi put up a face of indifference difference when the party leaders broke political ties with him. For he never sought power, like them, for the good things it brought to its possessor.

At the meeting of the Working Committee, and right under the nose of Gandhi, with an audacity not displayed before Rajagopalacharia refused to back him up any further. For he said: "I cannot go with Gandhi in his conception of the State. Ours is a political organization not working for non-violence but for the political ideal."[37] He was completely supported by Nehru, who believed nobody could function on the political plane in accordance with the idea of Gandhi.[38]

What the opponents of Gandhi had not taken into consideration seriously was the lack of interest of the British to set up a national government. With his icy reserve and impenetrable face, Linlithgow yet had a soft spot for the Muslim League. Therefore, delivering a vital policy statement in August he said that the British would not transfer power "to any system of government whose authority is directly denied by the large and powerful elements in India's national life. Nor could they be parties to the coercion of such elements into submission to such a government."[39]

In the sequel, the anti-Gandhi leaders realized how vain it was to build a movement without him; so the deserters one by one returned to Gandhi, and again looked at him for leadership; likewise, the leader of the short lived rebellion Rajagopalacharia, but he was still in a defiant mood, thinking that his policy was right and it was not the least wrong because the opposite side rejected it.[40] On the other hand, Gandhi said "Hitlers will come and go" but what mattered was the way people reacted to such a spirit embodied in tyranny. By violence that spirit was fed, while by the opposite method it was eliminated.[41]

As Gandhi stood by his word not to embarrass the British government when it was fighting for survival, and as there was no issue to rouse up the people, he was disinclined to go for mass action. But the Congress was open to the dangers of inactivity; to remove which he saw the Viceroy, and put before him the demand for freedom of conscience to speak against the war. During their conversation Gandhi observed that like a machine Linlithgow was precise and correct, but his disposition lacked that human touch which worked so much to the advantages of Irwin.[42] Moreover, his views on matters affecting both the countries stood so fixed and unalterable in his mind as the heavenly bodies up in the sky, and so Gandhi realized that there was little chance of influencing him.

Linlithgow told Gandhi that in England a conscientious objector to war was allowed to keep his distance from it, and even to profess his faith openly, but not to persuade others to give up their war efforts.[43] This much freedom was not enough for Gandhi, who asking for more said in justification that India was a subject country; therefore, comparison with another free country was not altogether proper. Their talks having achieved nothing Gandhi made lack of free speech a grievance, to redress which he intended to start civil disobedience.[44] Linlithgow could have spared his warning about the consequences, because he was no more capable of impressing Gandhi than he himself was prone to the other's influence.

Yet there was no ground for Linlithgow to look at Gandhi's intention with alarm, since he chose that kind of civil disobedience which had no cutting edge, and which kept the volatile masses in the background, only using lone individuals to break the law.[45] The first agitator Gandhi put in the field not only was schooled well in the ashram's hard life but also typified its sage-like virtues. He was Vinoba Bhave; he was expected to repeat parrot-fashion a slogan coined by Gandhi: "It is wrong to help the British war effort with either men or money."[46] He was taken to prison on the third occasion of his saying it before the public, and was given three months' imprisonment but this made no noise on account of tight censorship.[47] Later, it was the turn of prominent leaders, irrespective of the fact whether they got a chance to voice their dissent to the war or no, to fill the prisons. Gandhi did not go there because he wanted to oversee the movement which by the end of January 1941 sent into prison about three thousand agitators. However, after the movement completed one year there was widespread apathy; few of those who came out of prison wished to go in, again, in conformity with Gandhi's expectation, since the issues at stake were not clear to everyone, and publicity to set things right was not possible as censors came in the way.

Fear once more swept through India when the Japanese on 7th December 1941 entered the war after bombing the American naval base Pearl Harbour, and made rapid gains in Thailand, in Malaya (except Singapore Island), and in Burma where their troops were pushing towards Rangoon; in the process threatening the security of this country.[48] The leaders in the Congress owing to the proximity of danger again lost faith in Gandhi, and again repudiated his non-violence, thinking that it was good only in the field of religion although he pleaded that it was well tested political weapon. They got together at Bardoli on the 23rd and made known their resolve to side with Britain in the war, but to do any sort of help asked for liberty.[49] Gandhi let them go on their own way, and even persuaded his allies not to leave the party so as not to endanger its unity.[50]

To deny a rumour about his estrangement from Nehru he publicly made this statement: "I have always said that not Rajagopalacharia, nor Vallabhbhai Patel, but Jawaharlal Nehru will be my successor." What he said did not matter much then because if the Japanese got into India both he and Nehru would probably be consigned to oblivion.[51]

"If Central Government is placed in my hands," said Rajagopalacharia, "I would take it," thereby making it clear he did not fall in with Gandhi about his choice of Nehru.[52] Though he was clever in his trade of politics and though the British liked him better than Nehru, he kept an exaggerated view of himself and thought the circumstances were good for him to take a leap from provincial to national politics. "If I am a hunter," said he, "credit me with being big game hunter.[53] I will not be content with less."

Winston Churchill as the Prime Minister held the view that there would be no change in the constitutional sphere, particularly because the enemy was getting closer. But the unbelievable thing happened on February 15th 1942 when the strongly fortified Singapore fell, and about ninety thousand British, Australian and Indian troops surrendered. The British fell back to Burma; however on 8th March they abandoned Rangoon to the enemy.

The British empire, till now so impregnable to the attacks of Indian nationalism led by Gandhi, and so conscious of its strength based on the assumption of race superiority, was foundering suddenly before the fighting skill of Japan, the foremost Asian power. It seemed to many that Subhas Chandra Bose had been right after all, for non-violence had only checked to the progress towards freedom.[54]

True it is that war is a cruel teacher who so mended the ways of

Churchill as to force him to send the embassy of Sir Stafford Cripps to see whether a national government could be set up.

NOTES AND REFERENCES

1. Collected Works of Mahatma Gandhi, V. 70, p. 161.
2. *Ibid.*
3. *Ibid*, p. 162.
4. *Ibid*, p. 21.
5. Harijan, May 27th 1939, p. 138,
6. The Inner Circle, Memoirs of Ivone Kirkpatrick, p. 97.
7. Harijan, op cit, p. 138.
8. *Ibid.*
9. A Cultural History of India, A.L. Basham; Jainism, A.N. Upadhye, p. 109.
10. *Ibid.*
11. An Autobiography, M.K. Gandhi, p. 18.
12. Upadhye, p. 109.
13. The Wonder That Was India, A.L. Basham, p. 92.
14. A Cultural History of India, op. cit, Hinduism, S. Radhakrishnan, p. 75.
15. *Ibid.*
16. The Wonder That Was India, p. 123.
17. P. Moon, Gandhi and Modern India, p. 205.
18. *Ibid.*
19. Rajendra Prasad, Autobiography, p. 499.
20. The Rajaji Story, Rajmohan Gandhi, p. 49.
21. The Transfer of Power in India, V.P. Menon, p. 69.
22. *Ibid*, p. 70.
23. Foundations of Pakistan, S.S. Pirzada, V. 2, p. 325 & 341.
24. Mahatma, D.G. Tendulkar, V. 5, p. 332.
25. V.P. Menon, op cit, p. 83.
26. Tendulkar, p. cit, p. 334.
27. *Ibid*, p. 335.
28. *Ibid*, p. 333 & 334.
29. Encyclopaedia Britannica, 1979, World Wars, p. 982 & 983.
30. *Ibid*, p. 984.

31. A History of India, Percival Spear, V. 2, p. 218.
32. A Bunch of Old Letters, Jawaharlal Nehru, p. 443.
33. P. Moon, op cit,, p. 209.
34. Jawaharlal Nehru, An Autobiography, p. 610.
35. *Ibid.*
36. Tendulkar, p. 355.
37. C.W.M.G., V. 72, p. 237.
38. *Ibid.*
39. Tendulkar, p. 394.
40. C.W.M.G., V. 73, p. 56 & 57.
41. *Ibid*, p. 324.
42. *Ibid*, p. 78.
43. *Ibid*, p. 450 & 451.
44. V.P. Menon, P. 101.
45. C.W.M.G., V. 73, p. 103.
46. *Ibid*, p. 200.
47. Nehru, A Political Biography, Michael Edwardes, p. 136.
48. Encyclopaedia Britannica, op cit, p. 989 & 990.
49. V.P. Menon, p. 113.
50. C.W.M.G., V. 75, p. 223.
51. M. Edwardes, *op cit.*, p. 139.
52. The Transfer of Power, Nicholas Mansergh, V. 1, p. 37.
53. *Ibid.*
54. M. Edwardes, p. 140.

10

THE POWER BROKER

In the British Cabinet, Sir Stafford Cripps was the one member very fit enough to undertake the hazardous and thankless task of going to India in order to bring about a settlement.[1] This is because his reputation for sincerity was beyond suspicion, his relation with Gandhi as well as his heir apparent Nehru was cordial, and besides his partiality for India's freedom was well known. He did not come to India, however, as a plenipotentiary to negotiate the terms of an agreement; he carried with him a cut and dried plan which it was his business to impose upon the Indian leaders; but, before that he must exorcise the suspicions and fears they had of the British government.[2]

Such a task was too much even for Cripps, and his prestige as the emissary of the British Cabinet would not avail him much became evident when he met Gandhi, who gave a piece of his mind in this way: "Why did you come if this is what you have to offer? If this is your entire proposal to India, I would advise you to take the next plane home" He did not spurn the advice and in reply said: "I will consider that."[3]

It is true that Gandhi when he went through Cripps' proposal and saw that it offered genuine self-government after the war got satisfied on that score. Even Churchill, who had made known his opposition to the liquidation of the British empire, was in agreement with this offer: how he was forced by circumstances to go along with his colleagues he later gloomily revealed to the King in one of their luncheons, taking his listener by surprise as the royal diary makes it obvious: "He (the P.M.) amazed me by saying that his colleagues & both, or all 3, parties in Parliament were quite prepared to give up India to the Indians after the war. He felt they had already been talked into giving up India. Cripps, the Press & U.S. public opinion have all contributed to make their minds up that our rule in India is wrong & has always been wrong for India."[4]

Gandhi also perceived that the Cripps offer was contrived to prompt Jinnah to go with the task of building Pakistan in so far as it gave the provinces the right to opt out of the future Indian government.[5] From the period of Lord Curzon, successive British Viceroys adroitly made use of religious differences to further their political ends, and under Cripps that traditional policy realized its consummation.[6] It is true that Congress had not ruled out the idea of Pakistan, but it also kept hopes of preventing a split, and Cripps seemed to be encouraging the non-accession desires of the Muslim League, thereby making all efforts to preserve unity more difficult than before.

Over and above this, Gandhi, however much the British talked of the sacred nature of treaties, was against the continuance of princely rights, which Cripps took much pains to safeguard.[7] Their autocratic regimes, kept alive by British troops in opposition to democratic forces, were not at all acceptable to Gandhi.

Knowing that he stood for non-violence and was altogether opposed to his scheme, Cripps turned his attention toward those who principles did not come in the way of fighting the Japanese, especially because they were a dominant force in the Congress. Like Gandhi, they too saw the defects of the plan in respect of the provincial option and the rights of the princes; but since their effect would be felt at a distant and uncertain future, they were ready to overlook them at the present moment only if they got a share in power.[8] Indeed, Cripps was not out of sympathy with their aspirations; for he thought of handing over the Defence Ministry to an Indian subject to a written convention that he would not in any matter affecting the war act contrary to the policy of the War Cabinet.[9] He also wanted to change the complexion of the Viceroy's Executive Council by giving representation to political parties; his innovations by their very nature would shift power away from the Viceroy, but Linlithgow who had concluded that Cripps would fail ultimately wanted to retain all his decision making authority. If the British were going to transfer power completely after the war, a limited handling over of power could have taken place now in accordance with the suggestions of Cripps.[10] However Churchill as the Prime Minister would rather support the Viceroy than Cripps, who in consequence stood no chance of succeeding in spite of his determination to get over obstacles. Moreover, Stafford Cripps ability to do things in order to reach agreement was limited by his position in the Cabinet; he was the leader of the Labour Party, but the exigencies of war had made him an odd partner with Churchill in a coalition government; yet he was a rival to Churchill, whom it was thought he with the enormous prestige that would accrue to him should his diplomacy bring results in India would overshadow in the political arena.[11]

Cripps spared no efforts to succeed and went to the furthest extent to put power into the hands of the Indian leaders in conformity with the short-term objectives of his scheme: "During the critical period which now faces India and until the new Constitution can be framed, His majesty's Government must inevitably bear the responsibility for and retain the control and direction of the defence of India as part of their world war effort, but the task of organizing to the full the military, moral and material resources of India must be the responsibility of the Government of India with the co-operation of the peoples of India."[12] To carry this into effect he designed to reconstruct the Viceroy's Cabinet on a representative basis so as to make it approximate to the national government, always wanted by the party leaders.

At a press conference held by Cripps on 29th March he came to grips with the main issues, and the tenor of his speech raised their hopes. For he said: "You cannot change the constitution. All you can do is to change the conventions of the constitution. You can turn the Executive Council into a cabinet."[13]

This did not explain things clearly, and it was left to Congress President Azad to go to the bottom of the matter. "I asked Sir Stafford," says he. "what would be the position of the Viceroy in this Council. Sir Stafford replied that the Viceroy would function as a constitutional head like the King in the U.K. In order to remove any room for doubt, I asked him to confirm that this would mean that the Viceroy, as a constitutional head, would be bound by the advice of the Council. Sir Stafford said that this was the intention."[14]

But when Azad met him again, Cripps shifted his ground in a big way telling that the cabinet proposed by him could not arrive at decision through majority opinion because the constitutional power of the Viceroy would not be altered now.[15] It was not the desire of the War Cabinet to reduce the Viceroy's power during war time, and Cripps had exceeded his brief when he first spoke of a new cabinet with powers to do as it liked. Linlithgow, fighting every inch of the ground to maintain his authority from being undermined by populist leaders, made clear to Churchill this much: "The vital test of Cabinet Government, namely, responsibility to an Indian legislature, does not and cannot exist in the interim period."[16] His statutory powers to set aside the views of his Executive Council he would not give up, and he was accountable for all he did only to the British Parliament.

Gandhi had questioned why Britain should retain full authority over defence, and others too expressed the same view to Cripps; he therefore went ahead to create a new office for an Indian and to transfer to him any functions of the Defence Ministry which the Commander-in-Chief thought could be handed over without impairing his efficiency. He initially developed a plan by which the functions to be retained by the Defence Department were listed and the residue fell to the share of the commander.[17] This was changed later in order to help the Congress, after the intervention of President Roosevelt's representative in India Colonel Louis Johnson, so that the Indian minister would be known as Defence Minister with the exception of listed functions held by the commander. According to this Cripps-Johnson formula, the power of the commander as member of the Executive Council was to last "until the new constitution comes into operation." However, Cripps in order to please the Congress dropped the before quoted words so that the commander as war member seemed to lose his powers which would devolve upon, after the war, the Defence Minister; whose control of the Army during the time between the end of the war and the setting up of the new constitution "might be an absolutely decisive factor in the communal and party struggle which would inevitably precede the framing of a new constitution and the voting of the provinces on it."[18] Further, all disputes in regard to allocation of functions would be decided by the British government, and not by the Viceroy who in consequence believed that this aspect of the proposal was "a serious invasion" of his powers.[19]

Linlithgow was in a bad humour, had not yet made up his mind of accepting the formula, and on 8th April met Cripps, who unfortunately rubbed him the wrong way by telling that Congress would fall in with it. He was curious to learn how Congress came to know of the formula, and elicited the information from Cripps, that Johnson had carried it to that quarter.[20] Immediately, he protested against Congress leaders having been shown the formula, and the fact that Johnson had shown it to them made the situation very bad, in the light of United States involvement in the Indian theatre of war. "If I were now to differ from the draft, my position might well be rendered intolerable," said Linlithgow, "as I ran the risk of being held up to the U.S.A. as the obstacle to a settlement."[21]

At that point Johnson got in, and, in the discussion which continued, broke the news that Congress was going to settle on the formula drafted by him and Cripps. Then Johnson in the company of Sir Stafford got away. But Linlithgow called Sir Cripps back alone and made a direct complaint "about the manner in which I and the Commander-in-Chief had been passed over. We had neither of us had any opportunity of examining the formula before it had been shown to Colonel Johnson and to the Congress Working Committee."[22] Cripps no doubt was in a hurry to reach an agreement and replied "that the situation was getting hot and he had to do something."

Avoiding any further talk of a cabinet government, Cripps spoke to Azad and Nehru about a national government, which would be run by the Viceroy in conformity with appropriate conventions. Linlithgow felt that his position was threatened; while Cripps would go away with the credit of achievement, he the Viceroy would have to wrangle with the party leaders and to take the blame for wrecking the agreement, if it could not be put into practice. He was dissatisfied with the way things were proceeding, and had been writing behind Cripps back to Churchill to win him over to his way of thinking.

Churchill on 9th April met in his office Roosevelt's Special Adviser Harry Hopkins, to whom he apprised the recent happenings in India. The Viceroy's dispatches indicated that Cripps had offered a new proposal to Nehru, without consultation with Linlithgow, but presumably with the assistance of Colonel Johnson.[23] Had not Cripps and Johnson worked out this new arrangement the British could have got Nehru's consent to the original proposal.[24] Linlithgow was annoyed with the whole business of negotiation, and put stress on the fact that Johnson conducts himself as if his assignment to India was to mediate in the crisis there on behalf of Rooseelt.[25] It was apparent that this new proposal, known as Cripps-Johnson formula, might be rejected by the British Cabinet which was meeting that very day; in which case Roosevelt would lose face for having ostensibly made that proposal which was turned down.[26] To forestall such a development Hopkins loosened his tongue to good effect as the sequel would discover: "I told the Prime Minister that Johnson's original mission to India had nothing whatever to do with the British proposals and that I was very sure that he was not acting as the representative of the President in mediating the Indian business. That I believed Cripps was using Johnson for his own ends, Cripps being very anxious to bring Roosevelt's name into the picture. That it was to Cripps' interest to get Roosevelt identified with his proposals."[27]

Churchill immediately, in the presence of Hopkins, sent a message to Cripps making clear that "Colonel Johnson is not President Roosevelt's personal representative in any matter outside the specific mission dealing with Indian munitions."[28] Further, Churchill thought that Cripps in his desire to reach agreement was moving from the field of persuasion into that of negotiation, and that he was going beyond his brief and had to fall back upon the original scheme he took with him.

Such a view hurt Cripps at a moment, when, after many days of hard labour, determination rather than physical strength kept him going, and when trapped in the labyrinth of oriental negotiation he was on the point of achieving a breakthrough.[29] And seeing that his colleagues, especially Churchill, did not put faith in him he made it evident that unless he was trusted he could not carry on talks.[30] The futility of which was made clear to him when the Congress leaders demanded that the Viceroy should be turned into a constitutional monarch, and the reconstituted Executive Council should be endowed with real powers.[31] He himself had raised their hopes to a high pitch; but now they realized whatever ministerial portfolios he offered under the watchful eye of Churchill did not mean much because the overshadowing power of the Viceroy would undo their benefit. In fact, Cripps had anticipated the intransigence of the Viceroy, and, even before he set out for India, desired his removal from office; but he did not get the support of Churchill.[32]

NOTES AND REFERENCES

1. The Life of Richard Stafford Cripps, Colin Cooke, p. 285.
2. *Ibid.*
3. Conversations of Gandhi with Louis Fischer, C.W.M.G., V. 76, p. 427.
4. King George VI, John W. Wheeler-Bennett, p. 703.
5. The Transfer of Power, N. Mansergh, V.1, p. 499.
6. C.W.M.G., V. 76, p. 427 & 428.
7. The Transfer of Power, N. Mansergh, V.1, p. 498.
8. *Ibid*, p. 636.
9. *Ibid*, p. 638.
10. Nehru, a Political Biography, Michael Brecher, p. 282.
11. Churchill, Cripps, and India, 1939-1945, R.J. Moore, p. 82.
12. The Transfer of Power, N. Mansergh, V. 1, p. 567.
13. *Ibid*, p. 547.
14. India Wins Freedom, Abul Kalam Azad, p. 50.
15. *Ibid*, p. 52.
16. The Transfer of power, N. Mansergh, V. 1, p. 654.
17. *Ibid*, p. 716.
18. *Ibid*, p. 861.
19. *Ibid*, p.694.
20. *Ibid.*
21. *Ibid.*
22. *Ibid*, p. 695.
23. Roosevelt and Hopkins, R.E. Sherwood, V. 2, p. 102.
24. *Ibid.*
25. *Ibid.*
26. *Ibid.*
27. *Ibid.*
28. N. Mansergh, *op cit*, p. 704.
29. Colin Cooke, op cit, p. 291.
30. N. Mansergh, op cit, p. 717.
31. *Ibid*, p. 729.
32. The History of the Indian National Congress, B.P. Sitaramayya, V. 2, p. 328.

11

AN UPRISING

The direct and immediate effect of Cripps' failure was to enlarge the mistrust so obvious between the Congress and the British, in which background Gandhi tried to establish his control over the party. He was now certain that the British had no intention of leaving, and hence thought that they must be made to quit India under pressure, especially when the enemy was pushing through allied defence line. To be sure the Japanese on 23rd March 1942 captured the Andaman Islands, and launched a series of attacks on British ships.[1] Their preponderance in the Bay of Bengal was a threat to the towns on the Eastern seaboard; in fact, there was so much alarm in Madras of a Japanese invasion that the authorities ordered evacuation of the city which was partially abandoned in consequence.[2]

A similar fright overtook Orissa where the officers having put into execution a scorched-earth policy were all set to retreat to the hills, leaving the people exposed to the war's hard realities.[3]About this time the Indian communists were bent upon using people's energy to fight a guerilla war; likewise, Nehru got attracted to such a war against invading armies. Gandhi, however, knowing better than anyone else the man to whom he had bequeathed the crown said: "I am sorry he has developed a fancy for guerilla warfare. But I have no doubt that it will be a nine days' wonder."[4]

By contrast Rajagopalacharia was intensely practical, and perceiving how near Madras was to the theatre of war he desired to take certain steps even at the risk of breaking ties with the Congress.[5] Gandhi at any cost wished to prevent a break-up in the Congress, but the British eagerly looked for it and expected results from his rebel activities. Among the Congress leaders, he in fact had entertained great hopes in Cripps' ability to set up a national government, and when things did not go the way he expected he suffered from a mood of depression. Cripps left the country and with him was gone at least during the war the idea of a national government, but Rajagopalacharia still clung to it in order to relieve his gloom.

He like Cripps believed that Muslims were easy to deal with, if the Pakistan option was conceded to them; what is more, if the offer was made ungrudgingly, he thought that they were unlikely to take it. Hence, under his influence the Congress party in Madras, in order to pave the way for a popular government to face the enemy threat, accepted the right of the Muslim League to keep out of the Union.[6] This decision was taken, with a certain amount of precipitancy, in order to influence the opinion of the national Congress leaders who were to meet at Allahabad shortly.

Soon he realized that as a deviationist he was not acceptable to them, so that he begged them to put forward a different proposal which would break the communal deadlock. He failed to impress them mainly because his proposal towards the creation of Pakistan was treasonable in their eyes, and they were sensible of the fact that he was delivering a blow to their party already mauled by Cripps. After having embarked on a course in opposition to Gandhi, he took his defeat gracefully, and for the good of the party quit it.

Now and then, however, he turned his ire against Gandhi, and on the eve of the great struggle against the British said: "What you are now doing is not an adventure in non-violence though it may have that delusive appearance."[8] Of his detractors similar gibes were not lost upon Gandhi, who warned his followers that they must not give in to violence, and that "my blood will be on your head" if things happened otherwise.[9]

There still remained Azad and Nehru among the triumvirate to be dealt with, and they put up resistance to Gandhi's proposals delivered at the Allahabad meeting by Mira Behn, his emissary. While discussing the proposals in the Working Committee, the members having exchanged hot words were faced with the reality of divided loyalties.[10] In his proposals under consideration, Gandhi made a demand upon the British government to clear out of the country, and said "if Japan invaded India it shall meet with non-violent resistance."[11] On the whole, his proposals were in favour of Japan, and Nehru went so far as to say that Gandhi felt that the Axis Powers would win, and such a view unconsciously influenced his decision, with which he did not agree.[12] Finally, the committee approved his proposals in such a way that Gandhi had nothing much to complain of, and that in the party he got enough room for manoeuvre.[13]

Gandhi despite his moderation got exasperated at the British, perceiving that they could not defend the country but would not let the Indians do that task either.[14] Among the parties since discord prevailed, always the British professed not to know to whom they should hand over power. Not convinced by this excuse, however, Gandhi told them to leave India to anarchy, from which he expected some kind of new order phoenix like would arise, quite preferable to the existing dispensation. His once close associate, Subhas Chandra Bose backed Japan, and there were people in the country who out of animosity towards the British were ready to welcome enemy forces. Gandhi however thought that the right course for the British was to leave the country before the Japanese arrived, and the Indians invigorated by freedom could be expected to fight against enemy designs. Later, under pressure changing his stand he said, "I would tolerate British presence in India not in any sense as rulers but as allies," in order to repulse a Japanese attack.[15] Others guessed that the British would not so easily abandon the country, and what steps he would take to confront them with a crisis.

Both Nehru and Azad lacked enthusiasm to go along with him, and without qualms would have deserted him now had a third party effected a settlement with the British. Gandhi was so indifferent to their influence, and so confident of obtaining the approval of the All India Congress Committee to his measures, that on 13th July he sent a message to Nehru asking him to resign from the Working Committee, and, similarly, expected Azad to give up his position as head of the party.[16] Next day, the Working Committee in compliance with his wish asked Britain to leave, and made known its resolution to begin a non-violent mass struggle under Gandhi's leadership.[17] Gandhi, however, would not think of taking any action until the All India Congress Committee about to meet on 7th August at Bombay threw its weight behind him.

About his opponent's strength Linlithgow entertained no wrong notions and knew well that Gandhi had vast influence, had lost none of his political astuteness, and was unlikely "to engage in a battle in which he does not feel fairly confident of victory."[18] Not long ago, during Cripps' talks, Gandhi was very much in the background, but now "he has with singular success again focused attention in this country on himself."[19] He performed this feat, much to the concern of Linlithgow, by appealing to the people in order to turn them not against Japanese aggression, but against British presence. So Linlithgow having made up his mind to deal with the situation firmly observed every move of Gandhi, and "of course keeping Amery (Secretary of State for India) in the closest touch" in order to draw sustenance from him in the event of a big conflict.

His hard posture notwithstanding, the way he proceeded cautiously by taking into confidence the Executive Council, a body subservient to him, gave room for suspicion to his mentors abroad whether he was following a weak-kneed policy.[20] The foremost action contemplated by the British to suppress the upcoming revolt was to put Gandhi on board a ship going to Aden, from where he might be later shifted to another destination.[21] When the Viceroy however raised the issue of Gandhi's exile in the Executive Council, the members already agitated on account of the developing confrontation "were unanimously and without exception most strongly opposed to deportation."[22] They knew that once Gandhi was shut in prison he would sooner or later stage a fast, which would be easier to deal with in the country than abroad.[23] Moreover, if something bad happened to him in foreign lands, rumour-mongers would play it up in such a way that the British could not escape the imputation of guilt. So the plan to exile Gandhi was aborted for the aforesaid reasons, and he was destined to go no farther than his prison at Poona after he was held.

At the party meeting in Bombay Gandhi asked the people to show true courage, and he himself oozed confidence after having placed his trust in them. "At a time when I am about to launch the biggest fight in my life," Gandhi said, "there can be no hatred for the British in my heart."[24] Against the British, the battle cry of his followers was "Quit India" and over and above this they were fortified with his mantra "do or die" which was to spur them to action.

About this time Linlithgow presided over his Executive Council in order to create the impression he alone was not responsible for any invidious steps he took against Gandhi, but they had the support of Indian leaders as well. He was very pleased to see in the council C.P. Ramaswami Aiyer, because he was known for his intellectual abilities, and because he was never backward in supporting the government which was obviously passing through difficult times. Gandhi had made known he was unwilling to cross the Rubicon and move towards the zone of conflict, until he wrote a letter to the Viceroy to see whether a settlement was possible.[25] The suppositious letter of Gandhi was the subject of discussion in the council, and Linlithgow made it plain that there was nothing in fact to show that he might expect such a letter beyond rumours. Aiyer then broke in, and told an amusing anecdote of his epistolary involvement with Gandhi, and the delays, uncertainties and disappointment which fell to his lot in the sequel.[26] Finally, the council settled for action against Gandhi, and because it was under the thumb of the Viceroy dissent was not in issue.

The steps contemplated against Gandhi were to be carried out with the precision of a military operation, but complete secrecy could not be maintained. Gandhi, hours before he was apprehended, received a message from a source that revealed what was planned against him, but he hardly believed it especially because he had made it evident that he had not yet lost hope of a compromise.[27] His doubts, however, were removed in the morning of 9th August when the police chief carrying with him warrants of arrest descended upon his abode. And this highhanded action synchronized with the arrest of all the Working Committee members, besides some middle level party leaders.[28]

No sooner this was done than Linlithgow had to face a popular rebellion in which police stations, post offices, and railway system were the targets of attack in order to dislodge British power. As the leaders who mattered were out of the way, the rank and file of the party especially the Congress Socialists made no distinction between violence and non-violence, and the British too lost their usual sense of proportion when they sent low flying planes to attack the mobs. By the end of the year over sixty thousand people were held in different prisons, and about a thousand civilians were killed.[29] The Viceroy for many days had no authority over most of Bihar and some districts of the United Provinces; besides, the land connection between Delhi and Calcutta was cut off when it had great strategic value during the war against the Japanese.

Linlithgow knew that he was confronted with a most serious rebellion "since that of 1857," but for reasons of military security he thought it right to conceal from the world the extent and gravity of the trouble on his hands.[30] He sent to Churchill on 31st August the following message: "Mob violence remains rampant over large tracts of the countryside and I am by no means confident that we may not see in September a formidable attempt to renew this widespread sabotage of our war effort."[31] Churchill assured the House of Commons that the situation did not give room for despondency; that large reinforcements had been sent to India, and further said, doubtless haunted by memories of the 1857 Indian Mutiny, that more white soldiers were kept there than ever before.[32]

Amidst the crisis Linlithgow was relieved to think that his Executive Council held together, although several members lived in fear after having backed him in order to send Gandhi and his followers to prison. Soon the pride of the Executive Council, Ramaswamy Aiyer, came with a suggestion that it would be a good thing if he flew to Poona, saw Gandhi, and begged him to call off his movement. Linlithgow could not fathom the mind of the other, but he was astonished that a man of Aiyer's standing should think of making an approach to Gandhi without condemning his own government.[33] As he held the Information and Broadcasting portfolio, Aiyer thought that it was not inconsistent with his official position to see Gandhi; however, if that step did not find favour with the Viceroy, he wanted to leave the government so that he could do his work against violence at the private level. Both agreed in their talks that the usefulness of the step Aiyer had in mind turned upon "whether Gandhi did or did not sincerely and in his own heart abhor violence."[34] They disagreed on this fundamental issue when Aiyer backed Gandhi, and finally the Viceroy was left with no option but to accept the reality of his departure from an ornamental office that did not signify much to one who had tasted absolute power as Dewan of Travancore.

The British rulers after doing some research how Gandhi's mind worked had concluded that there would be for a long while no fast, but if it proved otherwise, they had made up their mind to release him as soon as his fast endangered his health. This was seen as weakness by Linlithgow's superiors, for they could not take the bitter truth, that Gandhi owned the power to come out of prison at any time he chose by means of fast. They thought that a principle was involved in dealing with the current impending fast, to uphold which they desired to see Gandhi fast himself to death. The Viceroy, however, wished to keep the business on the level of tactics, and not principles, knowing better the harsh ground realities than his superiors abroad.

Linlithgow in order to deflate Gandhi changed his position after all, and moved closer to Churchill, who by adopting an uncompromising posture towards Gandhi made himself a petty tyrant in the British Cabinet "which has no mind of its own and whose members are all terrified of saying anything which would draw his displeasure upon their heads."[35] Churchill did not give a jot about the supporters of the viceroy in the Executive Council, and he thought that in his hour of triumph when his war policy was meeting with success after initial setbacks it was wrong to stoop to defeat himself before the miserable figure of Gandhi whom he always hated as his enemy.[36]

So when Gandhi on February 10th 1943 began his fast, and his health deteriorated prompting three members of the Executive Council to tender their resignations, Linlithgow showed no concern. As the agitation to release Gandhi and save his life gained force, President Roosevelt's envoy in India William Phillips met the Viceroy in order to show a letter he had received from U.S. Secretary of State Cordell Hull. The letter which made no impression on Linlithgow ran as follows: "President Roosevelt and I suggest that you seek an informal interview with the Viceroy and convey to him an expression of our deep concern over the political crisis in India. Please express to His Excellency our hope that a means may be discovered to avoid the deterioration of the situation which would be almost certain to occur if Gandhi dies."[37]

Linlithgow mistrusted Gandhi, and questioned his motives to an extent that their friendship soured beyond the point of retrieval. In such a background, Gandhi's feeling towards the Viceroy were reflected in a letter he wrote to him not long after his fast:

> Dear Lord Linlithgow,
>
> On the eve of your departure from India I would like to send you a word. Of all the high functionaries I have had the honour of knowing, none has

> been the cause of such deep sorrow to me as you have been. It has cut me to the quick to have to think of you as having countenanced untruth, and that regarding one whom at one time you considered your friend. I hope and pray that God will some day put it into your heart to realize that you, a representative of a great nation, have been led into a grievous error.
>
> With good wishes,
> I still remain your friend,
> M.K. Gandhi.[38]

He who had thought that defeating Gandhi was a prerequisite for winning the war sent a reply as follows:

> Dear Mr. Gandhi,
>
> I am indeed sorry that your feelings about any deeds or words of mine should be as you describe. But I must be allowed, as gently as I may, to make plain to you that I am quite unable to accept your interpretation of the events in question.
>
> As for the corrective virtues of time and reflection, evidently these are ubiquitous in their operation, and wisely to be rejected by no man.
>
> Yours sincerely,
>
> Linlithgow.[39]

Linlithgow's dispensation to a certain extent could not escape blame for sheer inaction when food scarcity on account of war resulted in Bengal famine, in which more than a million people died either from starvation or consequent diseases. Had there been a responsible national government, Gandhi was sure that India-wide scarcity would not have been so deadly in its effect. Linlithgow came under attack for his failure to visit the devastated province; true, he was not insensitive to the miseries of the people there and brooded over the tragedy, "but he would not change his mind even though his wife herself begged him to go."[40] It is said that an excessive concern for provincial autonomy held him back, however, his immediate successor Lord Wavell in a few days after assuming office paid a visit to Bengal, and persuaded the ministry there to move the destitutes from Calcutta to food camps. Wavell thought that "Bengal famine was one of the greatest disasters that has befallen any people under British rule," and, by the force of his personality, goaded the higher authorities to action in order to mitigate the horrors of famine.[41]

NOTES AND REFERENCES

1. Encyclopaedia Britannica, 1979, Worlds Wars, p. 991.
2. The Spirit's Pilgrimage, Mira Behn, p. 231.
3. *Ibid.*
4. Harijan, 26th April 1942, p. 136.
5. The Rajaji Story, Rajmohan Gandhi, p. 84.
6. Mahatma, D.G. Tendulkar, V. 6, p. 96.
7. Rajmohan Gandhi, op cit, p. 84.
8. Collected Works of Mahatma Gandhi, V. 76, p. 462.
9. *Ibid*, p. 380.
10. Mira Behn, op cit, p. 229.
11. The Transfer of Power, N. Mansergh, V. 2, p. 158.
12. *Ibid*, p. 159.
13. Mira Behn, op cit, p. 230.
14. N. Mansergh, op cit, p. 83.
15. *Ibid*, p. 247.
16. Collected Works, op cit, p. 293.
17. *Ibid*, p.453.
18. N. Mansergh, op cit, p. 272.
19. *Ibid.*
20. *Ibid*, p. 606.
21. *Ibid*, p. 588.
22. *Ibid*, p. 596.
23. *Ibid.*
24. Collected Works, *op cit*, p. 379.
25. *Ibid*, p. 375.
26. N. Mansergh, op cit, p. 661.
27. Mira Behn, op cit, p. 239.
28. Tendulkar, op cit, p. 216.
29. *Ibid*, p. 226.
30. N. Mansergh, op cit, p. 853.
31. *Ibid.*
32. The War Speeches of the Rt. Hon. Winston, S. Churchill, V. 2, p. 320.

33. N. Mansergh, op cit, p. 720
34. *Ibid,* p. 721.
35. The Transfer of Power, N. Mansergh, V. 3, p. 632.
36. *Ibid.*
37. *Ibid*, p. 687 & 688.
38. Collected Works of Mahatma Gandhi, V. 77 p. 201.
39. The Transfer of Power, N. Mansergh, V. 4, p. 381.
40. The Viceroy at Bay, John Glendevon, p. 274 & 275.
41. Wavell The Viceroy's Journal, p. 54.

12

FREEDOM SANS JOY

Gandhi fell so ill that the new Viceroy Lord Wavell fearing the odium that would attach to his government if he died in prison, and knowing if he expired immediately after he came out he would get no credit for having released him lost no time to act. So on 6th May 1944, after spending twenty-one months in prison, he was out of it by the clemency of Wavell, who, in fact, had desired to let him out much earlier to break the ice in the political arena. But he who was thought dangerously ill having got back his health became (to use the expression of a poet) so "dangerously well" as to annoy Churchill. Gandhi, thwarted in his purpose to enter into talks with the Viceroy because of a hostile British Cabinet, turned his mind towards his "brother Jinnah" in order to mend political fences at least in that quarter.

The Muslim League took advantage of, especially in Muslim majority provinces where it had always been weak, the political vacuum caused by the imprisonment of Congress leaders.[1] It was easy for Jinnah to misrepresent the Congress move to drive the British out as an attempt to set up a Hindu government, and to build up the image of his party on the strength of the fact that it spoke only for the Muslims. Jinnah, with a strong party behind him, more passionately religious and more intensely suspicious of the Hindus than ever before, yet was ready to hold talks with Gandhi and invited him to his Bombay residence. Their conversation started on 9th September, and it proceeded in no friendly atmosphere as Jinnah tried to tax his patience and to exasperate him from which swordplay he gained nothing except the momentary satisfaction of having scored a point.

"I thought you had come here as a Hindu, as a representative of the Hindu Congress," said Jinnah.
"No," replied Gandhi.

Then Jinnah affirmed the obvious truth that he was the President of the League, and, if Gandhi spoke for nobody except himself, asked on what basis the talks could go on and who was to deliver the goods.

"The Muslims want Pakistan. The League represents the Muslims and it wants separation."

"I agree," replied Gandhi, "the League is the most powerful Muslim organization. I might even concede that you as its President represent the Muslims of India, but that does not mean that all Muslims want Pakistan. Put it to the vote of all the inhabitants of the area and see."

"Why should you ask non-Muslims?" Jinnah opined.

"You cannot," Gandhi said, "possibly deprive a section of the population of its vote. You must carry them with you, and if you are in the majority why should you be afraid?"[2]

Their talks lasting for many days finally broke down, since there was absence of common ground between them. Gandhi pressed for independence first, and the separation of the Muslims later, but Jinnah wanted things to go in reverse order as he did not desire the Muslims to come under a Hindu dominated government. Moreover, Gandhi never accepted the two-nation theory; never thought of complete severance of Pakistan from the rest of India, and the kind of separation he proposed safeguarded the common interests of both the people in the field of Defence, Foreign Affairs and certain other matters[3]. "I think he is suffering from hallucination," Gandhi said about Jinnah and his demand for viable Pakistan, "when he imagines that an unnatural division of India could bring either happiness or prosperity to the people concerned."[4]

Next, Gandhi having failed, it was the turn off one Bhulabhai Desai to try his hand at reconciliation. As the leader of the Congress in the Central Assembly, Desai had reputation, and besides he could easily ingratiate himself with people by lipping words that always sounded sweetly reasonable. But the unflattering side of his character was such that he was as slippery as an eel with the result his own party leaders might not have trusted him very far, neither did he trust them. For he expressed the view, quite dangerous and ominous of bad things to come according to Stafford Cripps, that he did not want the Congress Working Committee members to be released before his interim government came into existence as they would take an uncompromising position.[5]

The proposals of Desai required that he and Jinnah should be asked to form an interim government and to put forward names to the Viceroy of those to be included in it. Further, except the Viceroy and the Commander-in-Chief, it would be composed of Indians, with the Hindus and Muslims, getting equal representation, and with neither side committing on long-term constitutional problems.

On the whole, the initiative of Desai was thought of as good because if the two parties came together to run an interim government for a short time its effect might be to turn Jinnah's mind away from Pakistan, and to help things towards a constitutional settlement.[6] The British government too noted with satisfaction that, as Desai was prepared to ignore the Congress Working Committee, the influence of that party on the interim setup would be less potent, and the main actors put on the stage were Jinnah and Desai. About Jinnah, though Desai claimed his scheme he approved, the expectation was if the scheme met with success he would back it, otherwise he would disown any sort of connection with it. Certainly, Wavell was eager to know how Jinnah would react to the scheme, but he was under such tight control that to hold talks with him in order to know his mind he needed the permission of heads above him. Desai before long however, contrary to Gandhi's expectation that he should exhibit detachment in this matter, proved to be a braggart and his plan failed as the concerned leaders got alienated from him.

Now, after Desai too failed to reach agreement, Wavell redoubled his efforts to install a party based government, although Churchill was not receptive to his ideas and thought that Indian issues could be kept on ice in view of other pressing matters. He looking for guidance turned his attention to the wise heads of the Cabinet's India Committee who thought lowly of his ideas, since they believed that he seemed to have no idea of the implications of his scheme and of the risk attendant on it. He had now real powers and his Executive Council members were merely his creatures made respectable by him, but he was seized with a desire to replace them with politicians who represented parties so powerful that they would force him before long into a position in which dancing to their tunes he was nothing more than a constitutional monarch.

Not denying such a thing Wavell held the view that with the powers he had he could face the risk, which he believed was not "so great as the risks involved in sitting still and letting things get worse."[7] Furthermore, he said that the step he proposed involved no change in the constitution, but merely an alteration of personnel running the government. The India Committee, however, held contrary opinion because in its view induction into the Executive Council party leaders who would be trusted with authority due entirely to their representative capacity was indeed a big change. After it failed to hammer into his head that a change was involved it arrived at the conclusion "that the Viceroy cannot prudently be given the free hand which he desires," however, Churchill overturned this view by ostensibly reposing faith in him. Churchill with the election near at hand did not want to take the risk of India becoming a party issue and despite his misgivings approved Wavell's plan, but later revealed that the reason why he did so was the India Committee told him that it would fail.

Wavell back in India made a speech in which he recognized the uncontestable truth, that Gandhi and Jinnah controlled Indian politics and without their help nothing could be achieved. He said orders had been passed for the release of Congress Working Committee members, and messages were being sent to the two leaders mentioned above besides others inviting them to a conference on 25th June 1945 at Simla in order to set up a new Executive Council made up of caste Hindus and Muslims in equal proportions.[8]

Gandhi noted that the British wanted to separate the Hindus from the untouchables, and that the plan of Desai was superior in so far as it aimed at equality between the two big parties without bothering about caste.[9] It was Jinnah who wrecked the conference by insisting that all the Muslim members to the Council must be nominated by and from the League, and he himself as the head of that party should have the power of choosing them.[10] Wavell in order to please Jinnah even at the risk of alienating the Congress went so far as to exclude the claim of nationalist Muslims who were hated by the League for their supposed disloyalty, but his wish to bring one Muslim from the Punjab without strong party leanings into the government Jinnah opposed. It was believed that a member of the Executive Council plotted against the Viceroy by encouraging Jinnah whose policy was tailored to suit his demand for Pakistan, and to frustrate the efforts of the Congress to build a united India. Gandhi when the Viceroy broke the news of his lost hopes to him took it calmly, and then said that the British should accept either the Hindu or the Muslim point of view since nobody could reconcile their differences.[11]

The gloom of the failed conference was somewhat relieved when the Labour Party, known for its liberal outlook returned to power. As the war on both the fronts came to an end, the British knowing that this would release a lot of energies and thinking how to make use of them desired to hold elections in India. Wavell had seen Churchill too slow to move forward on India, but he found the new Prime Minister Attlee too fast with whom his differences were no less conspicuous than with his predecessor. He was also judged not to his advantage as Attlee began to feel that Wavell did not possess enough imagination, a deficiency about which during his command in North Africa Churchill had complained.

Wavell having returned home saw there Cripps for reasons of prestige intent upon the rehabilitation of his original offer, which had become obsolete by the passage of time. The purpose of Simla Conference was to bring the hostile parties together in order to avoid the creation of Pakistan, but now with no amity Wavell thought he had to face the Pakistan issue and bring its real implications to the light before he could go any further. His opinion, however, did not carry much weight, and so he concluded that the British leaders were bent upon ignoring the Muslim League and handing over India to the Congress, on behalf of which many especially Birla and Shiva Rao were in touch with Cripps as well as Attlee in order to influence their views. "I may have to decide whether to refuse to be a party to their plans to quit India," the Viceroy reflected, "or to go back and try to keep them out of disaster as much as possible."[12]

Next to Gandhi, the men who had influence in the congress were Nehru and Vallabhbhai Patel, and from what the two spoke either directly or obliquely reflecting the opinions of the rank and file of the party, Wavell believed that their party wished to make use of the Indian National Army as the spearhead of a revolt in order to seize power for itself after forcing the British out.[13] Though Gandhi was committed to moderation, he did not check extremism in the party and overlooked

Nehru's hot words aimed at revolution, saying they mattered not if the British were intent upon leaving the country but if the case was otherwise they ought to be more hot. He mixed his trust with caution because Britain in the past was less than honest, because nothing was achieved regarding a national government, and because many of his followers were still in prison thereby increasing extremism in the party.

That Gandhi distrusting violence was true to his faith became evident when at Bombay a pro-Indian naval mutiny broke out. At least one rebel warship Narbada endowed with rapid fire power aimed its guns at the yacht club in Bombay, and there were several ships with powerful guns under rebel control.[14] Soon the British were relieved to know that the bombers had arrived at Santa Cruz, and as their ability to launch an offensive improved Wavell said that if the rebel ships opened fire they would be sunk. While the moderate Congress leaders kept their distance from the mutineers, Gandhi himself never showed interest in the naval mutiny since it did not agree with his idea of mass action. Gandhi was ready to wait especially because Attlee had announced that a British Cabinet Mission, composed of Lord Pethick-Lawrence, the Secretary of State for India, Sir Stafford Cripps, President of the Board of Trade, and Albert V. Alexander, First Lord of the Admiralty, would come to India in order to help the Viceroy to grapple with the issue of a new Executive Council and a new Constitution.

There existed not much doubt that the Muslim League would emerge stronger from the elections, by insinuating into the favour of the Muslims to whom the choice given was to fall in with either Islam or Hinduism. Such an expectation its performance did not belie, since in the elections to the Central Assembly the League won all the Muslim seats, while the Congress obtained most of the other seats on the strength of its influence in the Hindu dominated areas.[15] At the provincial level, a great majority of non-Muslim seats went to the Congress, and a majority of Muslim seats to the League, with the exception of North West Frontier Province in which the influence of Ghaffar Khan and his brother Dr. Khan Sahib was decisive enough to swing the votes to the Congress. Since the Muslim parties other than the League bit the dust, Jinnah's claim that he alone represented the Muslims could not be set aside. On the whole, the election results proved beyond doubt that the Congress and the League were the parties that reflected in a large measure the popular will.

It is true that the League did not get absolute majority in the Punjab, so that Khizar despite his party's miserable show in the elections ran the coalition government as usual. This advantage however afforded him not much relief, in the face of League's improved strength in the Punjab together with its strong hold on Bengal, which made it inevitable that the Pakistan issue had to be tackled. For, so long as the bulk of the Muslims in these two strategic provinces was against dividing India, Jinnah had no courage to ask for what he greatly desired.[16]

The aforesaid British ministers having arrived the diplomacy of Stafford Cripps busied itself again to break the impasse; though he worked under favourable circumstances now, yet success eluded him mainly because Jinnah held fast to the two-nation theory, and because the late elections had intensified the struggle for ascendancy between parties which knew pretty well that power was slipping out of British hands.

Jinnah had amassed facts from history as well as contemporary life in order to prove before the ministerial delegation that the Hindus and Muslims had nothing in common to justify their living together in one nation. "The argument for the reality of a separate nationality," the historian Romila Thapar says, "is drawn from the writings of the theologians and court chroniclers, who consciously emphasized the distinctions between Hindus and Muslims because it was in their interests to do so."[17] Had the Turks and Afghans who ruled over India preserved their alien identity, and had they as foreigners constituted the majority of Muslims, then a separate nationality might have been possible. But the vast majority of the Muslims were proselytes at the expense of Hinduism, which fact Gandhi had always stressed, and which even Jinnah did not contradict before the ministers.

While Attlee still believed that it was possible to keep the unity of India and to hand over power to one central government, besides the opposition of the League, the princely states were not reconciled to that. Apart from the eleven British provinces ruled directly by the Viceroy, there existed 582 princely states which possessed only nominal power.[18] As the old treaties that did away with their real power would shortly come to an end when the British left India, the question naturally arose how they should carry on their existence. The princes having lived too long at the mercy of the British now yearned for sovereignty, especially because the ministers made it evident they could not transfer rights of paramountcy and treaty rights to a successor government. Further, Cripps backed the royal families saying that when the British gave up paramountcy the princes should own power, originally theirs before the English rulers entered into the picture.

After the princes made known their desire to have power on a level with independence, a deputation of the Sikhs met the ministers and told them that they had not so far talked about the matter of carving out a state for themselves, with their people.[19] Later, Stafford Cripps wished to know how Khalistan could be formed, and Sardar Baldev Singh enlightened him by telling that it would be the Punjab excluding the Multan and Rawalpindi divisions, with Lahore falling under its jurisdiction.[20] But he made it clear to Cripps that the Sikhs vigorously favoured one India, and looked upon its partition as not a wise step because the small states on the frontier would be under the shadow of big powers.

Amidst tense expectancy about the future shape of things, the Muslim League delegates to improve their bargaining strength and to influence the events met on 7th April 1946 in Delhi, and then delivered speeches rather in the style of feudal warlords intending to put armies into the battlefield, than democratic leaders constrained by the rule of law. Looking at futurity, the heavyweight politician of Bengal Suhrawardy talked of peace, yet having long pondered "whether the Muslims are prepared to fight" had war on his lips especially when he said that every Muslim in Bengal was ready to fight and die, thereby invoking the Malthusian spectre for depopulating a land already devastated by famine. Shaukat Hayat Khan boasted of his war community pedigree, and being more a man of action than words he spoke for the brave fighters in the Punjab, and declared that three-quarter million demobilized soldiers were committed to achieve Pakistan, and would fight till death if things went against their expectation. "You, sir," Hayat said turning his face towards his leader Jinnah, "are holding us back, and we beg of you to give the word of command." But Firoz Khan Noon, a discreet man wary of using words to inflame passion, brooding over the consequences of human action like a sage, forewarned the assembly: "We are on the threshold of a great tragedy."[21] Afterwards, they pledged themselves in the name of Him to work for the achievement of Pakistan, in which only rested the hopes of the Muslim nation yet to be born, and for which they were determined to fight "till the last ditch" and to undergo any danger, trial or sacrifice.

Cripps, meanwhile, by taxing his ingenuity had begotten two ideas: a small Pakistan, or alternatively a constitution made up of, at the bottom provinces, above them Groups or sub-federations of provinces, and above all of them a union. At first Jinnah was not inclined to take either, and Cripps despaired of winning him over, but later his cold and forbidding face showed a flicker of interest in the second idea mentioned above. For it was a union in which all the territories Jinnah was asking for would come under Muslim groups of provinces, which as a result obtained by Cripps' jugglery a semblance of big Pakistan. What is more, the right of a province to secede from the union might also be included in the constitution in order to make the proposal more attractive to Jinnah.

He was however pleased at the expense of the Congress, which did not like the federal idea as it weakened the center by concentrating at the middle level legislative power. In fact, the Congress Working Committee had already rejected it, nevertheless, Pethick-Lawrence was somewhat optimistic that a deal could be made with Gandhi.[22] For Gandhi had always opposed a sovereign Pakistan, but now Jinnah was in a mind to consider something less than that.

Now there was a basis for talks, the next stage was a conference at Simla, to which both the sides were ready to go without compromising their principles. On behalf of his party, Azad writing to Pethick-Lawrence made his position clear: "We consider it wrong to form groups of Provinces under the Federal Union and more so on religious or communal basis."[23] Gandhi was against any arrangement which would result in creating three layers of executive and legislative bodies as such a machinery would be cumbrous, and lacking in harmony,[24] however, he was available at Simla in order to guide the talks and to help those who needed his advice on several matters.

At the Simla conference, the main point of discord was over the question of union finance; the Congress wanted for the country an autonomous center with powers of direct taxation, but Jinnah said that it should be given a fixed amount, and if it needed more it should approach the middle level powers of the government.[25] Their disagreement continued when the issue of legislature was taken up;

the Congress wanted one at the center while Jinnah put up resistance to that and what he desired was legislature at the second-tier of the constitution in order to make it approximate to Pakistan. At one point in the talks when Jinnah was prepared for reciprocal concessions in order to attain his objective, and when Nehru responded by speaking in near favour of that, Vallabhbhai Patel, with his dress resembling a toga and besides with a Roman patriarch's face, normally hard, intelligent and uncompromising, but now suddenly flashed anger at the prospect of such a deal.[26] He doubtless backed Gandhi's view that India should not be divided on religious grounds, and doubtless suspected the ultimate intention of Jinnah, who at the conference seemed to claim the right of provinces to secede after five years, a claim that showed him in his true colours at least in the eye of Patel.

Further, in the scheme worked out by the three ministers, the Muslims to compensate for their inferiority in numbers would get equality of representation in the government, as well as in the legislature, at the central level. This was too much for Gandhi, and the fact that he was in close touch with Patel might have contributed to increase his mistrust at the way things were moving. With a candour that surprised Cripps, Gandhi told him to his face that his proposal was "worse than Pakistan" and so he could not recommend it to the Congress for consideration.[27] Gandhi probably was so much influenced by Patel's way of thinking as to make a firm stand against Jinnah's demands, and he seemed to be quite unmoved at the prospect of a civil war.

Further, Nehru and Jinnah held talks to see whether they could reconcile their differences, but in the background of mutual suspicion they achieved nothing. The Viceroy, leaving the difficult constitutional issue aside for a while, turned his attention to interim government; though this was a beaten path for him, and though his talks with the leaders of parties went on well initially, it was clear from his experience that success was difficult here too. Moreover, unless there was agreement on the constitutional issue, Jinnah and his party lacked interest to get into the interim government.[28]

After seeing the reluctance of the parties to agree, the ministers assisted by the Viceroy came out on 16th May with a proposal for settlement. Their document, in conformity with the desire of Gandhi, was not couched in the language of an award; for when the British were on the point of withdrawing power so decisively that they could not do anything to save the princes closely linked with them by treaties, they could not possibly dictate terms concerning what new power relationship should come after them.[29]

The ministers' document said that "voluminous evidence has shown an almost universal desire, outside the supporters of the Muslim League, for the unity of India."[30] This did not prevent them from taking up the question of a fully independent Pakistan made up of six provinces—that is in the west Punjab, Sind, North-West Frontier, and British Baluchistan; in the east Bengal and Assam—as claimed by the League. They rejected it pointing out that it would not solve the communal minority problem, since in Pakistan about 38 per cent of the population in the west and about 48 per cent in the east would be other than Muslims, while twenty million Muslims would remain as a minority in India. "Nor can we see any justification," the ministers said, "for including within a sovereign Pakistan those districts of the Punjab and of Bengal and Assam in which the population is predominantly non-Muslim."

Next, they considered a small or what is better known as truncated Pakistan confined to Muslim majority areas, but the Muslim League saw it as not practicable. They likewise believed that partition of the Punjab and Bengal would be against the wish of a big chunk of the inhabitants there, and against their cultural unity as each province had its own language, history and tradition. Moreover, splitting the Punjab would disperse the Sikhs on both sides of the boundary. Finally, the two halves of the proposed Pakistan would be separated by approximately seven hundred miles of alien territory.[31]

So the ministers fell back on the earlier idea of a three-tier constitution, already discussed at the Simla Conference, as the most suitable choice. At the top there would be a Union of India, embracing both British India and the States, with an Executive and Legislature empowered to deal with external affairs, defence and communications and to raise the finances needed for the above functions. The powers of the federal government in conformity with Muslim desires were abridged, and the provinces were to be free to make their own unions with executive and legislative authority. The problem of drawing up a constitution was left to the elected members of the provincial legislatures, and to the delegates from the States. After the constitution came into effect any province by a vote of its legislature could move out of any Group in which it had been placed.

Gandhi, observing that the ministers had not imposed an award, and that the provinces enjoy the latitude to keep out of grouping, favourably reacted to the new constitution. After he got a better picture of the situation he his initial hope not abandoning said: "my conviction abides that it is the best document the British government could have produced in the circumstances."[32] Jinnah, however, showed no enthusiasm because the Pakistan he was committed to achieve had been rejected. Further, opposition to the document came from several minority groups, particularly from the Sikhs, who had been on good terms with the Unionist Party, but in the late elections it had given way to the religious bigots constituting the leadership of the League. Now to the Sikhs, the new constitution came as a terrible blow, since the whole Punjab would be absorbed in a group of Muslim provinces, which if not exactly Pakistan might become so ultimately by the machinations of leaders inimical to them.[33]

The Sikhs harboured exaggerated idea of their importance in politics, though they formed about four million out of a total of twenty eight million people in the Punjab.[34]

It was Guru Nanak who founded the Sikh religion which preaches belief in one God, and denounces caste distinctions as well as idol worship, the twin pillars that support the Hindu faith. Nanak was an idealist in so far as he tried to bring the Hindus and Muslims together through his religion, and when he died both competed to have the honour of performing his obsequies.[35] The Sikhs despite their hostility to the Muslims had in the Granth Sahib a holy book like the Koran,and in the *Akalis* their holy warriors like the Muslim *ghazis*; further, their idea of martyrdom in battle resembled the Muslim concept of *jehad* or holy war.[36]

Well did Gandhi know the danger the Sikhs faced now, and against their wish he did not expect the Punjab, their "only home in India" to come under a Muslim dominated zone in the west, besides, he desired to prevent a similar fate to North West Frontier Province where a Congress ministry held power. Similarly, in the east, he did not wish to see Assam, a non-Muslim area, to be grouped with Bengal in accordance with the Cabinet delegation plan to form one more zone under Muslim influence. While the delegation thought that the concessions to the Muslim League in regard to dominant zones in the west and east were necessary to make it accede to a united India, Gandhi preoccupied himself with "the honourableness of opposition to grouping."

His position was based on the fact that after all the ministers' proposal was not compulsory, and had not the force of law. True, but still the authors of the scheme made it evident to Gandhi that there was no escape from grouping process, contrived to bring into existence one Hindu and two Muslim spheres of influence. Cripps took much pains to explain to him that "the proposals stand as a whole and it would get the country nowhere if different parties and communities could choose the pieces they like and reject those they do not like."[37]

Gandhi meanwhile turned his attack elsewhere, seeing the pernicious grouping scheme was hard to assail, and the fort could not be breached in that direction. "I would put on record my conviction," Gandhi said, "that independence would in fact be a farce, if the British troops are in India even for peace and order within, or danger from without."[38] What he meant was that with British troops close by, the constituent assembly could not boast of that sovereign power which the Founding Fathers of the United States of America had, before they put in writing their constitution. He thought that a national government responsible to the central legislature should precede the activities of the constituent assembly.

His outspoken views, however, had such a bad effect on the ministers, that First Lord Alexander was furious with Gandhi, Cripps was shaken to the core, and Pethick-Lawrence was sadly disillusioned.[39] Did Gandhi think of humiliating the British and securing power to his own party before a constitution came into existence? The ministers immediately sent a secret message to Attlee, telling him that the "situation has taken a turn for the worse." They let him know "that Congress propose to make an attack on the grouping proposal and that they object to parity in the interim Executive. These two points may be crucial in securing Muslim co-operation."[40] They expected that before long the Congress might resort to the threat of direct action, if the British did not give in.

As against this murky scenario, the Muslim League seemed to be in a mood to accept the British offer, and the thing that held it back was the fear of meeting with a repulse on the ground that the opposite party was not ready to take it.[41] So Liaquat Ali desired that Jinnah should formally be given a promise that if the League took the offer it would be asked to get into the interim government, whatever might be the response of the other party. The British, thinking that Muslim interests would be harmed, had refused to give such as assurance to the Congress to meet the reverse circumstances of the League rejecting and the Congress accepting their proposal.[42] Now Jinnah wanted it because it would help him to face the League Working Committee, and to pass a resolution in favour of the British offer. Later, he talked about this matter with the Viceroy, who told him that the British intention was "to go ahead with the scheme as far as possible with any party who would work for it."[43]

The Muslim League council met on 5th June and a report of the British Intelligence says: "Mr. Jinnah said that he and other members of the Working Committee were worried as to what would happen if the Muslim League accepted the proposals and the Congress did not. The Viceroy replied that he would brook no refusal from Congress and that if they decided against acceptance he would hand over the interim government to the Muslim League and give them all the support they required. This very point was raised by some members in the Council meeting and Mr. Jinnah took them into confidence and gave the same reply."[44]

Finally, the Muslim League council accepted the proposal, keeping in view that the basis and the foundation of Pakistan by virtue of the compulsory grouping of six Muslim provinces and the right of secession of provinces from the Union were inherent in it.[45]

Then the setting up of an interim government proved to be a herculean task. First, the League wanted parity with Congress, that is though the Muslims were a minority community they demanded equality with the Hindus concerning representation in the ministry. Second, as the League claimed that it alone represented the Muslims it desired to nominate all the Muslims to be inducted into the ministry. On both counts the Congress had always rejected the arguments of the rival party, and even now it did so.

Gandhi in this connection saw that the presence of the British encouraged the leaders to address rather to them than to the people, who could be depended upon to exert their moderating influence on the diehards in the party. Consequently, not pleased with the efforts of the British to bring about unreal agreement at the top among leaders, he suggested that power should be handed over to either party. Later, Stafford Cripps putting trust in Gandhi's words said that Congress was more likely to get into the constituent assembly if the interim government was formed on the advice of the League, rather than largely nominated by the Viceroy. Pethick-Lawrence, however, in spite of Gandhi's helpful attitude, was not sure that if Jinnah headed a government he would get the support of the Congress. Doubtless, it would be difficult for Jinnah to dominate a central government when the Congress in eight out of the eleven provinces held power.[46]

As no agreement could be reached between the two parties, the British abandoned further talks, and put forward on 16th June a list of fourteen persons to be included in the new government, which denied parity to the League and the right of proposing a nationalist Muslim to the Congress. Of these, six were Hindu members of Congress including a scheduled caste person, five members of the Muslim League, and three represented the minority communities of Sikhs, Indian Christians and Parsees.[47] The British in order to honour the pledge to move ahead with any party that accepted the May proposal and to help Jinnah who had already done so, while the Congress was still undecided, had included in the 16th June statement paragraph eight which in Wavell's later opinion "was put in, perhaps rashly," and which said: "In the event of the two major parties or either of them proving unwilling to join in the setting up of a coalition Government on the above lines, it is the intention of the Viceroy to proceed with the formation of an Interim Government which will be as representative as possible of those willing to accept the Statement of May 16th."[48]

It is difficult to believe that the British would have agreed to rule India, with the help of Muslims and other minority groups. After the list was made public, hope for a while was entertained that both sides might come together to run a ministry. It was thought that Jinnah was ready to accept the offer, but would not do so until the Congress made known its views. He was in the list of fourteen names, and had taken a fancy to Defence portfolio, showing for the first time in his life a desire to take part in the government, although the final say in the matter of getting that portfolio rested with the Viceroy. Though a Muslim from the Congress was not included in the projected ministry, both Nehru and Patel were believed to be favourably inclined towards the proposal.

Gandhi, however, observed that in the business of establishing a government the British had ignored his view that one or the other party should be asked to take initiative, and had decided to impose their ideas on the country. He thought that they could not help doing what they did because they were labouring under the long traditions of imperial domination, which they could not all of a sudden forgo. He was disturbed perceiving that his lifelong devotion to the ideals of communal unity had been undone in the maze of diplomacy to achieve temporary results, and got up in the night in order to dictate "for the Working Committee the draft of a letter to the Viceroy." In which he made it very clear that since Congress was a nationalist party it must have the right to include a Muslim in the government; that since League was purely a Muslim body it could not have any say in choosing names apart from its quota of five persons. Hence, if there was a vacancy among the seats allotted to the minorities, only the Congress had the right to fill it up.

Later, at the deliberations of the Working Committee, the draft letter of Gandhi did not receive much attention and was put into cold storage, mainly because the Congress did not worry too much about the failure of the Viceroy to give representation to a nationalist Muslim, thinking that this defect could be rectified by replacing a Hindu with a Muslim in its list of names. Gandhi, however, forced the party to take a decision on the matter quickly, by letting it know that if it did not do so "he would have nothing to do with the whole business and leave Delhi."[49] Patel when the committee met on 20th June backed Gandhi, and said that no agreement with the British was possible by repudiating his mentor; so it was decided to send his letter to the ministerial delegation. Carrying this hot news about Gandhi's ascendancy one Wyatt, meanwhile, broke into the conversation of the ministers with Wavell, in reference to certain assurances Jinnah had asked for. Wavell in his letter of 20th promised Jinnah not to effect a change in the principle involved in choosing ministers, without the consent of both the parties; so the option of the Congress to nominate a Muslim from its quota was barred. He further said that if minority seat including that of the Scheduled Castes fell vacant it would be filled after consulting the two parties, and this assurance tried to establish parity, although in theory it was set aside.

They learnt from Wyatt that Gandhi had put pressure on Azad to seek a position in the ministry on the strength of his being a nationalist Muslim, as well as the President of the Congress. They agreed that it was not possible to give way to the Congress on this point, and that they should make use of Cripps' diplomacy to checkmate Gandhi's influence, and to urge Azad not to look for a berth in the ministry; but if Cripps failed to achieve this purpose, then he should go to Gandhi to see whether he could influence him towards the same end.[50] So Cripss sallied out to meet Azad, who after having been sucked into the labyrinth of party politics compounded by religious animosity was up to his neck in troubles and therefore was not in a position to help him. He then as originally planned hurried off to see Gandhi who before him once again chanted his mantra: "this was the wrong way for forming a Government, that it should be left to one party or the other and not be a coalition forced on the two parties by the British." Apologetically, Cripps said that after having achieved so much it would be difficult to begin afresh.

The situation was past hope, but Sudhir Ghosh, well known as Gandhi's emissary, advised Pethick-Lawrence to see Vallabhbhai Patel, "the only man amongst the Congress leaders who was a practical statesman.[51]" He in accordance with the advice did see him, and heard from him the weak points of the British offer especially in regard to the promises made to the opposite party. In their talks, Patel contradicted the other by saying that the Congress had certainly accepted the May offer to which Pethick-Lawrence replied "that it was news to him." It was Cripps who after telling the Viceroy that Congress would never accept the May offer instigated it to do so by pointing out the tactical advantage it would gain as regard the interim government.[52] Cripps predisposed to favour the Congress, much to the disadvantage of Wavell in his relationship with Jinnah, was not too scrupulous especially when he was determined not to fail again.

Since both parties had now accepted the May offer relating to constitution, the British in conformity with paragraph eight of June proposal were precluded from establishing a government with the help of the League and without the other party. All the assurances given to Jinnah had disappeared, and the only alternative before everyone was to set up a new government on different principles. Obviously Jinnah was living on a hope that he would be asked to enter a government without congress participation, and the present situation would look to him suspicious because the ministers could not tell him that he had been outmanoeuvred by the rival party. Not reconciled to the existing situation he opined, that the British should float a government with those who accepted the June offer which it was wrong to set aside, and Pethick-Lawrence, allegedly more "non-violent" than Gandhi, replied that the ministers "were not asking for Jinnah's opinion of their conduct."

At this time Nehru mainly because Gandhi intervened on his behalf was elected the President of the Congress, though Vallabhbhai Patel was greatly favoured by the Provincial Congress Committees, and as the leader of the party was asked to head the interim government. Had it not been for Gandhi's opposition, Patel in 1946 would have been the first prime minister of India; he was deprived of the honour due to him, and the unfairness by which he was hammered into submission to Gandhi's way of thinking cut him to the heart. Nehru on 10th July declared that Congress would enter into the Constituent Assembly "completely unfettered by agreements and free to meet all situations as they arise," and further said that probably "there will be no grouping" and that provincial jealousies would work against it.[53] These words served Jinnah well who was always insisting that Congress acceptance of the British offer lacked sincerity, overlooking the fact that League's approval hedged about with qualifications was not as satisfactory as he made out to be.

The Cabinet Mission's treatment of Jinnah had vexed him, and efforts to soothe him had not met with much success, besides Nehru's undiplomatic words so much worsened matters that at the party meeting in Bombay he turned his ire against his foes. Again taking up the cause of Pakistan for abandoning which even temporarily he had been under attack in the party, Jinnah persuaded the League to have recourse to direct action, fixed on 16th August, and to revoke the acceptance of May offer. So there began a struggle for power between the Hindus and the Muslims, very deadly in its nature because the imminent departure of the British had weakened their authority to uphold the rule of law, and because the Muslims feared that they would soon come under the Hindu rule.

The focal point of disturbances was Calcutta, a predominantly Hindu city, but the seat of power of a Muslim ministry headed by

Suhrawardy, the most influential member of the Muslim League in Bengal.[54] On the day fixed for action the mobs dominated the city streets, and at first the Muslims had the upper hand, but later the tide turned against them as the Hindus and the Sikhs who "were every bit as fierce as the Muslims" launched a counterattack. About five thousand people were killed in the conflict, "but one shudders to think what would have been the result" if the British troops had not been there; true, without them the administration in Bengal would have collapsed, and it hurt the feelings of Gandhi to think that both the sides had to depend on them.

Wavell flew to Calcutta to see the effects of the late fighting, and among the people he saw one was "honest fat little Nazimuddin" who made an impression on him saying this much: if it was quite clear that a province could not move out of grouping scheme it might have a considerable effect on League policy.[55] Whether the events in Calcutta unnerved him or not, Wavell laboured under the apprehension that in the absence of amity between the two parties the communal strife would spread to other places as well. He summoned Gandhi and Nehru to a meeting, and, in order to make them fall in with the wishes of the opposite party, told them that he could not convene the Constituent Assembly until the controversial point in regard to grouping scheme was settled. When Gandhi talked about legal points to uphold his view, Wavell saying "I am a plain man and not a lawyer" rebutted him. The hard words of the Viceroy raised heat at the meeting, and without achieving anything their talks ended in acrimony. "As representative of the King," Gandhi later made it clear to the Viceroy, "you cannot afford to be a military man only, nor to ignore the law, much less the law of your own making. You should be assisted, if necessary, by a legal mind enjoying your full confidence."[56]

At home the policy makers were not prepared to face the consequences of a breach with the Congress; they found fault with Wavell for what he said what he said and in their view the right thing for him to have said was that he would have to postpone the meeting of the constitution writing body.

The interim government of Nehru assumed office on 2nd September, however, there was not much joy in the country because the Muslims felt they had been cheated of their due, and nourished anger especially against the Hindus. What prevented them from getting into the government was the nationalist Muslim issue which on the surface looked easy enough to reach agreement, but underneath there was the clash of the two Indian leaders. "Gandhi is determined," the Viceroy thought, "to leave Jinnah with the choice between humiliation and exclusion from the government."[57]

Wavell haunted by the fears of a civil war desired to forestall it through a coalition government; so, he tried to entice the League into the ministry, but Jinnah's main argument was he must have something with which to convince the Working Committee of the party that he on every issue had not been defeated. At last he yielded to the pressure of Wavell mainly because he did not want to see the Congress monopolize power, but made it evident by choosing a member of Scheduled Castes in his list that Congress right to nominate a nationalist Muslim was offset by his corresponding right. Although Wavell saw a coalition government, an achievement that had eluded the combined genius of the Cabinet Mission, he felt "no elation over it, rather depression over the difficulties still ahead." Gandhi too foresaw troubles, and any doubt about the intention of the League was cleared by Liaquat who declared that Muslims must continue to prepare to fight for "the winning of their goal, Pakistan."

About this time communal disturbances broke out at Noakhali in Bengal, and the League seemed to have chosen this area to prove that the Hindus and the Muslims could not live together. Facing the Bay of Bengal, Noakhali is situated amidst numerous creeks and watercourses, and at certain times of the year the tidal waves, foaming and writhing, shoot up to a height of about forty feet to lash the coast with sudden fury, sinking the islands and breaking into the farther land in the process.[58] True, here the Hindus were not killed on a vast scale, but there was widespread destruction of their property, and besides some of their women were raped and some were abducted. Soon many Hindus fled in terror, and came to Bihar with their tales of suffering which excited popular feelings against the Muslims. The violence against the Hindus reflected the impotency of the Nehru government, especially underscoring the fact that the British had now responsibility without the power while the Indian provincial ministries had the power but little or no sense of responsibility.

In Bihar, the eruption of savagery and bestiality was far more worst than the Calcutta killings, and far more terrible than the Noakhali riots; the victims were all Muslims whose population in comparison with the Hindus was small in this province. The Hindu crowds to whom revenge was made attractive by popular orators and whose movement "had an appearance of a spontaneous uprising" were seized with madness, when they burnt and killed not even sparing women and children.

Gandhi surmounting natural barriers visited Noakhali, and by his presence was able to put courage into the hearts of the Hindus so that he was needed in Bihar too in order to bring relief to the Muslims. After going there as well, he learnt to his astonishment that some believed the brutal killings in Bihar checked Muslim violence elsewhere.

After the disturbances in the two provinces the rival parties hardened their attitude to each other, and in such a background, the Viceroy's efforts to persuade Jinnah to bring the Muslims into the Constituent Assembly made no progress. Probably, Jinnah was honest in saying that he had much difficulty in putting across the British offer with his party; however, he raised the cry of Islam in danger originally to enhance his prestige and power which helped to increase the bargaining value of his party. He had now so inflamed his ignorant and impressionable followers with the idea of Pakistan as a Prophet's paradise on earth and as their only means of protection against Hindu domination, that it would be very difficult to satisfy them with anything else.[59]

A further difficulty was that the League, on the assumption it would revoke the late resolution which rejected the constitutional plan, had been taken into the government. Since Jinnah was not helpful in this matter the Congress believed that the League should not be represented in the government, however, the British did not show any interest to force the League to leave the Nehru dispensation because such a step would open the door to new disorders, perhaps leading the country to civil war in which they could not help getting involved.

They to break the stalemate held a conference in London, with Nehru and Jinnah representing their parties, and in the talks that followed Cripps and Pethick-Lawrence were partial to the Congress, while Alexander and Wavell backed the other party towards which Attlee tilted the balance after he came out on its side.[60] On the contentious issue of grouping provinces, the British after taking legal advice thought that they must support the League's opinion, and urged the Congress to agree with them. What would be the fate of the country in the background of League's intransigence, the British policy declaration of 6th December 1946 made very obvious: "There has never been any prospect of success for the Constituent Assembly, except upon the basis of an agreed procedure. Should a Constitution come to be framed by a Constituent Assembly in which a large section of the Indian population had not been represented, His Majesty's Government could not of course contemplate—as the Congress have stated they would not contemplate—forcing such a Constitution upon any unwilling parts of the country."[61]

Not long ago Attlee had said that the minorities would not be allowed to check the progress of the majority, but his current views distressed the Congress and bolstered the hopes of Jinnah in regard to Pakistan. The Congress under pressure, however, changed its attitude to grouping scheme and came very near to a genuine acceptance of May offer. This served no purpose as Jinnah by now had lost interest in the ministerial plan, and desired only the creation of Pakistan. "You don't realize," he in England told Major Wyatt, "how far the situation has gone in India since you were there," and he talked about the militancy of the opposite party especially what he called "the deliberate butchery of Muslims by Hindus in Bihar."

As the political situation became more confused, the British and Congress leaders blamed each other for the deadlock. Attlee speaking in the Cabinet made it evident that the two Indian parties lacked will to reach agreement between themselves, that Nehru seemed to be intent upon securing full power for his party at the expense of the other party. He thought that the Muslims might turn against the newly established power, and warned his colleagues that "the situation might so develop as to result in civil war in India, with all the bloodshed which that would entail." The view of the Cabinet was that the Indian leaders did not behave with enough sense of responsibility, because, however much they might abuse the British Raj, they harboured at the back of their minds the hopeful thought that the British Army was there to rescue them from the consequences of their misbegotten policies.[62] Such a confidence in the authority of the Army was no longer fully justified, partly because the strength of the British Force in India was not large, and partly because the Indian Army under circumstances similar to civil war could not be relied upon. The Cabinet was quite certain that the British could not put the clock back in India and take it into a new era of firm rule, since neither the military nor the administrative machinery there was any longer capable of facing that task.

The Viceroy's authority after it was made known that power would be handed over to the Indians inevitably declined, and a few British officials who supported him were tired and dispirited by political opposition. Almost without power to control events in India, the British now were running the government by relying upon their formerly earned prestige which however was fast depleting. In such a gloomy backdrop, and in the light of the fact that there was not much chance the League would sit in the Constituent Assembly, and that a constitution therefore could not be framed for the whole India, Wavell was forced to consider a method of retreat, known as the Breakdown Plan, from India. He thought that he was not "in a position to maintain British rule in India beyond March 31st 1948 and possibly not for so long," and, in accordance with his plan, he wished to abandon southern provinces first to be followed by complete withdrawal from India by the date mentioned above. His critics said that if the transfer of power to provinces merely meant the withdrawal of the British Governor and officials, it might be better to wait and withdraw all simultaneously.

Wavell needed authority to implement his well planned evacuation of India, and tried at London to influence ministerial opinion in his favour, but Attlee was hostile to the Breakdown Plan while some ministers were frightened of it because it would involve them in Parliamentary legislation. True, it was difficult to justify withdrawal when there was no political breakdown, but merely on an estimate that such a situation would arise within about one year.[63] Wavell persisted in his efforts to get sanction for his plan. Attlee had no alternative ideas to offer, nor had he the courage to tell him that he would get things done through somebody other than him. He told Attlee that, without some definite policy he could not go back to India, but the Prime Minister did not take him into confidence, and his mind, to Wavell, remained as unfathomable as the Martian field.

Attlee was inclined to accept the Viceroy's plan in principle if it was put in a different form, not requiring Parliamentary legislation, but dilated on the difficulties with regard to certain other matters. Then Lord Chancellor Jowitt, who seemed to be "knowledgeable, sensible and decided," gave an emphatic view that nothing could be done without legislation, but later agreed that it would be possible to proceed by a resolution, with legislation afterwards. Consequently, a draft Resolution was produced and this Wavell was assured would give him the powers he so urgently needed. Finally, the Viceroy took leave of Attlee, who was not at all gracious to him. "I am not sure," reflected Wavell, "that he has it in him to be so, or he doesn't like me, probably the latter." Two days before this ungracious event, Attlee, after taking the King into confidence but unknown to Wavell, had met Rear-Admiral Lord Mountbatten and asked him to take over as Vicerory.[64]

Obviously, Wavell was empty of new ideas, so the Prime Minister put his hopes in a new man and a new policy. There was a divergence of view between the Viceroy and the British ministers on the method of transferring power in India. The Viceroy saw the method as a withdrawal, planned on the lines of a military evacuation from hostile territory, while the British leaders wanted to hand over power in a friendly manner. His contemplated step was seen as the beginning of the liquidation of the British empire, and would have serious repercussions in other countries. Britain in the talks with Egypt had claimed that it would not be possible to withdraw troops from there before 1949, and it was not easy to reconcile this claim with British readiness to evacuate by the spring of 1948 the whole of India. The Cabinet felt that withdrawal from India need not appear to be forced upon the British by their weakness, nor to be the first step in the dissolution of the empire.

Soon after Wavell returned to India he received a letter from the Prime Minister telling him that the Cabinet had rejected his plan, and that withdrawal by stages was an encouragement to the fragmentation of India. Indeed, the logical sequence to retreat from the four southern provinces would be withdrawal from further provinces and this would lead straight in the direction of Pakistan.[65] Wavell the Viceroy received on 4th February 1947 a letter from the Prime Minister by special messenger dismissing him from his post, and he noted in his diary "not very courteously done" which concealed his indignation about the way he had been humiliated.

Though Attlee saw the Viceroy unfavourably for projecting a defeatist mentality, he found certain virtues in the idea of announcing a date for withdrawal, and besides Lord Mountbatten had agreed to take up his difficult assignment in the belief that a date would be put forward for demission of power. Attlee, therefore, while delivering a speech in Parliament on 20th February came up with a date, beyond which Britain would not rule India, but it was three months later than the date originally proposed by Wavell.

It became evident, when Mountbatten assumed powers as the Viceroy, that his immediate predecessor had not overreacted to the situation and that the Indian scene was one of unrelieved gloom. The whole country was in a unsettled condition, and even the capital Delhi was not spraed of trouble while in the Punjab all the parties were preparing for civil war. Among them the Sikhs by far the most warlike, and in fact had a plan on hand to seize certain strategic places so that they could exercise control over the Punjab.

Gandhi while touring violence-prone areas knew that events were moving fast now at the national level, but he could not guess how things would take their shape in the background of the fact that Attlee himself had not yet made up his mind whether power should be divided or not, before it was handed over to the Indian parties. Not giving up his optimism, Gandhi thought that the course of events would be influenced by the doings of the Constituent Assembly and the interim government.[66] Others put trust in the doings of Mountbatten, a scion of the British royal family, with enormous prestige, drive, and charm which at social gatherings was made to work to his advantage by his public-spirited wife Edwina; she helped him in diverse ways and established such good relationship with Indian leaders that Gandhi was fond of her.

Gandhi met the new Viceroy at Delhi, and staggered him by telling him to invite Jinnah to form a new central government to which he should turn over power. "I twitted him," Mountbatten observes, "that he really desired me to form a central government run by Congress, to which I would turn over power, and that the preliminary offer to Jinnah was merely a manoeuvre." Gandhi, however, made protestation of sincerity and volunteered to place his services at the Viceroy's disposal in trying to get the Jinnah government through by exercising his influence, firstly with the Congress, secondly with the masses, so as to make both accept it. After getting convinced of Gandhi's good intentions Mountbatten took interest in his proposal, but would not commit himself to its support till he knew the views of other leaders.

Considering that Gandhi's object was to retain the unity of India, and that he was basically right in this, it would not be very easy for Jinnah to refuse his offer. Gandhi honestly thought that the only hope of unity came from a coalition government, but the one under Nehru was functioning creakily as the ministers divided on party basis were at odds with each other. His viewpoint was that, since it was impossible to get the League to agree to Congress running the interim government, the only way to bypass the difficulty was to let Jinnah run it himself. Once the Muslims' fear was removed, and once a unified India became a reality after the British handed over power, Gandhi doubtless thought that the Indians themselves would be able to adjust matters and establish some sort of Pakistan, if necessary.[67]

On the contrary, it was said that the assurance of co-operation by the Congress was more a wishful thinking, and would certainly place Jinnah, if he presided over the interim government, in the position of having to adjust his views to those of the dominant party. This was perhaps "not unintended by Gandhi."

Mountbatten handled Jinnah with great dexterity in order to know whether he was inclined to accept the offer of Gandhi. He talked about the benefits of unity and portrayed the greatness India could achieve with it, and then said that it was a day-dream of his "to be able to put the central government under the Prime Ministership of Jinnah himself." Jinnah replied that he wished to see unity, and that it was indeed tragic that the behaviour of the Hindus made such a thing impossible. There was no doubt that the Viceroy's remark elevating him tickled the vanity of Jinnah who kept turning over the proposition in his mind, for he later made a reference out of the blue to it. So Mountbatten concluded that his suggestion had a far greater effect on him than he would have thought possible, and that Gandhi's famous scheme might yet go through on the strength of Jinnah's vainglory.

Gandhi's plan, however, never took off the ground, and he himself wrote to the Viceroy to drop his scheme owing to the opposition of Nehru and the Congress Working Committee members.

As Mountbatten desired to preserve the unity of India he fixed his thoughts on the Cabinet Mission plan; however, if he found that it would be not possible to impose such a plan without a recrudescence of bloodshed, leading perhaps to civil war, he felt the only alternative was to leave the decision in the hands of the people. He was certain of one thing: if he became convinced that partition was in the best interests of India, and decided on that step, he would apply the same principle both to the Punjab and Bengal so that the final solution would be either a "moth-eaten" Pakistan or united India.

However Jinnah wanted not only Pakistan but a "viable" one, and appeals to his reason did not prevail especially when he gave the impression that he was not listening, with the result Mountbatten might have felt he was talking to a whitewashed wall. The Viceroy's opinion was that, until he had met Jinnah, he had not thought it possible that a man with such a complete lack of sense of responsibility could hold the power that he did. He confessedly approached the problem with an open mind while Jinnah with a closed mind, a fact which explained why he was not able to put forward "one single feasible argument in favour of Pakistan." It was said that "the dominating feature in Jinnah's mental structure was his loathing and contempt of the Hindus," but Mountbatten pointed out that in any case the Muslims and Hindus would have to live together. Further, he believed that it was likely the Muslims in Bengal would not follow Jinnah's leadership, and his Pakistan in the end would consist only of Sind and part of the Punjab.

Mountbatten, when first formulating the principle that provinces should choose their own future, had not clearly realized the danger of encouraging too many independent nations.[68] It was said that if India was "Balkanised" more than was proposed by Jinnah the people would suffer, and so to get over this difficulty the Viceroy suggested that provinces might be asked in the first instance to join one or other Constituent Assembly.

The Muslim League in the late election had been defeated in the North Western Frontier Province on the Pakistan issue, but now under its influence an agitation began here to overthrow Dr. Khan Sahib's popular government as it was thought to be dominated by the essentially Hindu Congress. As a result property worth millions of rupees was destroyed, and the agitators had laid up bitter hatred "by massacres, forcible conversions and horrible atrocities."[69] Mountbatten in order to get a clear picture of the situation went to the province, and he was impressed by the mass demonstration and the strength of the movement behind it. The future of India concerned the tribes, especially the freedom loving Afridis who had already made claim on Khyber Pass when Wavell held power, and now "went to far as to make it clear that they felt themselves at perfect liberty to come to an accommodation with Afghanistan if they could not reach a satisfactory working arrangement with the successor government in India."

About the unrest in the province the Viceroy said that his conscience would not allow him to yield to force, and Jinnah too thought that it was wrong to give way to it but told him to his face "that His Excellency could not control the people nor could he." He wished to see the immediate dissolution of the frontier ministry, but the other was not willing to oblige him. The circumstances however somewhat favoured the Viceroy on account of this: if the Punjab as a whole or in part did not want to adhere to the Union, then the North West Frontier Province in view of its peculiar geographical position would be required to go through a referendum, under the supervision of the Governor General, to ascertain whether the people desired to join India or not.

The Afghan government too was concerned about the fate of the population of this province, if they were asked to choose between Pakistan or Hindustan. The British Foreign Office through diplomatic channel was made aware of the problem: "The Afghan government considered that the population of the former Afghan territories annexed by Great Britain to India during the last century should have the opportunity of deciding whether they wished to rejoin Afghanistan or to form a separate State enjoying complete independence." It blamed the British for what it called "an arbitrary dismemberment of Afghanistan" and further said that, in view of the change in the status of India, the obligations created by the Anglo-Afghan treaties in respect of the territories of this province would no longer be regarded as binding.

About this time when the British were struggling how to disentangle themselves from the Indian empire, an odd suggestion was made to them to the same end. Mountbatten came to know that Brigadier Cariappa, later Chief of Staff and Commander-in-Chief of the Indian Army, was carrying on propaganda among Indian officers at the staff college in favour of setting up military rule; however, Sir Claude Auchinleck, the Commander-in-Chief, was completely in the dark about this matter. Then Cariappa himself went to see Lord Ismay, the Viceroy's Chief of Staff, and volunteered the amazing suggestion that Indian Army with either Nehru or Jinnah as Commander-in-Chief should take over power, when the British left the country.[70] Lord Ismay told him that his proposal was not only impracticable but highly dangerous; that throughout history the rule of an Army had always proved incompetent and tyrannical, and begged him to put the idea right out of his mind never mentioning it again even in secrecy.

The Sikhs, meanwhile, in the Punjab felt much insecure, and Khizar, their one source of hope, unable to face the challenge of the League based on its mob strength, tendered on 3rd March 1947 his resignation. On the same day the capital of the Punjab Lahore saw great excitement after violent speeches were made at a anti-Muslim gathering, and the very idea of Pakistan was denounced. Next day rioting broke out in Lahore, and the ministers, who had been asked to carry on until a new government was set up, made it plain to the Governor that they could take no further responsibility for the situation.

Soon the conflict spread to other areas, and in the Rawalpindi and Attock districts as well as in part of the Jhelum district later "there was an absolute butchery of non-Muslims." The Nawab of Mamdot on behalf of the Muslim League was not in a position to form a ministry, and gave the impression that he was not anxious to take the burden of quelling violence. The Sikhs were highly combustible, the Muslims were openly provocative, and the British instead of playing their customary role as a buffer were too eager to shake off their imperial liability so that the Punjab rapidly slipped into the vortex of party inspired strife.

The Sikhs had the legal right to carry swords since 1924, and at the official level it was seen as not a wise step to deprive them of that privilege now. It was said that other inhabitants of the Punjab should be allowed to carry swords in order to defend themselves against sudden attacks by the Sikhs, but if the British allowed everyone to go armed in this province it was an invitation to civil war. The Sikhs harboured so much bitterness on account of Muslim cruelties that they were waiting for an excuse to take revenge, and the British thinking that it would be folly to let this occur proceeded with caution. The Nawab of Mamdot, however, was a dunce, and fixed his thoughts on the ephemeral advantages of power as he was under the influence of younger party fanatics, who believed that if the Muslim League could hold power that circumstance would help them to crush the Sikhs.[71] So he came forward to form a ministry, saw the Governor Evan Jenkins and then produced figures for his alleged majority consisting of 91 in a House of 175 members. It was obvious that a purely communal ministry would provoke the Sikhs, would be dislodged by a violent rebellion and might even be unable to hold its obligatory Budget session. Moreover, if the two big parties were able to reach an agreement, based on union or partition, then it would be easy to make a fresh start in a better environment.

Such considerations worked in the mind of the Governor, and perceiving that his solicitation to form a government had no chance of being taken seriously, Mamdot, who was rather sulky, hinted at the possibility of a mass agitation. The Governor said that he would sooner deal with it than a fight between a Muslim government and its opponents, but he hoped the other would see the need for moderation. Mamdot observed that this was all very well but the Muslims were not going to accept partition, and by this words a civil war in the Punjab seemed almost inevitable.

Mountbatten shortly before had talked with Jinnah, and, touching upon Sikh temperament, had advanced reasons to buttress his view that there should be no change in he Punjab; then he asked Jinnah whether he agreed with him.

> "Certainly not, I definitely do not agree," Jinnah said.
>
> "Do you entirely see my point of view and understand my reasons?" Mountbatten asked.
>
> "I entirely see your point of view and I respect your sincerity, though I do not agree with your decision," Jinnah replied.

"One day you will be thankful to me for saving you from getting into this mess that you would like to get into in the Punjab; it is mainly in the interests of the Muslim League that I am making this decision, and I am sorry not to have your agreement," Mountbatten said.[72]

Mountbatten talked in this manner because he thought that the Sikhs meant to come to terms with Pakistan, but one thing that would destroy such an eventuality would be a further bloodbath which was inevitable if Mamdot was allowed to form a ministry. But what would prompt the Sikhs to reach an understanding with Jinnah? This was their self-interest; they had much to lose by the partition of the Punjab as they would be split into two halves, and about half of their population would have to remain in Pakistan. Hence, it was said that the situation really called for a settlement between the Muslims and the Sikhs; their interests were not necessarily irreconcilable, and indeed had a good deal in common as appeared from the fact that they had for long worked together under the Unionist Party, or rather the coalition ministry of Khizar. The advantage of such a policy was that the Sikhs would avoid getting split up, and that the Muslims would get a larger and more viable Pakistan.

About this time Jinnah received a message from the Sikh leader Kartar Singh "suggesting that they should hold discussions about the Sikh state joining Pakistan after partition." Jinnah gratified by this move said that the Sikhs liked him personally, and had always trusted him, and that he had publicly stated he would support the Sikhs if any Muslims took unfair action against them.

Gandhi and Jinnah put their heads together on 5th May in order to reach agreement, and issued a statement which was self-explanatory: "We discussed two matters; one was the question of division of India into Pakistan and Hindustan, and Gandhi does not accept the principle of division. He thinks that division is not inevitable, whereas in my opinion not only is Pakistan inevitable, but is the only practical solution of India's political problem."[73] Further, Gandhi knew that Congress was not giving a clear lead in this matter, and, in his talks with Socialist leaders, said that it should "in no circumstance be party to partition."[74] He simplified the Viceroy's problem by telling the British to hand over power either to the League or to the other party, and then to quit with a clear conscience because the country was quite capable of taking care of itself.

About their position in the Punjab the Sikhs thought highly of themselves; such a view was due partly to their historical status as the rulers of the land traversed by the river Indus, partly to the rather flattering treatment they had received from the British as one of the great martial races, and partly to the fact that they considered that they had contributed out of proportion to their numbers to the economic wealth of the Punjab. During the visit of the British ministers the Sikhs were asked whether they wished to be all together in Pakistan or divided into two halves. The Sikhs refused to come to grips with the facts and so parried the difficult question saying, "if there were Pakistan there must be Sikhistan." However, in no single district of the Punjab did they constitute a majority of the population, and hence the British were scarcely in a position to help them.

Presently, the Sikh leaders, feeling insecure under the Muslim domination in the existing Punjab, asked for division of the province along the river Chenab with provision for exchange of population and property.[75] The Maharaja of Patiala appealed to the British to make the partition line on the basis of Sikh vested interests, but when it was made clear to him that it would not be possible to put Muslim majority areas under Sikh and Hindu domination merely on ownership of land and religious grounds, he said: "I greatly fear the Sikhs will fight." He was warned that the British would use massive force to put down any attempts at communal war, and, in the opinion of Mountbatten, the Maharaja was visibly shaken by this threat. Nevertheless, the Sikhs were prepared for war and it seemed that whatever was done short of deliberately putting Muslim majority areas under their control they would fight. Not taking any chances the British, meanwhile, took steps in order to pump additional forces into the Punjab, especially along the disputed territory between the Ravi and the Sutlej river.

Another Sikh leader Master Tara Singh, remembering the blood debt owed by the Muslims, said that he could never be friendly with them, and he would if necessary see that they were dealt with after the British moved out. The Sikhs were fortunate in one respect: though there were a number of Sikh shrines in Western Punjab their real Holy Land was in Amritsar, which would in any scheme of partition belong to them.

The communal strife began in the Gurgaon district of the Punjab when the Hindus attacked the area inhabited by Meos, the aborigines professing Muslim religion, and this led to reprisals by the Meos so that fighting raged across a fifty mile stretch of land for a while. Mountbatten could not help thinking that the renewed outbreak of violence, on the eve of his meeting with the leaders, might influence them to accept his plan which he was about to place before them.

Meanwhile, certain Sikhs in touch with Baldev Singh and Tara Singh were about to put forward, informally and privily, their conditions for joining Pakistan. If these offered a basis for negotiation they would approach informally certain Muslim League leaders, and the Sikhs were anxious that such contemplated talks should be kept secret. About this time one Penderel Moon wrote to Lord Ismay, suggesting that the Sikh demand should be encouraged and conceded, and the problem as he saw it was how to take the Sikhs away from the sphere of Hindu domination so that they would throw in their lot with Pakistan. It would considerably facilitate matters towards that end if the new Eastern Punjab had the strongest possible Sikh complexion, and therefore did not include four predominantly Hindu districts.[76] Already, the Sikhs had put this demand to the Congress which hesitated to accept it.

Such a plan for avoiding the future disaster in the Punjab did not work, since by and large "if the Sikhs were lukewarm about a settlement, the Muslims were icy cold." Once Jinnah got reconciled to a "truncated" Pakistan, which was more than the Sind desert but not so large as his ambition had visualized, he no more cared about the fate of the Sikhs. True, the Sikhs had asked for the partition of the Punjab, and now had to take the consequences of such a policy.

Mountbatten had sent his draft plan to London and was under the impression that the Indian leaders had implied that they would accept it; however, he gave Nehru the chance to read it who having done so vehemently rejected it; for, he thought that it would encourage people to realize that India was being balkanized, and that the Cabinet Mission's conception of a Union of India to begin with, was thrown away. Nehru wanted it to be fully established that India and the Constituent Assembly were the successors to, and Pakistan and the Muslim League the seceders from, British India.[77]

Mountbatten, in deference to the opinion of Nehru, omitted from his plan the choice to provinces for standing out independently. True, if it was the desire of all parties in a particular province to stand alone, and if the Legislative Assembly in Bengal voted for independence, the British could not prevent it but Mountbatten did not want to give openly that choice. He was thinking whether it would be right to transfer power to two central governments, India and Pakistan, on the basis of Dominion status.[78] Some leaders were confident that it would be possible for them to persuade the Congress to accept Dominion status provided they could say that, by this means, the actual transfer of power would be secured much earlier. If the future of the disputed provinces, Bengal and the Punjab, was settled by electoral means, the Hindus would co-operate with the Viceroy.

Any opposition from the Muslims would be on the ground that the Viceroy's plan did not grant them the whole of their wishes, in the form of the original and full-blooded Pakistan. In fact, Mountbatten failed in his efforts to get Jinnah agree to his plan, and then tested cautiously his reaction to the threat, failing agreement, of demitting power to the interim government on a Dominion status basis. Jinnah with a cool head said that he could not prevent such a step in any event and his response was both abnormal and disturbing the Viceroy ruminated. Later, he once again said that the "Muslim League cannot agree to the partition of Bengal and the Punjab," however, Mountbatten was right in his belief that the League would acquiesce to the plan.

The most perplexing question was how far Gandhi could or would resist the tidal flow of events towards the partition of India. The nationalists of the country said that until the League agreed to the division of the two provinces mentioned above its demand for Pakistan was not just, but Gandhi said: "If Pakistan is wrong, partition of Bengal and the Punjab will not make it right. Two wrongs will not make one right." Surely, the feelings engendered by Gandhi, at his prayer meetings when he was at his best as a saint, in the ordinary people were to the effect: "this partition is wrong; we must resist it; we must not give in."[79]

So Mountbatten faced the interview with Gandhi with considerable trepidation, but knowing well that his emotions were those of a man who had worked, lived, and prayed for the unity of India the Viceroy thoroughly understood him and responded to his feelings. Later, when the Viceroy got news that Gandhi was in a bad emotional mood and that some leaders feared he might at his prayer meeting denounce the plan, he immediately saw him. The upshot of their conversation was Gandhi felt that he had taken a far greater part in shaping the future of India than had at first sight appeared to him from the way the plan was worded, and that Mountbatten had honestly tried to follow his advice.

On the whole, Gandhi was in a melancholy situation, with less influence with the people than he had formerly, and besides the leaders who once adored him were now absorbed in grabbing power.

Power was almost certain to be demitted on 15th August 1947, and on that day paramountcy would come to an end; the princes at last divorced from British authority could taste the sweet nectar of freedom if they wished to do so. Aiyer, exercising autocratic power in Travancore, in order to improve the bargaining powers of the states and to enable them to negotiate on equal terms, appealed to the Viceroy that paramountcy should be loosened or allowed to lapse in advance of the date fixed for handing over power, and he replied that he would consider the premature lapse of paramountcy in special cases if it could be proved to him that its continuation was a handicap to negotiation.

Mountbatten with his royal pedigree could not be indifferent to the fate of the princes, who attached much significance to their ties with the British Crown.[80] The Nawab of Bhopal, with a predilection to be on good terms with everyone but unfortunately trusted by none, wanted to get Dominion status for his tribe of princes; however, the Viceroy lacked authority to discuss any project of that nature, and so did not take any steps to encourage his ambition. The Nawab of Bhopal sensible of the doom awaiting his tribe bemoaned his hard fate saying that the British had left the princes in the lurch, and that they could have joined the weak Centre envisaged by the Cabinet Mission. Now, because there would be a tight Centre, whichever side they preferred in order to form an alliance, the princes faced utter ruin.

The states represented more than one-third of India in area and more than a fourth in population, and in many ways princely rule compared favourably with the British India under the Viceroy. At least, in contrast to strife in the Punjab, in Bihar, and Bengal, not much blood had been shed in the domain of the princes.

The Nizam of Hyderabad had more inhabitants in his state than any British Dominion, including Canada, and in area it roughly approximated to France. He ruled over mostly Hindu subjects, but there were more than half million Muslims in the city of Hyderabad, and more than two million in the state—"they have the dynasty, the administration, the Army and the tradition of two hundred years' rule plus the treaties." The Nizam, Mir Osman Ali Khan, after seeing Clause 7 of the India Independence Bill was distressed to learn that the British had unilaterally repudiated the treaties. "I have been taught that," he wrote to the Viceroy, "I could safely rely on British arms and the British word and I have been persuaded, in consequence, right up to the present to refrain from increasing my army and from establishing in my state factories for the manufacture of arms and equipment."[81]

According to the Viceroy the legal position was that, without a shadow of doubt, the states would after 15th August be absolutely free. Mountbatten saw that, if the Nizam decided not to send representatives to the Legislative Assembly of India, Hyderabad would be depriving itself of a great opportunity. He thought the present chance was probably the last one too good to be missed lest it be lost forever, and if his advise was not taken prophesied calamity. The Nizam's Constitutional Adviser Sir Walter Monckton, however, talked bombastic nonsense when he said that Hyderabad might seriously consider the alternative of joining Pakistan. While the two parts of Pakistan could communicate by sea, this was not possible for Hyderabad which was completely enclosed by the territories of British India. The difficulty in the facts of geography was very real, comparable with Poland before the war, and the British did not feel that they could commit themselves to help a country which was thus surrounded. Late in 1945, there was suggestion that the Nizam might try to purchase Portuguese Goa or some part of it in order to get an outlet to the sea but nothing happened.

The Nizam kept up court traditions reminiscent of the now extinct Mogul dynasty, and he was such a shrewd as well as eccentric ruler that he would appoint his prime minister and then through a maze of intrigues he himself would overthrow him, thus exemplifying how much he was versed in statecraft. As Jinnah wanted Hyderabad state to be his close ally, he would not agree to the Nizam joining India even if he inserted a clause in the treaty to the effect that his forces must never be used to fight Pakistan. The Nizam's Muslim subjects formed a small proportion of the population, yet they filled almost all the government, police and military posts, and they would resent the idea of abandoning after all these centuries the southern bastion of the Muslim world in India to the Hindus, that too without a fight.

The situation in Kashmir was the opposite of Hyderabad, that is a Hindu king had power over largely Muslim subjects, and his army consisted almost entirely of Dogra Rajputs to which caste he himself belonged, and the people of Kashmir whether Hindu or Muslim were excluded from it. This state which borders Pakistan as well as India is composed of roughly three parts: Kashmir proper, Jammu, and Ladakh. The Muslim League had no influence in Kashmir, and a popular movement under the leadership of Sheikh Abdullah, a Kashmiri

Muslim, had taken root here. His party known as the Kashmir National Conference had captured the imagination of the masses, and, though Muslim in complexion, stood for joining the Constituent Assembly of India.

The Maharaja of Kashmir, Hari Singh, was not powerful, and a cabal headed by his Prime Minister Ramachandra Kak overshadowed him. The advice of Mountbatten to the ruler was that Kashmir should join one of the two nations, at least for defence, communications and external affairs. Both the prince and his minister Kak opined that, on account of the balance of population and the geographical position in which they found themselves, any premature decision might have a very bad effect. They wished to see no Congress or League leaders in their state until they made up their mind about its future, and they reasoned that it would add to their troubles if they were bombarded with political propaganda at a time when they, faced with the choice of Pakistan or India, were struggling to do the right thing and deliver themselves from the condition they were in.

Though the two potentates of Kashmir had their differences over policy issues, they were united in their animosity towards Nehru. Mountbatten who knew this could not appreciate the eagerness of Nehru, doubtless unhappy with the state of affairs in Kashmir, to go there now "to take up the cudgels on behalf of his friend" Sheikh Abdullah rotting in jail. He dreaded the prospect of the prince declaring adherence to Pakistan just before Nehru arrived in Kashmir, and Kak provoking an incident which would end up with the distinguished visitor shut in prison at a time when he should be taking over power in Delhi from the Viceroy. Because of his emotional state Nehru did not see the danger that lay ahead, and it was left to Mountbatten to bring him to his senses. It was wrong of him as the Prime Minister of a big nation which was on the verge of getting power to leave the capital, or rather to desert his responsibilities at the head of the government, and Mountbatten thought that he would be failing in his duty if he did not guide the other in the right way. So, he told Nehru that, until his new dispensation was firmly in the saddle and could spare his services, he should not go "running off to Kashmir" on what amounted to almost private business.

About this time Mountbatten informed Hari Singh as follows: "I am writing to tell Your Highness that I have had a talk with both

Mahatma Gandhi and Pandit Nehru, who are both still anxious to visit Kashmir. I pointed out to them that any visit from a big Congress leader in which speeches were made could not fail to cause the League to send speakers of the order of Jinnah to counter their propaganda. This would in effect produce the electioneering atmosphere which you so rightly wish to avoid, since, as you pointed out to me, there has been no bloodshed up to date and only violent political speeches could now bring about the bloodshed."[82] The Viceroy recommending Gandhi's visit to Kashmir told Hari Singh that he would like to meet people, especially Begum Sheikh Abdullah who was hostile to the prince, but had no desire to gather crowds around him.

Gandhi went there to please Nehru, who thought "nothing would be more natural than that Congress should send a high-level emissary" to put before the ruler of Kashmir the advantages of joining India. Kashmir, formerly bought by one Gulab Singh from the British, was a big state, had great strategic value to his possessor, and had four million people who were filled with local patriotism; on 15th August it would become an independent state, and that it could not remain in that condition for long was obvious.

While returning from Kashmir Gandhi made a halt at Lahore, and advised the people not to give way to fear, but it was like water off a duck's back. In this horror city, once the capital of Sikh Maharaja Ranjit Singh, the assassins stabbed their victims after choosing the moment carefully, bombs were extensively hurled at human targets with deadly result, and many empty houses testified to the fact that the Hindus and Sikhs had taken to their heels. The provisional boundary cutting the Punjab into two parts would give to the Sikhs and Hindus Ambala, Jullundur as well as Amritsar, and to the Muslims Rawalpindi, Multan and Lahore. True it was that fear and anger swayed the people everywhere in the Punjab, and this emotion was much more so among those who lived on the wrong side of the boundary. Hence, in Amritsar, the Muslims felt that they were doomed to a sordid existence, and might as well do as much mischief as they could before they fled or perished.[83] Likewise, the Sikhs and Hindus knew the hazard they faced in the Western Punjab especially when the Muslim League was bent upon establishing a theocratic state.

By now the Sikhs had collected vest quantities of arms, and looking at their offensive posture the Muslims too were making counter-preparation to meet them on equal terms. About this time Mountbatten came to know that some hot-headed Sikhs were involved in a plot to assassinate Jinnah in Karachi during the projected 15th August celebration.

In consequence of political extremism the Viceroy was fully sensible of danger, and thought that steps should be taken to ensure the fidelity of the Sikhs attached to his Bodygauard. He ordered his secretary to make arrangement so that the award of the Boundary Commission, which both the rival parties were sure to consider as unfair to them, "should not be put out in a communique from Viceroy's House, but rather published as a Gazette Extraordinary."[84] Further, in accordance with his express command one Major Massey should get in touch with the members of the Bodyguard, and, referring to the Boundary Commission award, make it clear to them that the Viceroy had nothing to do with it; he besides must see to it that Sikhs and others in the Bodyguard whose loyalty was open to suspicion did not attend the 15th August parades. About Sikhs in the Army, Lord Ismay had already spoken to the Commander-in-Chief Field Marshal Auchinleck who said there was a proportion of Sikhs in the Boundary Force, and the question of their loyalty had to be examined.

It was said in order to placate the Sikhs, that the boundary should be shifted so far west that Lahore as well as large tracts of country in which Muslims were in the majority would fall within India. Apart from weakening the principle which Mountbatten after so much labour had persuaded the parties to accept, this would not help matters was obvious: firstly, the Sikhs wherever they perceived themselves superior were intent upon attacking the Muslims, and juggling with the line of demarcation to please them now would not deflect them from their purpose; secondly, the muslims could not be expected to reconcile themselves to the loss of Lahore, and were certain to resort to violence on a far bigger scale than they did recently.

In North West Frontier Province the result of the Referendum was a decisive vote for Pakistan, thanks to all the infamous tactics adopted by Jinnah to rouse Muslim religious fanaticism, and to engender hatred of non-Muslims, the so-called enemies of Islam. The premier Khan Sahib originally indicated about his willingness to resign if the Referendum went against him, but now maintained, perhaps in conformity with the views of Congress High Command, that he saw no reason why his ministry should leave office especially when he had majority support in the House. Mountbatten came under considerable pressure to tell the Governor to ask the ministers to resign, and to dismiss the whole lot if they did not oblige; however, during his last fortnight as Viceroy, he did not want to take that extreme step which could later be held against him as an unconstitutional act. Jinnah was getting worried probably because Liaquat had evidence that Khan Sahib intended to declare a free "Pathanistan" on the morning of the 15th August, if he held power till then. The Viceroy, however, temporized leaving the decision to Jinnah, who after obtaining the powers of his new nation was expected to know how to tame Khan Sahib's restless energy.

At last the great day came in, or rather the greatest day in the annals of modern Indian history, 15th August 1947. The happiness of the day, born out of India's emancipation, was the culmination of efforts started about a hundred years ago, efforts in which many were killed, many were shut in prison and others were handled brutally, only because having loved their country they longed for this precious thing called freedom. At this historic moment Mountbatten did not forget the architect of Indian freedom through non-violence,—Mahatma Gandhi. While speaking on the memorable occasion, Mountbatten understood the true state of affairs when he said the joy of freedom was diminished to some extent because India went through partition. Further, he knew that Gandhi's absence from the ceremonies in Delhi was intentional; for, who could feel the pain of division more than him? Not for Gandhi therefore the gaiety of the day.

Even before power was handed over the Sikhs had moved for the attack, and unescorted Muslim refugees were butchered with extreme ferocity. How to get out of Lahore was the main worry of the Hindus, and their movement from the Western Punjab was more or less balanced by a similar exodus of Muslims from the eastern side. The Sikh leaders had two objectives: firstly, they wanted to take revenge on the Muslims for the outrages they had suffered at their hands; secondly, they desired to preserve at all cost the cohesion of their community by giving shelter to about two million Sikhs left high and dry on the other side of the border. So to make their settlement easy, the Muslims living within the Indian side of the border had to be ejected, and towards that end the Sikh militia fell upon them with considerable force unleashing terror to frighten their enemies so numerous in certain areas that they had no inclination to abandon their homes.[85] The contrast between the two sides in respect of their migration was striking; while the Sikhs with their flocks around them, and with their bullock carts closed up in defensive position pushed on from the west in good order, the Muslim refugees moving from the opposite direction were poor, ill-organized and dispirited, more like the stragglers of a broken army fleeing to escape ruin.

The whole countryside in the Punjab was involved in the conflict, whose intensity was evident from the fact that entire villages were often blotted out; but it was in central Punjab that the struggle went on with much cruelty, and the effusion of blood was more here as the people were temperamentally aggressive, and besides the forces pitted against each other were more or less evenly matched so that one side wishing to establish preponderance over the other most necessarily use decisive power.

In these times of unprecedented lawlessness, greed too played a role in accentuating the bitterness of the struggle; for even during normal times some could not help shooting an avaricious glance at others' affluence but now the stronger parties, hindered by no moral principles, exulting in their superiority over their opponents coveted their wealth and the ways by which they obtained it, either by fraud or downright plunder, exhibited human nature in the worst light.

When the towns in the Punjab were burning the heat was felt at Delhi, which overflowed with refugees and buzzed with rumours of a Muslim conspiracy as in the days of old to seize power. Such fears were not without some basis as the Muslim League had a strong presence in Delhi, and the police stood here divided on communal grounds while the army was not a powerful force yet. The mood of suspicion was heightened when a bomb exploded in a mainly Hindu area and then disturbances broke out in the capital as ruffian groups rambled through the streets looking for opportunities to shed human blood, and individuals too inflamed by a passion to settle account with their enemies killed them in a despicable manner. As night descended on, the continuous shooting, the dismal shrieking of the victims, and the lurid glow of fires on the horizon struck terror into the hearts of many.[86]

In this crisis, Mountbatten was away in Simla taking some well-deserved rest but immediately his service was in requisition, and the capital was saved from anarchy largely due to him as neither Patel nor Nehru had his experience and his knowledge to face this cataclysm. That the Indian leaders after some days of freedom were prepared to give him back power thus showing how much confidence they had in him redounded to his credit, but having understood the public mood Mountbatten did not want to go back to the previous era, and came up with the device of an Emergency Committee over which he would preside but which would be responsible to the Cabinet;[87] this device before long restored customary respect for law and order in Delhi.

There were signs, meanwhile, that the events in the Punjab were causing polarization of feelings in the armed forces. Massey, the commander of the last Viceroy's Bodyguard, which consisted of equal proportion of Sikhs and Muslims, reported to Lord Ismay that his men got "news of horrible happenings in they homes and of the murders of their kith and kin."[88] This had raised the level of their animosity, and Massey feared that their would take vengeance by falling upon each other. Ismay instructed the commander to parade the Bodyguard immediately, and to reason with the men especially about their responsibility as members of the oldest and most famous unit of the Indian Army "with two hundred years of unblemished tradition behind it." Surely, the two factions could live at peace carrying on their duty for the few days that remained. Further, Ismay warned the commander that, unless he was satisfied about the result of his talk, he should keep the men on the parade ground in order to let him speak to them in a more convincing way; however, Messey reported later that both the sides had promised to refrain from violence; in fact, both discharged their duty to the last but without speaking to each other.

From Lahore Gandhi went on his peace mission to Calcutta, now the seat of power of a Hindu ministry, and it was observed that, while the Punjab was embroiled in civil war despite the presence of large number of troops, he worked out such a miracle in Bengal that the independence day passed on quietly. Soon disturbances, however, broke out and Gandhi fearing that Bengal would be trapped in the feud on a level with the Punjab invoked his spiritual weapon, known as fasting, which till now had proved infallible in its effects. When Gandhi on 1st September began his fast, the Governor of West Bengal Rajagopalacharia came to see him; always a critic of Gandhi he was so even now on the ground that the fast could not be expected to bring a change in hardened ruffians and he was no mean critic as his intellectual abilities were such that later when Mountbatten for a while was away from India he was thought worthy enough to step into his shoes as acting Governor-General. While Mountbatten was dynamic, an extrovert, tackling events at the surface with feverish activity, Rajagopalacharia, being introspective and essentially a thinker, always probed into underlying causes of things.[89] Such was the personality to whom Gandhi now replied that the ruffians dared not act as they did shortly before without the passive support of the populace, whose hearts he intended to touch by his fast.

Another critic P.C. Ghosh, the Chief Minister of West Bengal, said that by asking the Hindus to give up violence when the opposite side had no such inhibitions Gandhi was unjust to them, and that at least some of them looked upon him as their enemy, in consequence. What is more, Ghosh himself was finding it difficult to run the government smoothly under the weight of Gandi's fast, but he the Mahatma by such arguments was not taken in, and rebutting him opined that in his efforts to check violence he in fact was helping the government.

Soon there was quiet in Calcutta, and meanwhile representatives of the people in successive batches met him as he was lying in bed and entreated him to desist, but until he saw a heart-change in them he had no inclination to oblige them. Finally, some well known leaders including the Governor and the Chief Minister of West Bengal put their heads together, and gave him the kind of assurances he needed to persuade himself that violence would not reappear, and to break his fast.

The refugees who had been forced out of Pakistan saw themselves unexpectedly reduced to a forlorn situation, and, at Delhi, thought that it was not an unprofitable business to vent their anger at the Muslims. When Gandhi entered the stage at this juncture, the pursuit of revenge became difficult for the Hindus, and precisely for that reason they did not like him and some were even angry at this moral gadfly. Whether Hindus or Muslims, he knowing well the rootless condition of the refugees, who for no fault of theirs had lost everything and so lived like vagrants, tried to pacify them so that he could bring peace to the capital. Not everyone he could win over to his side because it was his destiny to live at such a time that the conflict between the two communities was at its height; so, at his prayer meeting when Koranic poems were sung to underscore his wider outlook towards religion, some Hindu zealots cried out "death to Gandhi" and the disturbances that ensued forced the congregation to disperse abruptly.

After a long period of torpor under the weight of foreign domination, the Hindus to revivify themselves had started an organization briefly known as R.S.S. which represented Hindu militancy, and this body had highly respectable people at its head, but Gandhi was informed that it was egging on the mob in Delhi to violence. Its chief Golwalkar, however, denied the imputation of violence when Gandhi met him, and made it evident that the object of his organization was not a kill the Muslims but to protect the Hindus in general.

Thousands of Muslim refugees quartered at Purana Quila before they were to be sent off to Pakistan had to go through many privations, in consequence of the bad management of the camp. So they were in aggressive mood as Gandhi descended on them, and encircling him began to shout invective against him, but when they heard him talk and saw the agonized face of the Mahatma, a sensitive man who suffered only because others suffered, their bitter feelings left them so that they were swayed by his passionate emotions. He promised them that he would do everything in his power to bring down the level of their sorrow, and impressed by his words they escorted him away from their miserable habitations to his car to see him depart.[91]

Had the relation between the two just born independent nations been good, the troubles of Gandhi as the messenger of peace would have been much less a cause for worry. In fact, Mountbatten had thought that his main role in India was the promotion of cordial relations between the two inheritors of power, and did his utmost to achieve that, through a common Governor-General to both. Already, he had been told that Congress wanted him to be the first Governor-General of India, and that it would not raise objection if he were to accept the same position in the other country as well.[92] Jinnah put off the decision, giving the impression that he would ultimately invite Mountbatten to be Governor-General of Pakistan; however, at the eleventh hour, guided by his ego which advised him to be second to none he decided to elevate himself as Governor-General, and to make his Prime Minister Liaquat Ali Khan. This upset the calculation of Mountbatten, and put him in an extremely awkward position while Jinnah by his willful act lost much goodwill. He was disposed to wash his hands of the whole business, but the officers close to him thought that he should not turn down what was offered; if he did so the Congress would feel slighted which indeed was so partial to him that it believed no other Englishman except him and him only was fit enough for that exalted position. Further, if he departed from the scene, the British personnel from the Commander-in-Chief downwards not a whit concerned about the legacy of Clive would probably follow in his footsteps. Mountbatten ultimately made known his desire to serve India as its constitutional head, but he was in despair about the possibility of friendly relations with Jinnah who always seemed to be in opposition.

Thanks to Jinnah's warmongering, Mountbatten's abundant energy and shrewd judgement, well adapted to a challenge on the military front, were suddenly in demand and placed at the disposal of the country he was serving now. On 22nd October 1947, the frontier tribesmen including the warlike Afridis together with soldiers of the Pakistan Army pushed their way into Kashmir in what was obviously a full-scale invasion.[93] Such rapid progress they made after overrunning isolated frontier posts, that Jinnah at Abbotabad in North West Frontier Province was expecting to ride in triumph into Kashmir.

The Maharaja of Kashmir three days before the transfer of power had made known his resolve to sign standstill agreements with both the countries. "There is only one way for you to bring disaster to your country," Mountbatten had warned the prince, "and that is to do nothing."[94] Yet the Maharaja thought it expedient to procrastinate, perhaps, thinking that the two neighbours conflicting objectives would establish a kind of power balance which would give him enough room to manoeuvre. Patel, in fact, refrained from adopting any sort of measures to win him over, took no action which could be seen as forcing his hand and gave him even assurances that accession to Pakistan would not be taken amiss; on the other hand, it was Jinnah who forced him to act in such a way that the help he asked from India considerably enhanced its bargaining power with the prince.

His need for troops the Defence Committee on 25th presided over by Mountbatten considered, but he was not inclined to take a decision as preliminaries had to be gone through. Hence, a distinguished emissary rushed to Srinagar to look at the situation as it existed then, and his report was favourable to the prince in so far as it pointed out that his life, and his wealth kept in his palace, would be shortly at the mercy of avaricious tribesmen. There were besides British citizens in, and on the periphery of, his capital, and it was a reasonable guess that they would come to harm once the invading hordes got in.

Though the need of the moment was a quick response Mountbatten temporized, in the belief that in the background of Kashmir's independent status nothing could be done until that state acceded to India. The prevailing usage upheld the right of one country to obtain aid from another to increase its fighting potential when faced with external threat, but Mountbatten on account of his excessive preoccupation with legal niceties stuck to his point, that the only basis for sending troops was accession thereby either consciously or unconsciously promoting the interest of India. Again the same emissary hurried to Kashmir, and it did not take much effort on his part to squeeze out from the prince the document of accession with which he flew back to Delhi, and put it before Mountbatten. Then, the accession of Kashmir was accepted, on the understanding that a plebiscite would be held later.

On 27th, under the guidance of Mountbatten who was completely supported by Nehru, the military operation to rescue Kashmir began with the airlift of troops. Notwithstanding his experience as Supreme Allied Commander for South East Asia during the war, he was not familiar with this kind of operation effected in such a short time and with the help of a big fleet of planes. The First Sikh Battalion was in the air eager to meet on the battlefield the invaders, who were moving towards Srinagar but the airfield had not yet been captured so that the troops made an easy landing. The initial reports of the fighting were discouraging especially because there had been a withdrawal in consequence of the proportionately large number of invaders; heavy fighting raged about four miles west of Srinagar, which town the tribesmen in all probability would have overrun if they had been led by their own plundering instinct, but under British trained men they seemed to be cautious in their movement.

Gandhi, meanwhile, said he would not shed a tear if the Indian soldiers, in the footsteps of the brave Spartans at Thermopylae, died to the last man while defending the passes to Srinagar.

After learning that Kashmir had acceded to India and that its troops were on the move, Jinnah issued orders to General Gracey, the acting Commander-in-Chief of the Pakistan Army, to pump troops into Kashmir.[95] Gracey, however, was not ready to co-operate with him, and thought fit to refer the matter to Field Marshal Auchinleck. In the sequel, Auchinleck flew to Lahore to explain to Jinnah how impossible for the British to stage-manage in Kashmir a war in which victory and defeat being one and the same thing to them would be quite meaningless. After accession India had a perfect right to send troops; if Jinnah too did likewise, the British officers serving in Pakistan would be withdrawn. This threat of Auchinleck had the desired effect, and Jinnah's ambitious scheme of marching troops to Kashmir, conceived at a time of failure, similarly ended in failure.

Now, he in order to save face hit upon the device of holding a conference in Lahore where he would get the right platform for airing his grievances, and hence solicited the presence of both Nehru and Mountbatten. Nehru either was genuinely ill or had no interest to go there, with the result only Mountbatten elaborated the Indian point of view. Jinnah's face normally inclined to coldness now showed dejection at the turn of events; he did not accept the reality of accession, the foundation of which, in his view, rested on fraud and violence. That the accession had been brought about by violence Mountbatten agreed, but said that violence came from the tribes, for whom only Pakistan was responsible.[96] Beyond rhetorics and at the practical level, Jinnah was made to know that there was little chance of the tribesmen storming Srinagar, in the background of the Indian troops presence in strength there and their likely build-up in the future.

He in consequence made an offer: both sides should fall back at once and simultaneously. Since Pakistan had maintained that the tribal conquerors did not come under its influence, Mountbatten naturally asked how tribesmen could be induced to go back; to which Jinnah replied: "If you do this I will call the whole thing off," thereby betraying his involvement in the affair. Further, he thought that, with the Indian troops as well as Sheikh Abdullah dominating the Kashmir scene, the Muslims would be too frightened to support Pakistan in a plebiscite. Mountbatten suggested one under the United Nations auspices, "where upon Jinnah asserted that only the two Governors-General could organize it," but this found no favour with him for the simple reason that his constitutional position did not match well with the other's almost dictatorial powers. Their inability to reach any sort of understanding widened the breach between them, and Mountbatten who had entertained the thought "that it seemed hopeless to try to co-operate with Jinnah" might have felt he was right in his view after all.

Meanwhile, the pressure on the Muslims did not show any sign of abating, and the incoming refugees not only pitched camp in many enclosures which surrounded Delhi but also spilled over into the streets, and took over many mosques. Patel, in charge of Home Affairs, thought that there were many Muslims who a short while ago very actively supported the now defunct Muslim League, and that their mental predisposition came in the way of their manifesting loyalty to India. As power had conferred on him responsibilities he could not always oblige his mentor, and this made Gandhi all the more helpless to alleviate the sufferings of the Muslims, in whose cause, and at the hazard of his own life, he on 13th January 1948 started a fast. He a few days later ended it after having succeeded in pricking the conscience of the people, and forcing them to remember their duty to fellow human beings which was not to be discarded whatever might be the animus of the past.

In spite of Gandhi's sacrifice for the well-being of their community, the Muslim extremists were as irreconcilable with him as they always had been. About this time Gandhi came in possession of a book which was written by an eminent Muslim author, and which expounded the theory that the Hindus being unbelievers should be exterminated.[97] Such a view was expressed by hard-core members of that community even in the past, but the Muslim rulers during the meridian of their power did not give countenance to it knowing well its limitations as a guide to policy. Nevertheless the fact remained that Islam had traditionally been a fighting religion, and those who did not repose faith in it were looked upon by it as such a thoroughly bad lot that they even deserved annihilation.

In bygone times, when the Islamic religion was taking root in India, the Hindu masses, influenced by the custom and tradition of their forefathers, were indifferent to the reality of political power which was anyway out of their reach since it was appropriated by the upper caste leaders. Like Prometheus opened the eyes of man to the benefits of fire, Gandhi through the party system made known to the masses the advantages of power. Not unlike fire that was turned to destructive purpose, the masses during partition showed the ugly face of power. Gandhi recoiled in horror, and the Muslims who suffered much at the hands of mass power lost their pride and self-confidence for having belonged to India. Gandhi in order to tame the raw energy of the common people had recourse to fast, which restored to the Muslims a feeling of security. The Hindu extremists, however, like their counterparts among the Muslims, were on bad terms with Gandhi and thought that the time was right to put an end to his life.

Gandhi as he was going to his prayer meeting was assassinated on January 30th by a Hindu extremist, and he was "killed by his own people for whose redemption he lived. This second crucifixion in the history of the world has been enacted on a Friday—the same day Jesus was done to death one thousand nine hundred and fifteen years ago."[98]

NOTES AND REFERENCES

1. Gandhi and Modern India, P. Moon, p. 234 & 235.
2. Mahatma Gandhi, Pyarelal, V. 1, P. 84 & 85.
3. Collected Works of Mahatma Gandhi, V. 78, p. 126 & 127.
4. *Ibid*, p. 142.
5. The Transfer of Power, N. Mansergh, V. 5, p. 479.
6. Bhulabhai Desai, M.C. Setalvad, p. 256.
7. N. Mansergh, *op cit*, p. 745.
8. Collected Works of Mahatma Gandhi, V. 80, p. 441 & 442.
9. *Ibid*, p. 349.
10. The Viceroy's Journal, p. 149 & 152.
11. *Ibid*, p. 154.
12. *Ibid*, p. 170.
13. *Ibid*, p. 182 & 196.
14. Disastrous Twilight, Major-General Shahid Hamid, p. 26.
15. The Viceroy's Journal, p. 213.
16. The Transfer of Power, N. Mansergh,V. 6, p.771.
17. A History of India, Romila Thapar, V. 1, p. 319.
18. The Transfer of Power, N. Mansergh, V. 7, p. 68.

19. *Ibid*, p. 138.
20. *Ibid*, p. 142.
21. Foundations of Pakistan. S.S. Pirzada, V. 2, p. 520.
22. N. Mansergh, op cit, p. 342.
23. *Ibid*, p. 357.
24. Collected Works of Mahatma Gandhi, V. 84, p. 108.
25. The Viceroy's Journal, p.257.
26. *Ibid*, p. 258 & 259.
27. *Ibid*, p. 260.
28. N. Mansergh, *op cit*, p. 415.
29. Mahatma Gandhi, Lord Pethick-Lawrence, p. 271.
30. Collected Works, *op cit.*, p. 468.
31. *Ibid*, p. 470.
32. Collected Works, *op cit*, p. 169.
33. Divide and Quit, Penderel Moon, p. 49.
34. N. Mansergh, *op cit*, p. 141.
35. A History of the Sikhs, Khushwant Singh, V.1, p. 37
36. A History of India, Percival Spear, V. 2, p. 58.
37. N. Mansergh, *op cit*, p. 634.
38. Collected Works, op cit, p. 174.
39. The Viceroy's Journal, p. 274.
40. N. Mansergh, *op cit*, p. 644.
41. *Ibid*, p. 763.
42. *Ibid*.
43. The Viceroy's Journal p. 286.
44. N. Mansergh, op cit, p. 820.
45. *Ibid*, p. 837 & 838.
46. *Ibid*, p. 995.
47. Pethick-Lawrence, *op cit*, p. 277 & 278.
48. The Viceroy's Journal, p. 490.
49. Pyarelal, *op cit*, 222.
50. N. Mansergh, *op cit*, p. 988.
51. Gandhi's Emissary, Sudhir Ghosh, p. 167.
52. The Viceroy's Journal, p. 305.

53. India Wins Freedom, A.K. Azad, p. 164; the Transfer of Power, N. Mansergh, V. 8, p. 26.
54. N. Mansergh, *op cit*, p. 293.
55. The Viceroy's Journal, p. 340 & 419.
56. N. Mansergh, *op cit*, p. 322.
57. *Ibid*, p. 636.
58. The Geography of British India, George Smith, p. 81.
59. The Transfer of Power, N. Mansergh, V. 9, p. 242.
60. The Viceroy's Journal, p. 392.
61. N. Mansergh, op cit, p. 296.
62. *Ibid*, p.319.
63. The Transfer of Power, N. Mansergh, V. 8 p. 622 & 623.
64. The Great Divide, H.V. Hodson, p. 189; The Transfer of Power, N. Mansergh, V. 9, p. 396.
65. N. Mansergh, *op cit*, p. 477.
66. Collected Works of Mahatma Gandhi, V. 87, p. 12.
67. The Transfer of Power, N. Mansergh, V. 10, p. 127.
68. *Ibid*, p. 272.
69. *Ibid*, p. 682.
70. *Ibid*, p. 755.
71. *Ibid*, p. 758.
72. *Ibid*, p. 451 & 452.
73. Mission with Mountbatten, Alan Campbell-Johnson, p. 85.
74. Collected Works, *op cit,* p. 660.
75. N. Mansergh, *op cit*, pl. 660.
76. Penderel Moon, *op cit*, p. 85 & 86.
77. A.C. Johnson, p. 89.
78. The Transfer of Power in India, V.P. Menon, p.360.
79. The Transfer of Power, N. Mansergh, p.74.
80. Mountbatten, The Official Biography, Philip Ziegler, p. 405.
81. The Transfer of Power, N. Mansergh, V. 12, p. 31 & 32.
82. Collected Works of Mahatma Gandhi, V. 88, p. 488.
83. N. Mansergh, *op cit,* V. 11, p. 625.
84. *Ibid*, V. 12, p. 612.

85. Penderel Moon, *op cit*, p. 263 & 264.
86. V.P. Menon, *op cit*, p. 422.
87. H.V. Hodson, *op cit*, p. 413.
88. The Memoirs of Lord Ismay, p. 435.
89. A.C. Johnson, *op cit*, p. 238.
90. Collected Works of Mahatma Gandhi, V. 89, p. 177.
91. Mahatma Gandhi, The Last Phase, Pyarelal, p. 444.
92. Ismay, *op cit,* p. 428.
93. The Story of the Integration of the Indian States, V.P. Menon, p. 396.
94. A.C. Johnson, p. 240.
95. V.P. Menon, *op cit.*, p. 403.
96. A.C. Johnson, *op cit.*, p. 229.
97. Collected Works of Mahatma Gandhi, V. 90, p. 446.
98. A.C. Johnson, *op cit*, p. 281.

INDEX

B

C

N